America's Best Recipes

A 1988 HOMETOWN COLLECTION

America's Best Recipes

Oxmoor House®

©1988 by Oxmoor House, Inc.
Book Division of Southern Progress Corporation
P.O. Box 2463, Birmingham, Alabama 35201

ISBN: 0-8487-0737-0
ISSN: 0898-9982

Manufactured in the United States of America
First Printing 1988

Executive Editor: Ann H. Harvey
Production Manager: Jerry Higdon
Associate Production Manager: Rick Litton
Art Director: Bob Nance
Production Assistant: Theresa Beste

America's Best Recipes

Editor: Janice L. Krahn
Copy Editor: Mary Ann Laurens
Editorial Assistant: Pamela Whyte
Director, Test Kitchen: Julie Fisher
Test Kitchen Home Economists: Nancy C. Earhart,
    Lisa Glass, Gayle Hays Sadler, Paula N. Saunders,
    Jill Wills
Senior Photographer: Jim Bathie
Photo Stylist: Kay E. Clarke
Senior Designer: Cynthia R. Cooper
Assistants: Kay Hicks, D. Lynne Hopkins, and
    Melinda E. West

Project Consultants: Meryle Evans, Audrey P. Stehle

Scenic Illustrations by Dana Moore
Food Illustrations by Barbara Ball

Cover: Chicken-on-a-Skewer (page 248), Basque Sangría,
    (page 51), New York Cheesecake (page 93),
    Orange Rolls (page 68).

Frontispiece: Stiner Street, San Francisco, California

Oxmoor House, Inc., is also the publisher of *Cooking
Light* books. For subscription information for *Cooking
Light* magazine, write to *Cooking Light*®, P.O. Box C-549,
Birmingham, Alabama 35283.

Contents

Introduction

America's Best Recipes - A Hometown Collection celebrates our country's distinctive cuisine and the dedicated people who make America and American cooking unique. This national community cookbook salutes the special volunteers from non-profit organizations across the nation who through the creation of cookbooks have successfully raised the funds with which they enrich their communities. We would like to share this spirited collection of their winning recipes with you.

The creation of *America's Best Recipes* began with an experienced committee of food writers purveying literally hundreds of current community cookbooks from towns and cities across America. Over one thousand recipes were submitted as the best examples of traditional, regional, and just plain superb American cooking. Each recipe was rigorously tested, judged, and re-tested in our test kitchens by our staff of home economists to ensure that it was the best of the best from America's kitchens. The result is *America's Best Recipes*—a collection of over four hundred outstanding recipes from every region of the country.

The special entertaining section, "American Celebrations," features menus that reflect the diversity, unique local flavor, and family traditions of communities across America. Charming illustrations throughout the book invite you to take a scenic jaunt across the country from the Golden Gate Bridge in San Francisco to the windmills of Cape Cod.

America's Best Recipes is a unique recipe collection compiled in the spirit of sincere appreciation for the efforts of the past, in celebration of the present, and in hope for the future accomplishments of the organizations responsible for creating the fascinating community cookbooks that are featured in *America's Best Recipes - A Hometown Collection*.

The Editors

American
Celebrations

Everyone has a distinctive approach to cooking, and in the small, family-oriented community of Fredericksburg, Texas, a potluck supper out of doors is the perfect way to share treasured family recipes with friends and neighbors in a pitch-in social event—Texas style.

☆☆☆

Aloha Luncheon

Spicy Gazpacho with Garlic Croutons
Chinese Chicken Salad
Gougère
Glazed Almond Cookies
Macadamia Nut Brownies

Serves 8

A Taste of Aloha
The Junior League of Honolulu, Hawaii

Spicy Gazpacho with Garlic Croutons

**3 (28-ounce) cans whole
  tomatoes, drained**
1 cup chopped onion
1 cup chopped cucumber
½ cup chopped green pepper
1 clove garlic, minced
1 tablespoon salt
½ teaspoon ground cumin

**½ teaspoon freshly ground
  pepper**
2 cups tomato juice
**1 teaspoon Worcestershire
  sauce**
½ cup white wine vinegar
¼ cup olive oil
Garlic Croutons

Combine first 8 ingredients in container of an electric blender; top with cover, and process 1 minute or until finely chopped. Transfer mixture to a large bowl. Stir in tomato juice and Worcestershire sauce; cover and chill. Stir in vinegar and olive oil just before serving. Garnish with Garlic Croutons. Yield: 8 servings.

Garlic Croutons

6 slices white bread
2 large cloves garlic, minced

½ cup clarified butter

Trim crust from bread. Cut bread into ½-inch cubes. Sauté garlic in butter in a skillet over medium heat for 2 minutes. Add bread cubes; sauté until golden. Drain on paper towels. Yield: 3 cups.

Chinese Chicken Salad

5 cups shredded cooked
  chicken
2 cups cooked ham strips
1 cucumber, peeled, seeded,
  and cut into julienne strips

⅓ cup chopped peanuts
2 green onions, thinly sliced
Dressing (recipe follows)
1 small head iceberg lettuce,
  shredded

Combine chicken, ham, cucumber, peanuts, and green onions in a large bowl. Pour dressing over chicken mixture, and toss gently to coat well. To serve, arrange shredded lettuce on 8 individual serving plates. Divide chicken salad mixture evenly onto lettuce-lined plates. Yield: 8 servings.

Dressing

¼ cup peanut butter
3 tablespoons cider vinegar
3 tablespoons soy sauce
1 tablespoon dry mustard
1 teaspoon sesame seeds,
  toasted

3 cloves garlic, minced
½ teaspoon salt
¼ teaspoon white pepper
¼ teaspoon crushed red
  pepper

Combine all ingredients in a bowl; stir well. Yield: about ½ cup.

Gougère

½ cup butter or margarine
1 cup all-purpose flour
4 eggs
3 cups (12 ounces) shredded
  Cheddar cheese

1 cup (4 ounces) shredded
  Swiss cheese
¼ teaspoon salt
¼ teaspoon pepper

Melt butter in a medium saucepan; immediately add flour, and beat until mixture leaves sides of pan and does not separate. Remove from heat, and continue beating until mixture cools. Add eggs, one at a time, beating until mixture has a satiny sheen. Stir in cheeses, salt, and pepper.

Spoon into a greased 10-inch cast-iron skillet. Bake at 375° for 40 to 45 minutes or until golden brown. Cut bread into wedges to serve. Yield: 8 servings.

Note: This cheese bread will be heavy and dense.

Glazed Almond Cookies

1 cup butter or margarine,
  softened
1 cup sugar
2 eggs, separated
½ teaspoon almond extract
½ teaspoon vanilla extract

2⅔ cups sifted cake flour
½ teaspoon salt
¾ cup chopped blanched
  almonds
4 dozen whole almonds

Cream butter; gradually add sugar, beating until light and fluffy. Add egg yolks and flavorings, beating well. Add flour, salt, and chopped almonds, stirring well.

Shape dough into 1-inch balls, and place 2 inches apart on a greased cookie sheet. Place 1 whole almond in the center of each cookie; flatten slightly. Beat egg whites slightly, and brush over cookies. Bake at 350° for 13 minutes. Yield: 4 dozen.

Macadamia Nut Brownies

1½ cups sugar
⅔ cup butter or margarine
¼ cup water
1 (12-ounce) package
  semisweet chocolate
  morsels
2 teaspoons vanilla extract

4 eggs, beaten
1½ cups all-purpose flour
½ teaspoon baking soda
½ teaspoon salt
1 cup chopped macadamia
  nuts

Combine sugar, butter, and water in a large saucepan; cook over low heat, stirring constantly, until sugar dissolves and butter melts. Add chocolate morsels; cook, stirring constantly, until chocolate melts. Stir in vanilla; set mixture aside, and let cool.

Gradually add eggs to chocolate mixture in a slow steady stream, stirring constantly. Combine flour, soda, and salt; add to chocolate mixture, stirring until blended. Fold in nuts.

Pour batter into a greased and floured 15- x 10- x 1-inch jellyroll pan. Bake at 350° for 30 to 35 minutes. Cool and cut into 2-inch squares. Yield: 3 dozen.

Sporty Tailgate Picnic

Bloody Mary Soup
Zesty Nibbles
Pita Pockets with Steak and Mushrooms
Vegetable Grab Bag
Sauerkraut Salad
A No Chocolate Brownie
Cookie Chip Chocolates

Serves 8

Winners
The Junior League of Indianapolis, Indiana

Bloody Mary Soup

1 medium onion, diced
3 stalks celery, diced
2 tablespoons butter or margarine
2 tablespoons tomato puree
1 tablespoon sugar
5 cups vegetable juice cocktail
½ cup vodka
1 tablespoon salt (optional)
1 tablespoon lemon juice
2 teaspoons Worcestershire sauce
¼ teaspoon pepper

Sauté onion and celery in butter in a Dutch oven over medium heat. Add tomato puree and sugar; cook 1 minute. Add vegetable juice cocktail; bring to a boil, reduce heat, and simmer 8 minutes. Stir in vodka, salt, if desired, and remaining ingredients; strain. Serve hot or chilled. Yield: 8 to 10 servings.

Zesty Nibbles

6 cups oyster crackers
⅓ cup vegetable oil
1 (0.4-ounce) envelope ranch salad dressing mix
½ teaspoon lemon-pepper seasoning
½ teaspoon dried whole dillweed
¼ teaspoon garlic powder

Place crackers in a large container. Heat oil in a small saucepan over low heat just until warm. Pour oil over crackers, tossing to coat.

Combine salad dressing mix, lemon-pepper seasoning, dillweed, and garlic powder in a small bowl. Add mixture to crackers, tossing to mix well. Let stand in an airtight container for 24 hours, shaking container occasionally. Yield: 1½ quarts.

Pita Pockets with Steak and Mushrooms

1½ pounds boneless sirloin steak
½ cup vegetable oil
¼ cup Chablis or other dry white wine
2 tablespoons vinegar
2 teaspoons sugar
1 teaspoon dried whole basil
¼ teaspoon salt
½ pound fresh mushrooms, sliced
2 tomatoes, peeled and chopped
½ cup sliced green onions
6 ounces fresh spinach
1 (8-ounce) carton commercial sour cream
½ teaspoon dried whole dillweed
4 (6-inch) pita bread rounds, cut in half

Place steak on rack in broiler pan. Place pan 10 inches from heat. Broil 10 to 12 minutes on one side. Turn steak, and broil 10 to 12 minutes. Slice steak into thin strips; set aside.

Combine vegetable oil, wine, vinegar, sugar, basil, and salt in a large bowl; stir well. Add mushrooms, tomatoes, green onions, and steak to marinade. Let stand at room temperature 2 hours, stirring occasionally. Drain well.

Remove stems from spinach; wash leaves thoroughly, and pat dry. Tear into bite-size pieces. Add to steak mixture; stir well. Combine sour cream and dillweed, stirring well.

Spread sour cream mixture evenly inside each pita bread half; fill each with equal portions of marinated steak mixture. Serve immediately. Yield: 8 servings.

Vegetable Grab Bag

1 (8-ounce) carton
   commercial sour cream
1 cup mayonnaise
½ cup prepared horseradish
1 tablespoon fresh lemon
   juice
2 teaspoons dry mustard
½ teaspoon salt
1 (8-ounce) can sliced water
   chestnuts, drained

1 (6-ounce) can ripe olives
4 cups cherry tomatoes
½ pound fresh mushrooms,
   quartered
3 medium cucumbers,
   unpeeled and cubed
2 avocados, peeled and cubed

Combine sour cream, mayonnaise, horseradish, lemon juice, mustard, and salt in a large bowl. Add water chestnuts and remaining ingredients, tossing gently to coat. Serve, using bamboo skewers to spear vegetables. Yield: 8 to 10 servings.

Sauerkraut Salad

1 (27-ounce) can sauerkraut,
   rinsed and drained
2 onions, chopped
1 cup chopped celery
⅔ cup chopped green pepper

1 (4-ounce) jar sliced
   pimiento, drained
½ cup sugar
½ cup cider vinegar
¼ cup vegetable oil

Combine sauerkraut, onion, celery, green pepper, and pimiento in a large bowl. Toss gently.

Combine sugar, vinegar, and oil; stir with a wire whisk. Pour over sauerkraut mixture. Toss gently. Cover and marinate in refrigerator at least 24 hours. Yield: 8 to 10 servings.

A No Chocolate Brownie

¼ cup butter or margarine,
   melted
1 cup firmly packed brown
   sugar
1 egg, beaten
¾ cup all-purpose flour

1 teaspoon baking powder
½ teaspoon salt
½ teaspoon vanilla extract
¼ cup shredded coconut
½ cup chopped pecans
Frosting (recipe follows)

Combine butter and brown sugar, beating well at medium speed of an electric mixer. Add egg, and beat well. Combine flour, baking powder, and salt; add to creamed mixture, mixing well. Stir in vanilla, coconut, and pecans.

Spread batter in a greased and floured 8-inch square pan. Bake at 350° for 20 to 25 minutes. Cool; spread with frosting. Cut into squares. Yield: 16 brownies.

Frosting

¼ cup butter or margarine
¼ cup firmly packed brown
  sugar

2 tablespoons half-and-half
½ teaspoon maple flavoring
1 cup powdered sugar

Melt butter in a saucepan over medium heat. Add brown sugar. Reduce heat to low, and cook 3 minutes. Stir in half-and-half. Cool slightly; stir in maple flavoring. Add powdered sugar, and beat until blended. Yield: enough for 16 brownies.

Cookie Chip Chocolates

4 cups broken
  medium-size
  sugar cookies

2 (12-ounce) packages
  semisweet chocolate
  morsels

Break cookies into small pieces in a large bowl. Set aside.

Place chocolate morsels in top of a double boiler; bring water to a boil. Reduce heat to low, and cook until chocolate melts. Pour chocolate over cookie pieces; stir gently to coat. Drop by rounded tablespoonfuls onto wax paper-lined baking sheets; chill until firm. Store in a cool place. Yield: about 3 dozen.

Country Jamboree

Roasted Peanuts
Popcorn
Bar-B-Q Country Ribs
Homemade Baked Beans
Coleslaw
Sweet Water Rolls
Susie's Lemon Ice Cream
Granny's Sugar Cookies
Keg of Beer

Serves 10

Silver Soirees
The Service Guild of Birmingham, Alabama

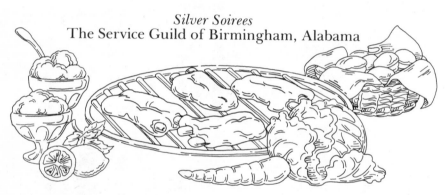

Bar-B-Q Country Ribs

1 cup minced onion
1 cup catsup
1 cup pineapple juice
⅔ cup vinegar
½ cup vegetable oil
½ cup Worcestershire sauce
1 tablespoon plus 1 teaspoon salt

2 teaspoons hot sauce
2 teaspoons chili powder
1 teaspoon red pepper
½ teaspoon dried whole oregano
10 pounds country-style ribs

Combine first 11 ingredients in a large Dutch oven; stirring well. Bring mixture to a boil. Reduce heat; simmer, uncovered, 10 minutes, stirring frequently. Remove from heat. Add ribs to sauce; cover and marinate in refrigerator for at least 8 hours.

Remove ribs from sauce, reserving sauce for basting. Place ribs 4 to 6 inches from slow to medium coals. Grill ribs, basting frequently with sauce and turning every 5 to 10 minutes for 1 to 1½ hours or until ribs are no longer pink. Yield: 10 servings.

Homemade Baked Beans

1 pound dried navy beans
2½ quarts water
1 small ham hock
1 pound ground beef, cooked
  and drained
2 cups catsup

1½ cups firmly packed light
  brown sugar
3 tablespoons Worcestershire
  sauce
1 tablespoon dry mustard
1 large onion, thinly sliced

Sort and wash beans; place in a large Dutch oven. Cover with water 2 inches above beans; let soak overnight.

Drain beans; add 2½ quarts water and ham hock; simmer 1 to 2 hours or until beans are tender. Drain, reserving liquid. Remove meat from ham hock, and coarsely chop. Return chopped ham to beans; add ground beef. Set aside.

Combine catsup, brown sugar, Worcestershire sauce, and mustard, stirring well; add sliced onion. Pour catsup mixture over bean mixture; stir gently. Pour into a 5-quart baking dish. Cover with reserved liquid 1 inch above mixture in dish. Bake at 350° for 3 hours. Yield: 10 to 12 servings.

Coleslaw

2 small heads cabbage,
  shredded
2 medium carrots, shredded
2 cups mayonnaise
¼ cup plus 2 tablespoons
  sugar
¼ cup red wine vinegar

2 teaspoons grated onion
1½ teaspoons celery seeds
½ teaspoon dry mustard
¼ teaspoon curry powder
⅛ teaspoon salt
⅛ teaspoon pepper

Combine cabbage and carrots in a large bowl; set aside. Combine mayonnaise and remaining ingredients; stir well. Pour mayonnaise mixture over vegetables; toss gently. Cover and chill. Yield: 10 to 12 servings.

Sweet Water Rolls

2 packages dry yeast
2 tablespoons sugar
1 cup warm water (105° to 115°)
9 to 9½ cups all-purpose flour
1 cup instant non-fat dry milk powder

¾ cup sugar
2 tablespoons baking powder
1 tablespoon salt
1 cup shortening
2 cups warm water (105° to 115°)
½ to ¾ cup melted butter or margarine

Dissolve yeast and 2 tablespoons sugar in 1 cup warm water; let stand 5 minutes.

Combine flour, milk powder, ¾ cup sugar, baking powder, and salt in a large bowl; cut in shortening with a pastry blender until mixture resembles coarse meal. Add 2 cups warm water and yeast mixture, stirring to make a soft dough. Cover dough, and refrigerate 2 hours or until dough is doubled in bulk.

Turn dough out onto a well-floured surface. Roll to ½-inch thickness. Cut with a 2-inch cutter. With dull edge of knife, make a crease just off center on each round. Brush rolls with melted butter. Fold over so that top overlaps slightly; press edges together. Dip rolls in butter. Place in four ungreased 9-inch square baking pans; cover and let rise in a warm place (85°), free from drafts, 40 minutes or until doubled in bulk. Bake at 350° for 20 minutes or until golden. Yield: 5 dozen.

Susie's Lemon Ice Cream

1 cup fresh lemon juice
¼ cup grated lemon rind
5 cups sugar

6 cups half-and-half
1 cup whipping cream
Milk

Combine lemon juice, lemon rind, and sugar in a medium bowl; refrigerate for 24 hours.

Pour mixture into freezer can of a 5-quart hand-turned or electric freezer. Add half-and-half and whipping cream. If necessary, add milk until mixture reaches fill line in freezer can. Freeze according to manufacturer's instructions. Let ripen at least 30 minutes before serving. Yield: 5 quarts.

Granny's Sugar Cookies

1 cup butter or margarine
1½ cups sugar
2 eggs
2¾ cups all-purpose flour

1 teaspoon cream of tartar
1 teaspoon baking soda
½ teaspoon salt
Sugar

Cream butter; gradually add 1½ cups sugar, beating until light and fluffy. Add eggs, one at a time, beating well after each addition. Combine flour, cream of tartar, soda, and salt; add to creamed mixture, beating until blended. Chill dough at least 1 hour.

Shape dough into 1-inch balls; roll in sugar. Place on lightly greased cookie sheets, and bake at 400° for 6 to 8 minutes or until lightly browned. Let cool on wire racks. Yield: 5 dozen.

Fourth of July

Popcorn Soup
Grilled Steaks
Friggione (Pepper, Tomato, and Onion Stew)
Frybakers
Meringue Shells with Blueberries

Serves 12

Carnegie Treasures Cookbook
Women's Committee,
The Carnegie Museum of Art
Pittsburgh, Pennsylvania

Popcorn Soup

8 medium-size ears fresh
corn
2 onions, sliced
3 bay leaves
8 cups chicken broth, divided

6 egg yolks
½ cup unsalted butter, melted
4 quarts freshly popped
popcorn, divided
¼ teaspoon pepper

Remove corn from cob. Cook corn in a small amount of boiling water 5 minutes or until tender. Drain; rinse and drain again.

Combine onions, bay leaves, and 2 cups chicken broth in a large skillet. Bring to a boil; reduce heat, and simmer 15 minutes or until onions are tender. Remove from heat. Discard bay leaves.

Transfer onion mixture to container of an electric blender. Add corn and 2 cups broth. Cover and process until pureed; reserve 2 cups. Pour remaining mixture into a large bowl. Set aside.

Place egg yolks in blender container. Cover and process at high speed 5 seconds. With blender on high, add melted butter in a slow steady stream. Add 2 cups pureed mixture. Process 30 seconds or until thickened and smooth. Add to mixture in bowl.

Combine 1 quart popcorn and 2 cups broth in blender container; puree. Strain mixture to remove coarse hulls. Add strained mixture to mixture in bowl. Repeat procedure with 1 quart popcorn and remaining 2 cups broth. Add pepper; stir well. Soup may be served hot or cold; garnish with remaining popcorn just before serving. Serve immediately. Yield: 12 servings.   Edith H. Fisher

Grilled Steaks

12 (8-ounce) filets mignons, 2 inches thick
or
12 (10-ounce) strip steaks, 1¼ inches thick
or

4 (2-pound) boneless top sirloin steaks, 3 inches thick
1 tablespoon dried whole rosemary
1 tablespoon dried whole thyme

Place steaks on grill 5 inches from hot coals. Sprinkle rosemary and thyme over steaks and coals. Grill steaks 8 to 12 minutes on each side or to desired degree of doneness. Place steaks on a wooden plank; slice diagonally. Yield: 12 servings.

Friggione (Pepper, Tomato, and Onion Stew)

4 pounds tomatoes, peeled and seeded
2 teaspoons salt, divided
½ cup olive oil
¼ cup unsalted butter
2 pounds green peppers, chopped
2 pounds sweet red peppers, chopped

2 pounds pearl onions, peeled
4 bulbs garlic, minced
2 tablespoons dried whole basil
½ teaspoon freshly ground pepper

Cut tomatoes in half; scoop out pulp, and reserve for use in other recipes. Sprinkle insides of tomatoes with 1 teaspoon salt. Place tomato shells upside down on paper towels to drain. Let stand for 30 minutes. Chop and set aside.

Combine olive oil and butter in a large skillet over medium heat; add green peppers, red peppers, onions, and garlic. Cook, stirring frequently, until onions are translucent. Add reserved tomatoes and basil. Reduce heat to low, cover and cook for 10 minutes. Add remaining salt and pepper.

Increase heat to high, and cook, uncovered, until most of the liquid has evaporated, stirring frequently. Yield: 12 servings.

Frybakers

¼ cup vegetable oil
1 small onion, finely chopped
1 teaspoon dried whole
  dillweed
½ teaspoon dried whole
  rosemary
½ teaspoon dried whole
  thyme
¼ teaspoon salt
¼ teaspoon pepper
6 medium baking potatoes

Cover bottom of a 13- x 9- x 2-inch baking dish with vegetable oil. Combine remaining ingredients, except potatoes; sprinkle evenly over bottom of baking dish. Set aside.

Wash potatoes, and cut in half lengthwise. Place potatoes, cut side down, in prepared baking dish. Bake at 350° for 45 minutes or until potatoes are tender. Yield: 12 servings.   Mrs. John T. Morris

Meringue Shells with Blueberries

6 egg whites
½ teaspoon cream of tartar
⅛ teaspoon salt
2 teaspoons vanilla extract
2 cups sugar
4 cups fresh blueberries
1 cup orange juice
  concentrate, thawed
2 teaspoons grated orange
  rind
2 cups whipping cream,
  whipped

Cover 2 baking sheets with unglazed brown paper. Draw one 9-inch circle on each paper-lined baking sheet. Set aside.

Beat egg whites (at room temperature) in a large bowl at high speed of an electric mixer until foamy; sprinkle cream of tartar, salt, and vanilla over egg whites; continue beating until soft peaks form. Gradually add sugar, one tablespoon at a time, beating until stiff peaks form. Spoon half of meringue onto each circle. Using the back of a spoon, shape mixture into circles, mounding sides 1¼ inches higher than centers.

Bake at 275° for 1 hour. Turn oven off, and let meringue shells cool at least 2 hours before opening oven door. Carefully remove baked meringue shells from brown paper. Use immediately or store in an airtight container.

Combine blueberries, orange juice, and orange rind in a large mixing bowl; stir gently. Carefully fold whipped cream into blueberry mixture. Spoon fruit mixture into meringue shells. Serve immediately. Yield: 12 servings.   Pat Barnett

Northwest-Style Grilled Dinner

Savory Cheese Spread
Stuffed Salmon
Baked Potato Wedges
Corn on the Cob
Spinach Salad with Radishes
Hot Sourdough Bread
Blackberry and Cream Pie

Serves 8

The Overlake School Cookbook
The Overlake School Parents Club
Redmond, Washington

Savory Cheese Spread

1 cup crumbled feta cheese
1 (8-ounce) package cream cheese, softened
1 tablespoon whipping cream
2 tablespoons chopped chives

1 clove garlic, crushed
¼ teaspoon freshly ground pepper
Dash of red pepper

Position knife blade in food processor bowl; add feta cheese. Top with cover, and process until smooth. Add cream cheese and whipping cream; process until smooth. Spoon mixture into a serving bowl; stir in chives, garlic, pepper, and red pepper.

Cover cheese mixture, and chill several hours. Serve with crackers. Yield: 8 servings.

Stuffed Salmon

1 (4-pound) salmon, cleaned
  and dressed
2 tablespoons chopped onion
2 tablespoons chopped
  mushrooms
2 tablespoons chopped ripe
  olives
1 tablespoon finely chopped
  green pepper
1 tablespoon finely chopped
  fresh parsley

½ teaspoon salt
¼ teaspoon dried whole basil
¼ teaspoon freshly ground
  pepper
1 cup soft whole wheat
  breadcrumbs
¼ cup butter or margarine,
  melted
4 slices bacon

Carefully wash salmon, and pat dry; set aside.

Combine chopped onion and next 9 ingredients, mixing well.
Place stuffing in fish cavity. Lay bacon slices on top of salmon; place
fish on a large piece of heavy-duty aluminum foil.

Place salmon on grill over medium coals. Close lid, and grill for 30
to 40 minutes or until fish flakes easily when tested with a fork.
Yield: 8 servings.

Baked Potato Wedges

4 large baking potatoes
¼ cup butter or margarine,
  melted
¼ cup catsup
1 teaspoon prepared mustard

½ teaspoon paprika
¼ teaspoon salt
¼ teaspoon freshly ground
  pepper

Wash potatoes, and pat dry. Quarter each potato. Cut each
quarter crosswise into ¼-inch slices, cutting to, but not through,
bottom of potato to resemble a fan. Place each potato wedge, skin
side down, on a large baking sheet. Set aside.

Combine butter and remaining ingredients; stir well. Brush tops
and sides of potatoes with one-third of butter mixture. Bake, uncovered, at 425° for 35 to 40 minutes, basting occasionally with remaining butter mixture. Yield: 8 servings.

Spinach Salad with Radishes

1 pound fresh spinach, torn
  into bite-size pieces
1 (6-ounce) package radishes,
  sliced
⅓ cup olive oil
Juice of 1 lime

1 teaspoon Dijon mustard
1 clove garlic, minced
⅛ teaspoon anchovy paste
Dash of freshly ground
  pepper

Combine spinach and radishes in a large bowl; toss gently. Combine olive oil and remaining ingredients; stir, using a wire whisk, until well blended. Pour oil mixture over spinach and radishes, and toss gently. Yield: 8 servings.

Blackberry and Cream Pie

1½ cups all-purpose flour
¾ teaspoon salt
⅔ cup shortening
3 tablespoons cold water
4 to 5 cups fresh or frozen
  blackberries, thawed and
  drained

1 teaspoon lemon juice
  (optional)
1 cup commercial sour cream
½ cup firmly packed brown
  sugar
1 tablespoon all-purpose flour
Whipping cream

Sift 1½ cups flour and salt into a large bowl; reserve ¼ cup in a small bowl. Cut shortening into mixture in large bowl with a pastry blender until mixture resembles coarse meal. Add cold water to ¼ cup flour mixture, stirring until smooth. Add to shortening mixture. Stir with a fork just until dry ingredients are moistened. Shape into a ball. Roll dough to ⅛-inch thickness on a lightly floured surface. Place in a greased 9-inch pieplate; trim off excess pastry along edges. Fold edges under and flute.

Remove excess moisture from blackberries, using paper towels. Arrange blackberries in pastry shell. Sprinkle with lemon juice, if desired. Combine sour cream, brown sugar, and 1 tablespoon flour, stirring well. Pour sour cream mixture over blackberries in pastry shell. Bake at 425° for 10 minutes. Reduce heat to 325°, and bake 35 to 40 minutes or until pie is set. Pour whipping cream into a pitcher, and serve with warm pie. Yield: one 9-inch pie.

Bayfront Buffet

Spinach Balls
Marinated Vegetable Appetizer
Grilled King Mackerel Steaks
or
Char-Broiled Shrimp
Creole Salad
Ann's Potato Salad
Hopkins Boarding House Squash Casserole
Hush Puppies
Hummingbird Cake
Mississippi Mud Cake

Serves 8

Some Like It South!
The Junior League of Pensacola, Florida

Spinach Balls

2 (10-ounce) packages frozen chopped spinach
3 cups herb-seasoned stuffing mix
1 large onion, finely chopped
6 eggs, beaten
¾ cup butter or margarine, melted
½ cup grated Parmesan cheese
1½ teaspoons garlic salt
1 to 1½ teaspoons pepper
½ teaspoon dried whole thyme

Cook spinach according to package directions; drain. Press between layers of paper towels to remove excess moisture.

Combine spinach and remaining ingredients in a large bowl; stir well. Shape mixture into ¾-inch balls. Place on lightly greased baking sheets. Bake at 325° for 15 to 20 minutes. Serve immediately. Yield: about 10 dozen.

Marinated Vegetable Appetizer

½ cup wine vinegar
½ cup olive oil
¼ cup water
2 tablespoons sugar
1 tablespoon salt
½ teaspoon dried whole
   oregano
¼ teaspoon pepper
2 medium carrots, scraped
   and sliced
2 stalks celery, sliced
1 small head cauliflower,
   broken into flowerets

1 medium-size green pepper,
   cut into 1-inch pieces
1 (6-ounce) jar button
   mushrooms, drained
1 (6-ounce) can ripe olives,
   drained
1 (4-ounce) jar pitted green
   olives, drained
1 (3-ounce) jar cocktail
   onions, drained

Combine first 7 ingredients in a large skillet; cook over medium heat until mixture simmers. Add carrots; cover and simmer 2 minutes. Add celery and cauliflower; cover and simmer 2 minutes. Add green pepper, mushrooms, olives, green olives, and onions; cover and simmer 1 minute.

Pour mixture into a large container; cover tightly, and chill 24 hours. To serve, drain vegetables, and place in a serving dish. Yield: 8 to 10 servings.

Grilled King Mackerel Steaks

2 pounds king mackerel, cut
   into 1-inch-thick steaks
   (leave skin on)
¼ cup orange juice
¼ cup soy sauce
2 tablespoons chopped fresh
   parsley

2 tablespoons vegetable oil
2 tablespoons catsup
1 tablespoon lemon juice
1 clove garlic, crushed
½ teaspoon dried whole
   oregano
½ teaspoon pepper

Place mackerel steaks in a large shallow dish. Combine orange juice and remaining ingredients; mix well. Pour marinade over fish. Cover and marinate in refrigerator 30 minutes, turning once.

Drain steaks, reserving marinade; place steaks in a wire grilling basket. Place basket 4 inches from medium-hot coals. Grill 8 minutes on each side or until fish flakes easily when tested with a fork, basting often with marinade. Yield: 8 servings.

Char-Broiled Shrimp

3 pounds large fresh shrimp
1 cup olive oil
⅓ cup chopped fresh parsley
2 tablespoons fresh lemon
  juice

2 cloves garlic, crushed
1 teaspoon salt

Peel shrimp, leaving tails intact. Combine olive oil and remaining ingredients in a 13- x 9- x 2-inch baking dish; stir well. Add shrimp, stirring gently. Cover and marinate in refrigerator at least 8 hours, stirring occasionally.

Remove shrimp from marinade, using a slotted spoon; reserve marinade. Place shrimp on nine 14-inch skewers. Grill kabobs over medium-hot coals 3 to 4 minutes on each side, basting frequently with marinade. Yield: 8 servings.

Creole Salad

8 small zucchini, thinly sliced
4 medium tomatoes, chopped
1 green pepper, finely
  chopped
1 medium avocado, peeled
  and cubed

1 small onion, grated, or 3
  green onions, chopped
1 teaspoon sugar
1 teaspoon salt
½ teaspoon freshly ground
  pepper

Combine all ingredients, tossing well. Let stand at room temperature at least 1 hour before serving. Yield: 8 to 10 servings.

Ann's Potato Salad

6 medium-size baking
  potatoes, peeled
8 small sweet pickles, finely
  shredded
4 to 6 hard-cooked eggs,
  finely shredded

1 medium onion, finely
  chopped
1 stalk celery, finely chopped
1 carrot, scraped and finely
  shredded
Dressing (recipe follows)

Cook potatoes in boiling salted water to cover 25 minutes or until tender. Drain and cool slightly. Shred potatoes. Combine shredded potatoes, pickles, eggs, onion, celery, and carrot in a large bowl. Stir gently. Add dressing, and toss gently. Yield: 8 to 10 servings.

Dressing

1 cup mayonnaise
3 tablespoons vinegar
3 tablespoons sweet pickle
  juice
½ teaspoon salt

½ teaspoon sugar
⅛ teaspoon paprika
Dash of freshly ground
  black pepper

Combine all ingredients in a bowl; stir well. Yield: 1⅓ cups.

Hopkins Boarding House Squash Casserole

3 pounds yellow squash,
  sliced
½ cup chopped onion
½ cup butter or margarine

2 eggs, beaten
¾ cup cracker crumbs
1 teaspoon salt
½ teaspoon pepper

Cook squash, covered, in a small amount of boiling salted water 10 to 15 minutes or until tender. Drain well, and mash. Set aside.

Sauté onion in butter until tender. Add onion, eggs, cracker crumbs, salt, and pepper to squash; stir well. Spoon mixture into a lightly greased 2-quart casserole. Bake, uncovered, at 350° for 20 minutes. Yield: 8 to 10 servings.

Hush Puppies

1 cup self-rising cornmeal
½ cup self-rising flour
1 medium-size green pepper, chopped
1 medium onion, chopped

1 (8.5-ounce) can cream-style corn
½ cup buttermilk
Vegetable oil

Combine cornmeal, flour, green pepper, onion, and corn. Add buttermilk, stirring until dry ingredients are moistened.

Carefully drop batter by rounded tablespoonfuls into deep hot oil (375°). Fry 3 to 5 minutes or until hush puppies are golden brown, turning once. Drain well on paper towels. Yield: about 2 dozen.

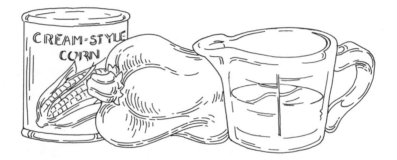

Hummingbird Cake

3 cups all-purpose flour
1 teaspoon baking soda
1 teaspoon salt
2 cups sugar
1 teaspoon cinnamon
3 eggs, beaten
1½ cups vegetable oil

1½ teaspoons vanilla extract
1 (8-ounce) can crushed pineapple, undrained
1 cup chopped pecans
2 cups mashed banana
Frosting (recipe follows)

Combine first 5 ingredients in a large bowl; add eggs and oil, stirring just until dry ingredients are moistened. Do not beat. Stir in vanilla, pineapple, pecans, and banana.

Pour batter into 3 greased and floured 9-inch round cakepans. Bake at 350° for 30 to 35 minutes or until a wooden pick inserted in center comes out clean. Cool in pans 10 minutes; remove from pans, and let cool completely on wire racks.

Spread frosting between layers and on top and sides of cake. Yield: one 3-layer cake.

Frosting

1 (8-ounce) package cream
  cheese, softened
⅓ cup butter or margarine,
  softened

1 (16-ounce) package
  powdered sugar, sifted
2 teaspoons vanilla extract
1 cup chopped pecans

Combine cream cheese and butter, beating until smooth. Add powdered sugar and vanilla; beat until light and fluffy. Stir in pecans. Yield: enough for one 3-layer cake.

Mississippi Mud Cake

1 cup butter or margarine
½ cup cocoa
2 cups sugar
4 eggs, slightly beaten
1½ cups flour
Pinch of salt

1½ cups chopped pecans
1 teaspoon vanilla extract
1 cup miniature
  marshmallows
Frosting (recipe follows)

Melt butter in a small saucepan over medium heat; add cocoa, mixing well. Remove from heat.

Combine cocoa mixture, sugar, and eggs in a large mixing bowl; mix well. Stir in flour, salt, pecans, and vanilla.

Spoon batter into a greased 13- x 9- x 2-inch baking pan. Bake at 350° for 35 to 45 minutes. Sprinkle miniature marshmallows over warm cake, and spread with frosting. Cut into squares to serve. Yield: 15 servings.

Frosting

½ cup butter or margarine
¼ cup plus 2 tablespoons
  cola-flavored carbonated
  beverage

3 tablespoons cocoa
1 (16-ounce) package
  powdered sugar, sifted
1 cup chopped pecans

Combine butter, cola, and cocoa in a small saucepan; cook over medium heat, stirring frequently, until mixture boils. Pour hot mixture over powdered sugar in a medium mixing bowl. Add chopped pecans; mix well. Yield: about 2 cups.

Home on the Range

Margaritas by the Gallon
Mexican Cheese Ball
Brisket in a Bag
Jalapeño Baked Potatoes
Congealed Avocado Salad
Mexican Chocolate Cake with Praline Frosting

Serves 10

Plain & Fancy
The Junior League of Richardson, Texas

Margaritas by the Gallon

1 (12-ounce) can frozen
lemonade concentrate,
thawed and undiluted
1 (6-ounce) can frozen
limeade concentrate, thawed
and undiluted
2 cups fresh lime juice

1 cup commercial lime juice
1 (25.4-ounce) bottle tequila
1½ cups Triple Sec or other
orange-flavored liqueur
Lime wedges
Salt

Combine first 6 ingredients in a 1-gallon container. Add water to equal 1 gallon. Stir well. Chill several hours or overnight.

Rub rim of cocktail glasses with wedge of lime. Place salt in saucer; spin rim of each glass in salt. Pour chilled beverage into prepared glasses. Yield: 20 (6-ounce) servings.

Mexican Cheese Ball

1 tablespoon water
1 (1-ounce) package onion
dip mix
4 cups (16 ounces) shredded
sharp Cheddar cheese
1 (4-ounce) can chopped
green chiles, drained

1 (2-ounce) jar diced
pimiento, drained
½ cup mayonnaise
¼ cup butter or margarine,
softened
¼ to ½ teaspoon red pepper
Additional red pepper

Combine water and onion dip mix in a small mixing bowl; stir well, and set aside.

Combine Cheddar cheese, green chiles, and pimiento; stir well. Add mayonnaise, butter, and ¼ to ½ teaspoon red pepper; stir well. Chill; shape into a ball, and sprinkle with additional red pepper. Serve with taco chips. Yield: 4 cups.

Brisket in a Bag

1½ cups water
1 cup catsup
½ cup cider vinegar
¼ cup Worcestershire sauce
¼ cup butter or margarine
2 tablespoons chopped onion
1 clove garlic, minced
1 teaspoon sugar
¼ teaspoon salt
1 teaspoon paprika
1 teaspoon chili powder
Pepper to taste
1 cup vegetable oil

½ cup vinegar
¼ cup liquid smoke
1 large onion, chopped
2 cloves garlic, crushed
1 celery stalk, chopped
1 tablespoon prepared
  mustard
1 tablespoon pepper
1 (8- to 10-pound) untrimmed
  beef brisket
¼ cup water
2 tablespoons all-purpose
  flour

Combine first 12 ingredients in a large saucepan. Bring mixture to a boil; reduce heat, and simmer, uncovered, 15 minutes, stirring occasionally. Remove from heat, and strain.

Combine 1 cup strained catsup mixture (reserving remainder of strained mixture to be used in the barbecue sauce), vegetable oil, ½ cup vinegar, liquid smoke, onion, garlic, celery, mustard, and 1 tablespoon pepper; mix well, and set aside.

Place brisket, fat side up, in a large roaster or cooking bag. Pour vegetable oil mixture over brisket. If using roaster, cover pan. If using cooking bag, force air from bag, seal, and cut a slit in top of bag. Place in a large shallow pan. Marinate in refrigerator 1 to 3 days. Bake at 175° for 27 hours. Slice and trim meat.

Combine ¼ cup water, flour, and remaining strained catsup mixture in a small saucepan. Cook over medium heat, stirring constantly with a wire whisk, until thickened and smooth. Serve barbecue sauce with brisket. Yield: 10 servings.

Jalapeño Baked Potatoes

6 large baking potatoes
12 jalapeño peppers, halved
  and seeded

Shortening
Butter or margarine
Commercial sour cream

Scrub potatoes thoroughly. Core 4 holes in each potato, one on each end and one on each side. Place a jalapeño pepper half in each hole. Rub potatoes with shortening. Wrap each potato in aluminum foil. Bake at 450° for 1 hour. Split potatoes lengthwise, and serve with butter and sour cream. Yield: 12 servings.

Congealed Avocado Salad

1 (3-ounce) package
  lemon-flavored gelatin
1 cup boiling water
2 large avocados, peeled and
  cubed

1 (8-ounce) package cream
  cheese, softened
1 (8-ounce) can crushed
  pineapple, drained
1 cup chopped pecans

Dissolve gelatin in boiling water. Chill until consistency of unbeaten egg white.

Combine avocado and cream cheese; beat at medium speed of an electric mixer until blended. Stir in pineapple and pecans.

Combine avocado mixture with gelatin mixture; beat well. Pour into a lightly oiled 8-inch square pan. Cover and chill until firm. Yield: 10 to 12 servings.

Mexican Chocolate Cake
with Praline Frosting

3 (1-ounce) squares
  unsweetened chocolate
1 cup boiling water
½ cup butter or margarine,
  softened
1¾ cups firmly packed
  brown sugar
2 eggs
1 teaspoon vanilla extract

1¾ cups plus 2 tablespoons
  all-purpose flour
1 teaspoon baking soda
¼ teaspoon salt
½ cup commercial sour
  cream
Praline Frosting
½ cup finely chopped pecans

Combine chocolate and boiling water in a small bowl; stir until chocolate melts. Set aside.

Cream butter; gradually add brown sugar, beating well at medium speed of an electric mixer. Add eggs, one at a time, beating well after each addition. Stir in vanilla.

Sift together flour, baking soda, and salt. Add sifted dry ingredients to creamed mixture; mix until blended. Stir in sour cream and melted chocolate.

Pour batter into a greased 9- x 5- x 3-inch loafpan. Bake at 350° for 1 hour and 15 minutes or until a wooden pick inserted in center comes out clean. Cool in pan 10 minutes; remove from pan, and let cool on wire rack. Spread Praline Frosting over cake; sprinkle with pecans. Yield: 1 loaf.

Praline Frosting

½ cup butter or margarine
1 cup firmly packed brown
   sugar
¼ cup milk

1 to 2 cups sifted powdered
   sugar
½ teaspoon vanilla extract

Combine butter and brown sugar in a heavy saucepan; bring to a full boil, and cook 2 minutes, stirring constantly. Add milk, and return to a boil. Remove from heat, and let cool. Gradually add powdered sugar, beating until light and fluffy. Stir in vanilla. Yield: enough for 1 loaf.

Celebration Dinner

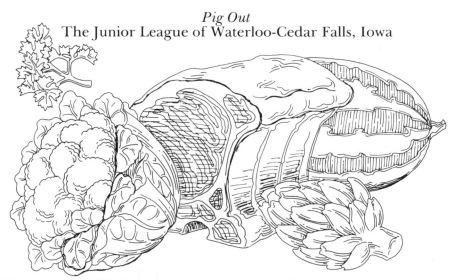

Lemon Champagne Punch
Cream of Broccoli Soup
Mixed Greens and Artichoke Salad
Pork Loin Roast with Orange Glaze Cups
Cauliflower Pie
Swedish Rye Bread
Valentine Tarts
Watermelon Granite

Serves 8

Pig Out
The Junior League of Waterloo-Cedar Falls, Iowa

Lemon Champagne Punch

1½ quarts cold water
2 (12-ounce) cans frozen lemonade concentrate, thawed and undiluted
2 (12-ounce) cans frozen pineapple juice concentrate, thawed and undiluted
6 (25.4-ounce) bottles champagne, chilled
2 (33.8-ounce) bottles ginger ale, chilled
1 (33.8-ounce) bottle sparkling water, chilled

Combine cold water, lemonade, and pineapple juice concentrates in a large container; cover and chill. Just before serving, add chilled champagne, ginger ale, and sparkling water to juice mixture. Yield: 10½ quarts.   Margie Lahey Skahill

Cream of Broccoli Soup

3 (10¾-ounce) cans chicken
  broth, undiluted
1 medium carrot, scraped and
  chopped
1 stalk celery, chopped
1 medium onion, chopped
1 small potato, peeled and
  finely chopped
2 bay leaves

1 (1½-pound) bunch fresh
  broccoli, broken into
  flowerets, or 2 (10-ounce)
  packages frozen chopped
  broccoli
1½ cups half-and-half,
  scalded and divided
Salt and pepper to taste

Combine chicken broth, carrot, celery, onion, potato, and bay leaves in a large Dutch oven. Bring to a boil. Cover, reduce heat, and simmer 25 minutes or until vegetables are tender. Remove and discard bay leaves.

Chop fresh broccoli; add to broth mixture. Bring to a boil; cover, reduce heat, and simmer 20 minutes or until broccoli is tender.

Remove from heat; pour half of broccoli mixture into a large container, and set aside. Pour remaining broccoli mixture into container of an electric blender or food processor. Cover and process until smooth. Add ¾ cup half-and-half. Process until smooth. Return pureed mixture to Dutch oven. Repeat procedure with reserved broccoli mixture and remaining half-and-half. Heat soup thoroughly. Add salt and pepper to taste. Yield: 8 servings.

Susan Kersten Cortright

Mixed Greens and Artichoke Salad

1 cup vegetable oil
½ cup tarragon vinegar
2 teaspoons Italian salad
  dressing mix
2⅔ cups torn iceberg lettuce
2⅔ cups torn spinach
1⅓ cups torn leaf lettuce

2 (6-ounce) jars marinated
  artichoke hearts, drained
  and quartered
16 cherry tomatoes, halved
Salt and freshly ground black
  pepper to taste
1 teaspoon sesame seeds

Combine oil, vinegar, and salad dressing mix in a jar. Cover tightly, and shake vigorously. Chill. Combine iceberg lettuce and next 4 ingredients; toss well. Shake salad dressing, and pour over salad; toss gently. Sprinkle with salt, pepper, and sesame seeds. Yield: 8 servings.

Connie Stroh Werner

Pork Loin Roast
with Orange Glaze Cups

1 teaspoon grated orange rind
1 cup orange juice
2½ teaspoons cornstarch
½ teaspoon ground ginger
½ teaspoon ground mace
1 (5½-pound) center loin
   pork roast
1 teaspoon salt

½ teaspoon pepper
4 oranges
1 (10½-ounce) can pineapple
   chunks, drained
2 tablespoons Grand Marnier
   or other orange-flavored
   liqueur
Fresh parsley sprigs

Combine first 5 ingredients in a small saucepan. Cook over medium heat, stirring constantly, until mixture thickens.

Place roast, fat side up, on a rack in a roasting pan. Rub with salt and pepper. Insert meat thermometer into thickest part of roast, making sure it does not touch fat or bone. Bake, uncovered, at 325° for 1½ to 2 hours. Brush with juice mixture. Continue baking for 30 minutes or until thermometer registers 170°.

Cut oranges in half crosswise. Clip orange membranes, and carefully remove pulp (do not puncture bottom). Reserve orange shells. Dice orange pulp; drain. Combine orange pulp, pineapple chunks, and Grand Marnier; chill. Spoon fruit mixture into orange shells.

Place roast on a serving platter. Garnish with parsley sprigs and orange cups. Yield: 8 servings.   Ruth Lutz Buck

Cauliflower Pie

¾ cup (3 ounces) shredded
   sharp Cheddar cheese,
   divided
½ cup fine, dry breadcrumbs
2 tablespoons all-purpose
   flour
1 medium head cauliflower,
   broken into flowerets

1 (8-ounce) carton
   commercial sour cream
2 eggs, beaten
¾ teaspoon salt
¼ teaspoon white pepper

Combine ½ cup cheese, breadcrumbs, and flour, stirring well. Spread half of breadcrumb mixture in bottom of a well-greased 9-inch pieplate. Add remaining cheese to remaining breadcrumb mixture. Stir well. Cook cauliflower in a small amount of boiling water 8 minutes or until tender. Drain, and arrange in pieplate.

Combine sour cream, eggs, salt, and pepper; stir, using a wire whisk. Pour over cauliflower; top with breadcrumb mixture. Bake at 375° for 20 minutes. Yield: 8 servings.   Carol Hayes Steckelberg

Swedish Rye Bread

2 packages dry yeast
2 cups warm water (105° to 115°), divided
½ cup sugar
3 tablespoons molasses
2 cups rye flour
4 cups all-purpose flour
½ cup shortening, melted
2 teaspoons salt

Dissolve yeast in 1 cup warm water; let stand 5 minutes. Combine remaining 1 cup water, sugar, and molasses in a large bowl; add yeast mixture, mixing well. Add rye flour, mixing well. Gradually add all-purpose flour. Add shortening and salt, mixing well.

Turn dough out onto a lightly floured surface, and knead until smooth and elastic. Place dough in a well-greased bowl, turning to grease top. Cover and let rise in a warm place (85°), free from drafts, 1 hour or until doubled in bulk.

Punch dough down, and divide in half; shape each half into a loaf. Place in two well-greased 8½- x 4½- x 3-inch loafpans. Cover and let rise in a warm place, free from drafts, 45 minutes or until doubled in bulk. Bake at 375° for 40 minutes or until loaves sound hollow when tapped. Remove from pans, and let cool on wire racks. Yield: 2 loaves.   Peg Zeis McGarvey

Valentine Tarts

2 ounces semisweet chocolate
2 baked 9-inch heart-shaped
  tart shells
2 (3-ounce) packages cream
  cheese, softened
1 cup sifted powdered
  sugar
⅓ cup whipping cream

1 tablespoon Grand Marnier
  or other orange-flavored
  liqueur
½ teaspoon vanilla extract
1 quart fresh strawberries,
  washed and hulled
½ cup seedless raspberry
  jam, melted

Melt chocolate in a small saucepan over low heat. Spread melted chocolate over bottom of each tart shell; set aside.

Beat cream cheese and powdered sugar at medium speed of an electric mixer until smooth. Add cream, liqueur, and vanilla, beating until smooth. Spoon cream cheese mixture over chocolate in tart shells.

Combine strawberries and jam in a large bowl, tossing berries gently to coat. Arrange berries over filling in each tart. Cover and chill thoroughly. Yield: 8 servings.   Jane Rife Field

Watermelon Granite

2½ cups water
2½ cups sugar
2½ cups diced, seeded
  watermelon

½ cup lemon juice
1 teaspoon almond extract

Combine water and sugar in a saucepan; bring to a boil and cook, stirring constantly, 5 minutes or until sugar dissolves. Cook over low heat 5 minutes. Let cool.

Stir in watermelon, lemon juice, and almond extract. Pour mixture into container of an electric blender; process until smooth. Spoon mixture into a 2-quart ring mold; freeze until firm, stirring several times during freezing process.

Unmold onto a serving dish, and cut into slices to serve. Yield: 8 to 10 servings.   Leila Clark Girsch

Appetizers & Beverages

Pre-revolutionary construction lends colonial charm to the Pink House at 21 Chalmers Street in South Carolina. Thought to be one of Charleston's oldest taverns or coffee houses, it has been the source of rest and refreshment for generations of weary travelers.

☆☆☆

Sugar and Spice Pecans

1 egg white	½ teaspoon salt
1 tablespoon butter or margarine, melted	1½ teaspoons ground cinnamon
2 cups pecan halves	¾ teaspoon ground nutmeg
½ cup sugar	¾ teaspoon ground allspice

Beat egg white (at room temperature) until stiff peaks form; fold in butter. Add pecans, tossing gently to coat well.

Combine sugar, salt, cinnamon, nutmeg, and allspice in a small bowl. Sprinkle 2 tablespoons sugar mixture on an ungreased baking sheet. Dredge pecans, ¼ cup at a time, in remaining sugar mixture. Spread pecans on baking sheet, and sprinkle with any remaining sugar mixture. Bake at 300° for 20 minutes, stirring after 10 minutes. Separate pecans with a fork. Let cool. Store in an airtight container. Yield: 2 cups.   Betty Garrett Mansfield

Perennials
The Junior Service League of Gainesville, Georgia

Stuffed Endive

⅔ cup uncooked wild rice	⅓ cup mayonnaise
2 cups water	⅓ cup commercial sour cream
4 heads Belgian endive	
½ cup golden raisins	¼ teaspoon curry powder
⅓ cup chopped pine nuts, toasted	

Wash wild rice in 3 changes of hot water; drain. Combine rice with 2 cups water in a medium saucepan; bring to a boil. Cover, reduce heat to low, and simmer 30 to 45 minutes or until rice is tender and water is absorbed. Fluff rice with a fork, and chill.

Separate endive into leaves. Combine wild rice, raisins, pine nuts, mayonnaise, sour cream, and curry powder; mix well. Stuff endive leaves with rice mixture. Yield: 3 dozen.

Wild Rice, Star of the North
The 1006 Summit Avenue Society
St. Paul, Minnesota

Sun-Dried Tomatoes with Cream Cheese and Basil

1 (8-ounce) package cream
  cheese, softened
48 (¼-inch-thick) slices
  French bread

1 (6-ounce) jar sun-dried
  tomatoes, drained and
  quartered
Small fresh basil leaves

Spread softened cream cheese on one side of each piece of French bread. Top each with tomato quarter, and garnish with fresh basil leaves. Yield: 4 dozen.

California Fresh
The Junior League of Oakland-East Bay, California

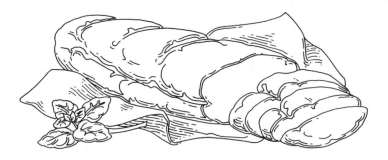

Cheese Bennes

½ cup butter or margarine,
  softened
2 cups (8 ounces) shredded
  sharp Cheddar cheese

1¼ cups all-purpose flour
½ teaspoon salt
½ cup sesame seeds, toasted
⅛ teaspoon red pepper

Cream butter and cheese until smooth. Combine flour, salt, sesame seeds, and red pepper; add to creamed mixture, blending well.

Shape dough into four 1-inch-wide rolls. Roll each in wax paper, and chill several hours. Slice rolls into ¼-inch-thick rounds. Place on lightly greased baking sheets. Bake at 350° for 10 minutes or until lightly browned. Let cool on wire racks. Store in an airtight container. Yield: 10 dozen.   Peggy Simons Cathcart

Charleston Receipts Repeats
The Junior League of Charleston, South Carolina

Savory Cheesecake

1 (10-ounce) package frozen
  chopped spinach, thawed
¼ cup plus 1 tablespoon
  butter or margarine, melted
1⅓ cups fine, dry
  breadcrumbs
3 (8-ounce) packages cream
  cheese, softened
¼ cup whipping cream
½ teaspoon salt
¼ teaspoon ground nutmeg
⅛ teaspoon red pepper

4 eggs
1 cup (4 ounces) shredded
  Gruyère cheese
3 tablespoons minced green
  onions
1 cup finely chopped ham
3 tablespoons butter or
  margarine
½ pound fresh mushrooms,
  chopped
¼ teaspoon salt
¼ teaspoon pepper

Drain spinach well, pressing between paper towels until barely moist. Set spinach aside.

Combine melted butter and breadcrumbs, mixing well. Press into bottom and up sides of a well-greased 9-inch springform pan. Bake at 350° for 8 minutes; let cool.

Combine cream cheese, whipping cream, ½ teaspoon salt, nutmeg, and red pepper in container of an electric blender or food processor; cover and process on low speed 1 minute or until smooth. Add eggs, and process until smooth. Combine Gruyère cheese and half the cream cheese mixture in a medium bowl; set aside. Combine spinach, onions, and ham with remaining cream cheese mixture, stir well; set aside.

Melt 3 tablespoons butter in a medium saucepan; add mushrooms, ¼ teaspoon salt, and pepper. Cook over low heat, stirring frequently, 5 to 8 minutes or until mushrooms are tender. Set aside.

Pour spinach mixture into prepared crust. Layer mushrooms over spinach mixture. Carefully pour remaining Gruyère mixture over mushrooms. Place cheesecake on a baking sheet. Bake at 325° for 1 hour and 15 minutes. Turn oven off, and partially open oven door; leave cheesecake in oven 1 hour. Let cool to room temperature on a wire rack. Yield: 12 servings.

Brunch Basket
The Junior League of Rockford, Illinois

Spicy Lemon Shrimp

1 cup water
1 cup dry white wine
1 bay leaf
1 pound medium-size fresh shrimp, peeled and deveined
1 sweet red pepper, thinly sliced
1 small red onion, thinly sliced and separated into rings
½ cup halved pitted ripe olives, drained
1 lemon, thinly sliced
½ cup lemon juice
½ cup olive oil
1 tablespoon red wine vinegar
1 clove garlic
1 tablespoon chopped fresh parsley
1 tablespoon dry mustard
½ teaspoon salt
¼ teaspoon red pepper
⅛ teaspoon cracked pepper
Lettuce leaves

Combine water, wine, and bay leaf in a 2-quart saucepan; bring to a boil over medium heat. Add shrimp; cook 3 to 5 minutes. Transfer shrimp to a large bowl, using a slotted spoon; reserve liquid in saucepan. Simmer sweet red pepper in liquid 1 minute; drain. Add red pepper, onion, olives, and lemon slices to shrimp. Set aside.

Combine lemon juice, oil, vinegar, garlic, parsley, mustard, salt, red pepper, and cracked pepper in container of an electric blender; process until smooth. Pour marinade over shrimp mixture; toss gently. Cover and refrigerate 8 hours, stirring occasionally.

Drain shrimp mixture, reserving ¼ cup marinade. Spoon shrimp mixture into a lettuce-lined bowl; pour ¼ cup marinade over top. Serve immediately. Yield: 6 servings.

Tidewater on the Half Shell
The Junior League of Norfolk-Virginia Beach, Virginia

Bacon-Marmalade Rounds

4 cups (16 ounces) shredded Cheddar cheese
1 (8-ounce) package cream cheese, softened
3 egg yolks
½ cup orange marmalade
60 melba rounds
½ pound bacon, cooked and crumbled

Combine cheeses and egg yolks in a large bowl; stir well. Stir in marmalade. Spread 1 heaping teaspoon mixture on each melba round. Sprinkle with crumbled bacon. Place on baking sheets, and broil 4 to 5 inches from heat 1 minute or until bubbly. Serve immediately. Yield: 5 dozen.

Uptown Down South
The Junior League of Greenville, South Carolina

Chinese Pot Stickers

¼ **pound ground round**
¼ **pound ground pork**
¼ **pound cabbage, finely shredded**
1 **small zucchini, shredded**
2 **tablespoons soy sauce**
1 **teaspoon grated fresh gingerroot**
½ **teaspoon sesame oil**
¼ **teaspoon salt**
3 **cups all-purpose flour**
1 **cup water**
2 **to 3 tablespoons vegetable oil**
½ **cup water**
Soy sauce
Chili oil
Vinegar

Combine first 8 ingredients in a large bowl, stirring well. Set aside.

Place flour in a large bowl; make a well in center. Add 1 cup water, and stir until mixture forms a stiff dough. Turn dough out onto a lightly floured surface, and knead 8 to 10 times or until smooth and elastic. Cover dough, and chill 30 minutes. Divide dough into thirds. Roll each portion of dough into a 1-inch-wide log. Set 2 logs aside. Slice remaining log into ½-inch-thick slices. Roll each slice on a floured surface to a 3-inch circle. Place one teaspoon of meat mixture in center of each circle. Moisten edges of circles with water. Fold circles, and press edges together with a fork dipped in flour. Repeat procedure with remaining logs and meat mixture.

Place 2 tablespoons vegetable oil in a skillet over medium heat. Add one-third of dumplings, and brown on all sides. Add ½ cup water to dumplings in skillet; cover and simmer 10 minutes or until water evaporates. Add remaining tablespoon vegetable oil to skillet, and cook, uncovered, 5 minutes. Repeat procedure with remaining dumplings and additional vegetable oil and water. Serve with a mixture of soy sauce, chili oil, and vinegar to taste. Yield: 3 dozen.   Tom Chen, M.D.

Chord en Bleu
The Orchestra of Illinois Guild
Glenview, Illinois

Pizza Bread

3 eggs
3 tablespoons grated
  Parmesan cheese
1 tablespoon dried whole
  oregano
2 (16-ounce) loaves frozen
  bread dough, thawed

3 (3½-ounce) packages sliced
  pepperoni
2 cups (8 ounces) shredded
  provolone cheese

Combine first 3 ingredients; beat well. Set aside.

Roll dough to two 14- x 8-inch rectangles. Spread egg mixture evenly over each rectangle, reserving 3 tablespoons. Top each with half of pepperoni and provolone cheese.

Starting at long end, roll up dough, jellyroll fashion; pinch seams and ends of rolls to seal. Place each roll, seam side down, on a large baking sheet. Brush with remaining egg mixture. Bake at 350° for 20 to 30 minutes. Yield: 2 loaves.

The Market Place
The Augusta Junior Woman's Club, Inc.
Augusta, Georgia

Brie en Croûte

½ cup pine nuts
2 tablespoons butter
1 (2.2-pound) round fully
  ripened Brie

11 sheets frozen phyllo
  pastry, thawed
½ cup butter, melted

Sauté pine nuts in 2 tablespoons butter until browned. Drain on paper towels.

Remove rind from top of cheese, cutting to within ¼ inch of outside edges. Arrange pine nuts over top. Brush 2 sheets of phyllo with melted butter; place Brie in center. Fold sides over, and place seam side down on 2 sheets of phyllo brushed with butter. Repeat procedure with remaining phyllo and melted butter.

Place on an ungreased baking sheet; chill 10 minutes. Brush the top with butter; bake at 400° for 15 to 20 minutes. Serve hot with crackers. Yield: one 8-inch cheese round.

San Francisco Encore
The Junior League of San Francisco, California

Dot Kiely's Yankee Meatballs

3 pounds hot Italian sausage
1 pound bulk pork sausage
4 eggs, beaten
1½ cups soft breadcrumbs
3 cups catsup

¾ cup firmly packed brown
    sugar
½ cup wine vinegar
½ cup soy sauce
½ cup strong coffee

Combine sausages, eggs, and breadcrumbs in a large bowl; mix well. Shape into 1-inch balls. Brown half of meatballs on all sides in a nonstick skillet over medium heat. Remove meatballs; drain on paper towels. Repeat with remaining meatballs. Combine catsup and remaining ingredients in a saucepan. Simmer 15 minutes, stirring occasionally. Add meatballs; stir to coat. Simmer 30 minutes. Yield: 12½ dozen.   Brownie Burton McGehee

Vintage Vicksburg
The Junior Auxiliary of Vicksburg, Mississippi

Oriental Meatballs

1 pound ground beef
2 eggs, slightly beaten
1 medium onion, chopped
½ cup seasoned, dry
    breadcrumbs
½ teaspoon salt
½ teaspoon pepper
1 teaspoon soy sauce
1 teaspoon Worcestershire
    sauce

Dash of ground oregano
¼ cup shortening
1 (6-ounce) can pineapple
    chunks, undrained
¾ cup sugar
⅓ cup cider vinegar
2 tablespoons cornstarch
2 tablespoons dark soy sauce

Combine first 9 ingredients; mix well, and shape into 1-inch balls. Brown in hot shortening in a skillet over medium heat; drain well.
   Drain pineapple, reserving juice; add water to make ⅓ cup liquid. Combine ⅓ cup liquid, sugar, vinegar, cornstarch, and dark soy sauce in a saucepan. Cook over medium heat until thickened and bubbly. Add pineapple and meatballs; stir to coat. Serve in a chafing dish. Yield: 3½ dozen.   Sandy McDeed

Culinary Arts & Crafts
The Park Maitland School
Maitland, Florida

Apple Wedge Dip

1 (8-ounce) package cream
  cheese, softened
1 tablespoon mayonnaise
1 (8-ounce) can crushed
  pineapple, drained

1 cup chopped dates
½ cup chopped pecans
2 apples, unpeeled and cut
  into wedges

Combine cream cheese and mayonnaise; beat well. Stir in pineapple, dates, and pecans. Cover and chill. Serve with apple wedges. Yield: about 2 cups.

Sassafras!
The Junior League of Springfield, Missouri

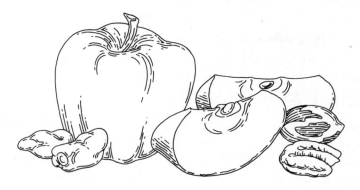

Perpetual Cheese Dip

2 (8-ounce) packages cream
  cheese, softened
3 ounces blue cheese,
  crumbled

5 tablespoons olive oil
5 to 6 tablespoons brandy
1 tablespoon dry mustard

Combine all ingredients; stir well. Store in refrigerator in a small covered crock.

Replenish dip by adding more of each ingredient as the dip is used. Serve with crackers or fresh vegetables. Yield: 3 cups.

Oregon Sampler: Resorts & Recipes
The Assistance League of Corvallis, Oregon

New Year's Day Dip

1 large onion, minced
2 stalks celery, finely
chopped
4 jalapeño peppers, seeded
and finely chopped
½ cup catsup
¼ cup finely chopped green
pepper
1 teaspoon salt
1 teaspoon coarsely ground
pepper
1 teaspoon hot sauce
3 teaspoons chicken-flavored
bouillon granules

¼ teaspoon ground cinnamon
¼ teaspoon ground nutmeg
2 (16-ounce) cans black-eyed
peas, rinsed and drained
1 (14-ounce) can whole
tomatoes, drained and
chopped
1 teaspoon garlic powder
½ cup bacon drippings,
melted
3 tablespoons all-purpose
flour

Combine first 11 ingredients in a saucepan. Cook over low heat until mixture begins to simmer. Stir in black-eyed peas, tomatoes, and garlic powder. Simmer 30 minutes, stirring frequently. Combine bacon drippings and flour. Add to mixture in saucepan. Simmer 10 minutes. Serve dip with tortilla chips. Yield: 4 cups.

Out of Our League, Too
The Junior League of Greensboro, North Carolina

Gullixson Crab

4 (3-ounce) packages cream
cheese, softened
1 small onion, chopped
2 tablespoons butter, softened
1 tablespoon lemon juice
1 tablespoon Worcestershire
sauce

¾ cup chili sauce
1 to 1½ tablespoons prepared
horseradish
½ pound fresh lump
crabmeat, drained
Fresh parsley sprigs

Position knife blade in food processor bowl; add first 5 ingredients. Top with cover, and process until smooth. Shape cheese mixture into a 1-inch-thick circle on a platter. Combine chili sauce and horseradish; pour over cheese round. Top with crabmeat, and garnish with parsley. Serve with crackers. Yield: 10 servings.

Private Collection 2
The Junior League of Palo Alto, California

Caviar Pie

6 hard-cooked eggs
1 (8-ounce) package cream
cheese, softened and
divided
1 (8-ounce) carton
commercial sour cream,
divided
1 medium onion, grated

Dash of hot sauce
1 (3½-ounce) jar black caviar
2 tablespoons fresh lemon
juice
Lemon slices
Fresh parsley sprigs
Paprika

Separate egg whites and egg yolks; set egg yolks aside. Mash egg whites. Combine one-third of cream cheese and one-third of sour cream with egg whites; mix well. Spoon into a 9-inch glass pieplate.

Mash egg yolks. Combine one-third of cream cheese and one-third of sour cream with egg yolks; mix well. Spread egg yolk mixture over egg white mixture.

Combine remaining cream cheese, sour cream, onion, and hot sauce. Spread over egg yolk mixture. Cover and chill.

Place caviar in a strainer, and sprinkle with lemon juice. Drain caviar on paper towels. Spread caviar over pie just before serving. Garnish with lemon slices, parsley, and paprika. Serve with crackers. Yield: 14 to 16 appetizer servings.

Artist's Palate Cookbook
Women's Volunteer Committee, New Orleans Museum of Art
New Orleans, Louisiana

Liptovsky Syr (Liptauer Cheese)

1 (8-ounce) carton small-curd
cottage cheese
½ cup unsalted butter or
margarine, softened
¾ cup commercial sour
cream
1 tablespoon sweet Hungarian
paprika
1 tablespoon finely chopped
onion

2 teaspoons caraway seeds
1 teaspoon dry mustard
1 teaspoon chopped capers
¼ teaspoon salt
Freshly ground black pepper
to taste
3 tablespoons chopped chives

Press cottage cheese through a sieve into a small mixing bowl; set aside. Cream butter in a medium mixing bowl. Add cottage cheese, sour cream, paprika, onion, caraway seeds, mustard, capers, salt, and pepper; beat until smooth. Garnish with chives. Serve with crackers. Yield: 2¼ cups.

Fest of All Worlds
The American Lebanese Christian Women's Society of Illinois
Chicago, Illinois

Smoked Trout Mousse

1 pound smoked trout
2 tablespoons chopped green onions
2 teaspoons chopped fresh dillweed
⅛ teaspoon salt (optional)
¼ teaspoon white pepper
¼ teaspoon ground nutmeg
1½ teaspoons fresh lemon juice

1 tablespoon unflavored gelatin
1½ cups whipping cream
½ cup plain yogurt
Vegetable cooking spray
Fresh dillweed sprigs (optional)
Toast points (optional)

Carefully remove and discard skin and bones from trout; cut trout into 2-inch pieces. Position knife blade in food processor bowl. Combine trout, onions, chopped dillweed, salt, if desired, pepper, nutmeg, and lemon juice in processor bowl. Top with cover; process 30 seconds or until smooth.

Combine gelatin and whipping cream in a small saucepan; let stand 1 minute. Cook over low heat, stirring constantly, until gelatin dissolves; remove from heat. Stir in yogurt. Add gelatin mixture to food processor bowl; top with cover. Process 30 seconds or until mixture is smooth.

Pour trout mixture into a 3-cup mold coated with cooking spray. Refrigerate 4 hours or until firm. Unmold mousse onto a serving plate; garnish with dillweed sprigs, and serve over toast points, if desired. Yield: 3 cups.

Noteworthy
The Ravinia Festival
Highland Park, Illinois

Apricot Slush

2 cups sugar
2 cups boiling water
6 cups water
1 (12-ounce) can frozen
orange juice concentrate
1 (12-ounce) can frozen
lemonade concentrate

1 (25.4-ounce) bottle
apricot-flavored brandy
1 (33.8-ounce) bottle ginger
ale

Dissolve sugar in 2 cups boiling water in a large Dutch oven. Add 6 cups water and remaining ingredients, except ginger ale; stir well, and freeze until firm. Just before serving, partially thaw apricot mixture. Place in punch bowl, and break into chunks. Add ginger ale; stir until slushy. Yield: about 5 quarts.   Dorothy Marchezak

The Great Entertainer Cookbook
The Buffalo Bill Historical Center
Cody, Wyoming

Citrus Frappé

½ cup fresh orange juice
¼ cup fresh lemon juice
½ teaspoon grated lemon
rind

1 cup lemon or lime sherbet
10 ice cubes, crushed
2 tablespoons dry sherry
(optional)

Combine orange juice, lemon juice, and lemon rind in container of an electric blender. Cover and process 5 seconds. Add sherbet and crushed ice. Process 1 minute or until foamy. Add sherry, if desired. Process 5 seconds. Serve immediately. Yield: 3 cups.

Winners
The Junior League of Indianapolis, Indiana

Mint Juleps

12 (4-inch) fresh mint sprigs,
slightly crushed
3 cups water
1 cup sugar

3 gallons crushed ice
3 quarts bourbon
Fresh mint sprigs

Combine crushed mint and water in a saucepan. Bring to a boil, reduce heat, and simmer 15 minutes; remove and discard mint. Add sugar; return to a boil, reduce heat, and simmer 10 minutes. Remove from heat, and set aside.

For each serving, fill a glass with 1 cup crushed ice. Add ¼ cup bourbon and 1 tablespoon mint syrup, stirring gently. Garnish with a fresh mint sprig. Yield: 48 servings.

Mrs. Waldo Lambdin, W. Chandler Mosley

Taste of the South
The Symphony League of Jackson, Mississippi

Irish Cream Liqueur

1¾ cups Irish whiskey
1 (14-ounce) can sweetened condensed milk
1 cup whipping cream
4 eggs

2 tablespoons chocolate syrup
2 teaspoons instant coffee granules
1 teaspoon vanilla extract
½ teaspoon almond extract

Combine all ingredients in container of an electric blender; process until smooth. Serve over ice. Yield: 5 cups.   Jeannie Smith

Lone Star Legacy II
The Junior Forum of Austin, Texas

Mrs. Yancey's Tallahassee Eggnog

15 eggs, separated
1 cup sugar
1½ cups rye whiskey
½ cup dark rum
Pinch of salt

Dash of ground nutmeg
Dash of ground mace
2 cups whipping cream, whipped

Beat egg yolks and sugar in a large mixing bowl. Gradually add liquor, beating well at medium speed of an electric mixer; set aside.

Beat egg whites (at room temperature) in a large bowl until stiff. Gently fold egg whites into egg yolk mixture, blending well. Sprinkle eggnog with salt, nutmeg, and mace. Fold in whipped cream just before serving. Yield: 1½ gallons.   Jack Champion

Best of Friends
Friends of the Maitland Public Library
Maitland, Florida

Cranberry Snap Punch

1 quart cranberry juice
2 cups fresh orange juice
½ cup fresh lemon juice
1 cup pineapple juice
½ cup crushed pineapple,
  drained

1 cup water
⅓ cup sugar
1 teaspoon almond extract

Combine all ingredients in a large container, stirring well; chill. Serve over crushed ice. Yield: 2 quarts.

Palette to Palate
The Junior League of St. Joseph and Albrecht Art Museum
St. Joseph, Missouri

Hot Cranberry Punch

¾ cup firmly packed brown
  sugar
1 teaspoon whole cloves
4 (1½-inch) sticks cinnamon

1½ quarts cranberry juice
  cocktail
1 quart apple juice

Assemble an electric percolator according to manufacturer's instructions. Place sugar, cloves, and cinnamon sticks in filter basket. Combine cranberry juice cocktail and apple juice; add to percolator, and brew. Serve immediately. Yield: 10 cups.   Connie Irwin

Armour Centennial Cookbook
The Armour Centennial Committee
Armour, South Dakota

White Wine Punch

1 (25.4-ounce) bottle white
  wine, chilled
1 (25.4-ounce) bottle
  champagne, chilled

3 cups ginger ale,
  chilled

Combine wine, champagne, and ginger ale in a punch bowl; stir gently. Serve immediately. Yield: 3 quarts.   Terry Routman

Temptations
Presbyterian Day School
Cleveland, Mississippi

Basque Sangría

1 (25.4-ounce) bottle dry red
  wine
1 cup orange juice
¼ cup Cointreau or other
  orange-flavored liqueur

1 cup club soda
1 lemon, thinly sliced
1 orange, thinly sliced

Combine wine, orange juice, and Cointreau in a large pitcher; stir gently. Cover and refrigerate for several hours. Stir in club soda, lemon slices, and orange slices just before serving. Serve over ice. Yield: 1½ quarts.

Bound to Please
The Junior League of Boise, Idaho

No-Hassle Wassail

1 gallon apple cider
2 quarts apricot nectar
3 cups dark rum
1½ cups firmly packed brown
  sugar

¼ cup lemon juice
6 (3-inch) sticks cinnamon
3 small oranges
1½ teaspoons whole cloves

Combine cider, nectar, rum, brown sugar, lemon juice, and cinnamon sticks in a large Dutch oven. Bring to a boil; reduce heat, and simmer, uncovered, 1 hour. Stud oranges with cloves, and add to cider mixture. Serve hot. Yield: 1½ gallons.   Jim Holton

Cooking with Class
Frederick Community College
Frederick, Maryland

Dunedin Junior Service League "Bundles Coffee" Punch

1 gallon strong, hot coffee
5 (3-inch) sticks cinnamon
3 cups whipping cream, whipped and divided
½ gallon coffee ice cream, softened
1¼ cups brandy
⅓ cup sugar
1½ tablespoons vanilla extract

Combine coffee and cinnamon sticks. Let coffee cool. Remove cinnamon sticks, and pour coffee into a punch bowl. Stir in 2¼ cups whipped cream and remaining ingredients. Serve with dollops of remaining whipped cream. Yield: about 24 cups.   Jeanette Hale

Suncoast Seasons
The Dunedin Youth Guild, Inc.
Dunedin, Florida

Velvet Hot Chocolate

½ cup semisweet chocolate morsels
3 cups milk
1 cup half-and-half
½ cup sugar
½ cup light rum
½ cup amaretto
Whipped cream
Cinnamon sticks

Place chocolate in top of a double boiler; bring water to a boil. Reduce heat to low; cook until chocolate melts. Set aside.

Combine milk, half-and-half, and sugar in a saucepan. Scald mixture over medium heat. Gradually add 1 cup milk mixture to melted chocolate, stirring until smooth. Add chocolate mixture to remaining milk mixture. Stir in rum and amaretto. Top each serving with whipped cream, and garnish with a cinnamon stick. Serve immediately. Yield: 5 cups.

Sounds Delicious!
The Volunteer Council of the Tulsa Philharmonic Society, Inc.
Tulsa, Oklahoma

Breads

The Amish community in Tunas, Missouri, sees the beauty of a fine horse and buggy, a well-tended farm, and a simple way of life. Settling in Pennsylvania, Ohio, and the Midwest in the eighteenth century, the Amish preserve simplicity of dress and habits while rejecting worldy concerns.

☆☆☆

Almond-Lime Bread

3 cups all-purpose flour
1 tablespoon baking powder
½ teaspoon baking soda
1 teaspoon salt
1 cup plus 2 tablespoons
  sugar, divided
¾ cup plus 2 tablespoons
  sliced almonds, divided
1 to 2 tablespoons lime rind

1 egg
1 cup milk
¼ cup plus 1 tablespoon
  butter or margarine, melted
  and divided
3 tablespoons lime juice,
  divided
1 tablespoon grated lime rind

Sift together flour, baking powder, soda, salt, and 1 cup sugar in a bowl. Stir in ¾ cup almonds and 1 to 2 tablespoons lime rind. Beat egg and milk; stir in ¼ cup butter and 2 tablespoons lime juice. Add to flour mixture; stir until blended. Pour into a greased 9- x 5- x 3-inch loafpan. Combine remaining sugar, almonds, and butter; spoon over bread. Bake at 350° for 1 hour and 10 minutes. Cool 10 minutes; remove from pan. Drizzle remaining lime juice over bread; sprinkle with remaining lime rind. Let cool completely. Yield: 1 loaf.

The Stenciled Strawberry Cookbook
The Junior League of Albany, New York

Apricot Bread

1¼ cups chopped dried
  apricots
1 cup apricot nectar
½ cup butter, softened
1 cup sugar
2 eggs

2¼ cups all-purpose flour
1 teaspoon baking powder
1 teaspoon baking soda
½ teaspoon salt
¾ cup chopped walnuts

Combine apricots and nectar in a saucepan; bring to a boil. Remove from heat; cover and let stand 1 hour.

Cream butter and sugar; add eggs, and beat well. Combine flour, baking powder, soda, and salt; add to creamed mixture alternately with apricot mixture. Stir in walnuts. Pour into a greased 8-inch loafpan. Bake at 350° for 40 minutes; reduce heat to 325°, and bake for 20 minutes or until a wooden pick inserted in center comes out clean. Cool 10 minutes; remove from pan, and let cool completely on wire rack. Cover and chill 8 hours. Yield: 1 loaf.

Clock Wise Cuisine
The Junior League of Detroit, Michigan

Buttermilk Chocolate Bread with Honey Chocolate Butter

½ cup butter or margarine, softened
1 cup sugar
2 eggs
1 cup buttermilk
1¾ cups all-purpose flour

½ cup cocoa
½ teaspoon baking powder
½ teaspoon baking soda
½ teaspoon salt
⅓ cup chopped walnuts
Honey Chocolate Butter

Cream ½ cup butter; gradually add sugar, beating well at medium speed of an electric mixer. Add eggs, one at a time, beating after each addition. Stir in buttermilk. Combine flour and next 4 ingredients; add to creamed mixture, mixing well. Fold in walnuts.

Pour batter into a greased 9- x 5- x 3-inch loafpan. Bake at 350° for 1 hour or until a wooden pick inserted in center comes out clean. Cool in pan 15 minutes; remove from pan, and let cool completely on wire rack. Serve with Honey Chocolate Butter. Yield: 1 loaf.

Honey Chocolate Butter

½ cup butter or margarine, softened

2 tablespoons chocolate syrup
2 tablespoons honey

Combine all ingredients; beat until light and fluffy. Yield: 1 cup.

First There Must Be Food
Northwestern Memorial Hospital
Chicago, Illinois

Cracklin' Cornbread

¼ cup bacon drippings
2 cups cornmeal
2 teaspoons baking soda
1 teaspoon salt

2 eggs, beaten
2 cups buttermilk
¾ cup cracklings

Heat drippings in a 10-inch cast-iron skillet until hot. Combine dry ingredients; stir in eggs and buttermilk. Add cracklings and hot drippings; mix well. Pour batter into hot skillet. Bake at 450° for 20 to 25 minutes. Yield: 8 servings.   Patsy Spiers Mercer

Perennials
The Junior Service League of Gainesville, Georgia

Herbed Cheese Bread

1 (1-pound) round loaf
  sourdough or French bread
½ cup butter or margarine,
  melted
1 tablespoon chopped fresh
  parsley

1 teaspoon minced onion
1 teaspoon poppy seeds
8 ounces Monterey Jack
  cheese, thinly sliced

Score bread in a diamond design, cutting to, but not through, bottom of bread. Combine butter, parsley, onion, and poppy seeds. Place cheese slices in slits in bread. Drizzle butter mixture over bread. Wrap bread in aluminum foil. Place on a baking sheet, and bake at 350° for 15 minutes. Uncover and bake an additional 15 minutes. Serve immediately. Yield: 1 loaf.

Private Collection 2
The Junior League of Palo Alto, California

Cranberry Festive Bread

4 cups all-purpose flour
1 cup sugar
1 teaspoon baking powder
1 teaspoon baking soda
¼ teaspoon salt
1 cup buttermilk
¾ cup vegetable oil
3 eggs, beaten

2 teaspoons grated orange
  rind
2 cups fresh or frozen
  cranberries, thawed
1 cup chopped dates
1 cup walnuts, chopped
½ cup sugar
½ cup orange juice

Combine first 5 ingredients in a bowl. Combine buttermilk, oil, eggs, and orange rind; stir well. Add to dry ingredients; beat until smooth. Fold in cranberries, dates, and walnuts. (Batter will be thick.) Pour batter into a greased 10-inch tube pan. Bake at 350° for 1 hour or until a wooden pick inserted in center comes out clean. Cool in pan 10 minutes. Remove from pan; let cool to touch.

Pierce bread at 1-inch intervals, using a wooden pick. Combine ½ cup sugar and orange juice; spoon half over bread. Invert bread, and repeat piercing and glazing procedure. Invert again. Yield: one 10-inch loaf.   Mrs. William M. Hendry

Acornucopia
The Valley Hospital Auxiliary
Ridgewood, New Jersey

Cranberry Coffee Cake

½ cup butter or margarine
1 cup sugar
2 eggs
2 cups all-purpose flour
1 teaspoon baking powder
1 teaspoon baking soda
½ teaspoon salt
1 (8-ounce) carton
   commercial sour cream
1 teaspoon almond extract
1 (16-ounce) can whole
   cranberry sauce
½ cup chopped pecans
Glaze (recipe follows)

Cream butter and sugar, beating at medium speed of an electric mixer until well blended. Add eggs, one at a time, beating well after each addition.

Combine flour, baking powder, soda, and salt; add to creamed mixture alternately with sour cream, beginning and ending with flour mixture. Stir in almond extract.

Spoon one-third of batter into a greased and floured 10-inch tube pan. Spread one-third of cranberry sauce over batter. Repeat layers twice, ending with cranberry sauce. Sprinkle with pecans. Bake at 350° for 1 hour or until a wooden pick inserted in center comes out clean. Let stand 5 minutes; invert cake onto a serving plate, and drizzle with glaze. Yield: one 10-inch coffee cake.

Glaze

¾ cup sifted powdered sugar
1 tablespoon warm water
½ teaspoon almond extract

Combine powdered sugar, water, and almond extract in a small mixing bowl; mix well. Yield: ¼ cup.   Pam Robinson

A Great Taste of Arkansas
The Arkansas Sesquicentennial
Pine Bluff, Arkansas

Sinful Sour Cream Coffee Cake

1 cup butter or margarine, softened	2 cups all-purpose flour
2 cups sugar	1 teaspoon baking powder
2 eggs	½ teaspoon salt
1 (8-ounce) carton commercial sour cream	1 cup chopped pecans
	⅓ cup sugar
1 teaspoon vanilla extract	2 teaspoons ground cinnamon

Cream butter; gradually add 2 cups sugar, beating until light and fluffy. Add eggs, one at a time, beating well after each addition. Fold in sour cream and vanilla. Combine flour, baking powder, and salt; fold into creamed mixture. Pour half of batter into a greased and floured 10-inch springform pan. (Batter will be thin in pan.)

Combine pecans, ⅓ cup sugar, and cinnamon in a bowl. Sprinkle three-fourths of pecan mixture over batter in pan. Top with remaining batter. Sprinkle with remaining pecan mixture. Bake at 325° for 1 hour and 10 minutes or until a wooden pick inserted in center comes out clean. Let cool on a wire rack 10 minutes. Remove sides of pan; let cool completely. Yield: one 10-inch coffee cake.

Unbearably Good!
The Junior Service League of Americus, Georgia

Butter Dips

2 cups all-purpose flour	½ cup cold butter or margarine, divided
1 tablespoon baking powder	
1 teaspoon salt	1 cup milk

Position knife blade in food processor bowl. Add flour, baking powder, salt, and ¼ cup cold butter. Process until mixture resembles coarse meal. Add milk; process until dry ingredients are moistened.

Turn dough out onto a floured surface, and knead lightly 4 or 5 times. Melt ¼ cup butter in an 8-inch cast-iron skillet. Roll dough to ½-inch thickness; cut with a 2-inch biscuit cutter. Coat biscuits with melted butter, and place in skillet with sides touching. Bake at 425° for 25 minutes. Yield: 1 dozen.

Gulfshore Delights
The Junior League of Fort Myers, Florida

Sweet Potato Biscuits

2 cups cooked, hot, mashed
  sweet potatoes
½ cup shortening
¾ cup sugar
¼ cup plus 2 tablespoons
  buttermilk

3 to 4 cups all-purpose flour
1 tablespoon plus 1 teaspoon
  baking powder
½ teaspoon baking soda
1 teaspoon salt

Combine sweet potatoes and shortening, stirring until shortening melts. Add sugar and buttermilk, stirring well. Add flour, baking powder, soda, and salt, stirring until blended.

Roll dough to ½-inch thickness; cut with a 2-inch biscuit cutter. Place biscuits on ungreased baking sheets. Bake at 450° for 8 to 10 minutes or until biscuits are lightly browned. Yield: 3 dozen.

Mary Esther Herget

Celebration: A Taste of Arkansas
The Sevier County Cookbook Committee
Lockesburg, Arkansas

Morning Glory Muffins

2 cups all-purpose flour
2 teaspoons baking soda
½ teaspoon salt
2 teaspoons ground cinnamon
1¼ cups sugar
1½ cups finely shredded
  carrot
2 large cooking apples,
  peeled, cored, and shredded

¾ cup flaked coconut
½ cup raisins
½ cup chopped pecans
1 cup vegetable oil
3 eggs, slightly beaten
½ teaspoon vanilla extract

Combine flour, soda, salt, and cinnamon in a large bowl. Stir in sugar. Add carrot, apples, coconut, raisins, and pecans. Stir well. Make a well in center of mixture. Combine oil, eggs, and vanilla; add to dry ingredients, stirring just until moistened. Spoon batter into greased muffin pans, filling three-fourths full. Bake at 375° for 18 to 20 minutes or until golden brown. Yield: 2 dozen.

Taste the Seasons
Woodside-Atherton Auxiliary to Children's Hospital at Stanford
Menlo Park, California

Lemon-Dipped Blueberry Muffins

1¾ cups all-purpose flour
½ cup sugar
2½ teaspoons baking powder
¾ teaspoon salt
1 egg, slightly beaten
¾ cup milk
⅓ cup vegetable oil
1 cup fresh or frozen
blueberries, thawed

2 tablespoons sugar
2 teaspoons grated lemon
rind
2 tablespoons butter or
margarine, melted
¼ teaspoon lemon juice
Sugar

Combine flour, ½ cup sugar, baking powder, and salt in a large bowl; make a well in center of mixture. Combine egg, milk, and oil; add liquid mixture to dry ingredients, stirring just until dry ingredients are moistened. Set aside.

Toss blueberries with 2 tablespoons sugar and lemon rind; fold berries into batter. Spoon batter into greased or paper-lined muffin pans, filling two-thirds full. Bake at 400° for 18 minutes or until golden brown. Remove from pans; set aside.

Combine melted butter and lemon juice. Dip tops of warm muffins in butter mixture, then in sugar. Yield: 12 muffins.

To Market, To Market
The Junior League of Owensboro, Kentucky

Lemon Muffins

½ cup butter or margarine,
softened
½ cup sugar
2 eggs, separated
¼ cup lemon juice

1 teaspoon grated lemon rind
1 cup all-purpose flour
1 teaspoon baking powder
Powdered sugar

Cream butter; gradually add ½ cup sugar, beating until light and fluffy. Add egg yolks, lemon juice, and rind; beat well. Add flour and baking powder; beat well.

Beat egg whites (at room temperature) until stiff peaks form. Fold egg whites into batter. Fill greased miniature muffin pans three-fourths full. Bake at 350° for 15 minutes. Remove from pans; dip tops of warm muffins in powdered sugar. Yield: 2½ dozen.

Uptown Down South
The Junior League of Greenville, South Carolina

Hotel Peabody Vanilla Muffins

2 cups sugar
2 eggs, beaten
4 cups all-purpose flour
1 tablespoon plus 1 teaspoon
  baking powder

2 cups milk
½ cup butter, melted
1 tablespoon vanilla extract

Combine sugar and eggs, beating well at medium speed of an electric mixer.

Combine flour and baking powder. Add to sugar mixture alternately with milk, beginning and ending with flour mixture, and beating well after each addition. Stir in butter and vanilla.

Spoon into greased muffin pans, filling two-thirds full. Bake at 400° for 20 minutes. Remove muffins from pans immediately. Yield: 3 dozen.   Hazel Dakin, Ginger Pepper

Temptations
Presbyterian Day School
Cleveland, Mississippi

Cheddar Corn Muffins

2½ cups cornmeal
¾ cup all-purpose flour
1 tablespoon baking powder
1½ teaspoons salt
2¼ cups shredded sharp
  Cheddar cheese

2¼ cups buttermilk
¾ cup milk
3 eggs, beaten
¼ cup plus 2 tablespoons
  vegetable oil

Combine first 5 ingredients in a bowl; set aside. Combine buttermilk, milk, eggs, and oil, mixing well. Add to dry ingredients; stir until moistened. Spoon into greased and floured muffin pans, filling two-thirds full. Bake at 425° for 20 minutes. Yield: 2 dozen.

Polly Simms

Offerings Past and Present
St. Luke's Episcopal Church Women
Salisbury, North Carolina

Skipper's Bread

2 cups boiling water
1 cup cracked wheat
3 packages dry yeast
1 cup warm water (105° to 115°)
2 cups milk
1 cup unbleached flour

⅓ cup sugar
¼ cup vegetable oil
¼ cup molasses
2 tablespoons salt
2 tablespoons anise seeds
1 (5-pound) bag unbleached flour

Combine boiling water and cracked wheat; set aside.

Dissolve yeast in 1 cup warm water in a large mixing bowl. Stir in cracked wheat mixture, milk, and next 6 ingredients. Beat at medium speed of an electric mixer 5 minutes. Stir in enough unbleached flour to make a stiff dough.

Turn dough out onto a lightly floured surface. Knead and add flour until smooth and elastic. Shape dough into a ball, and place in a well-greased bowl, turning to grease top. Cover and let rise in a warm place (85°), free from drafts, 1 hour or until doubled in bulk.

Punch dough down; shape into a ball. Cover and let rise in a warm place, free from drafts, about 40 minutes or until doubled in bulk.

Punch dough down; turn out onto a lightly floured surface, and knead lightly 4 or 5 times. Divide dough into fifths; shape each portion into a loaf. Place in five greased 9- x 5- x 3-inch loafpans. Cover and let rise in a warm place, free from drafts, 40 minutes or until doubled in bulk.

Bake at 325° for 50 minutes to 1 hour or until loaves sound hollow when tapped. Remove from pans, and let cool on wire racks. Yield: 5 loaves.

Cornsilk
The Junior League of Sioux City, Iowa

Refrigerator White Bread

2 packages dry yeast
1 cup cold water
1 cup boiling water
1 cup butter or margarine,
  softened

⅔ cup sugar
1½ teaspoons salt
3 eggs, beaten
8 cups bread flour, divided

Dissolve yeast in cold water. Combine boiling water, butter, sugar, and salt in a bowl; mix well. Cool to 105° to 115°. Add eggs and yeast mixture to butter mixture. Stir in 6½ cups flour; mix well. Cover and refrigerate 8 hours.

Punch dough down. Turn dough out onto a floured surface. Add 1½ cups flour, and knead 8 to 10 minutes or until smooth and elastic. Place in a well-greased bowl, turning to grease top. Cover and let rise in a warm place (85°), free from drafts, 1 hour or until doubled in bulk.

Punch dough down, and divide into thirds; shape each into a loaf. Place in three well-greased 9- x 5- x 3-inch loafpans. Cover and let rise in a warm place, free from drafts, 50 minutes to 1 hour or until doubled in bulk. Bake at 350° for 30 minutes or until loaves sound hollow when tapped. Remove from pan, and let cool on wire racks. Yield: 3 loaves.

Palette to Palate
The Junior League of St. Joseph and Albrecht Art Museum
St. Joseph, Missouri

Wild Rice and Three-Grain Bread

2 cups milk
1 package dry yeast
⅓ cup warm water (105° to
  115°)
½ cup honey
2 tablespoons butter or
  margarine
2 teaspoons salt
½ cup regular oats, uncooked

½ cup rye flour
2 cups whole wheat flour
4 cups all-purpose flour,
  divided
1 cup cooked wild rice
1 egg, beaten
1 tablespoon water
½ cup sunflower kernels

Scald milk; let cool. Dissolve yeast in ⅓ cup warm water in a large bowl. Add milk, honey, butter, and salt. Stir in oats, rye flour, whole wheat flour, and 2 cups all-purpose flour. Stir in wild rice. Cover and let rest 15 minutes. Gradually add enough remaining flour to make a stiff dough. Turn dough out onto a lightly floured surface, and knead 8 to 10 minutes or until smooth and elastic. Place in a well-greased bowl, turning to grease top. Cover and let rise in a warm place (85°), free from drafts, 2 hours or until doubled in bulk.

Punch dough down, and divide in half; shape each half into a loaf. Place in two greased 9- x 5- x 3-inch loafpans. Cover and let rise in a warm place, free from drafts, 45 minutes or until dough is doubled in bulk. Combine egg and 1 tablespoon water; beat well. Brush loaves with egg mixture. Sprinkle with sunflower kernels. Bake at 375° for 45 minutes or until loaves sound hollow when tapped. Remove from pans, and let cool on wire racks. Yield: 2 loaves.

Wild Rice, Star of the North
The 1006 Summit Avenue Society
St. Paul, Minnesota

Anadama Bread

1 tablespoon yellow cornmeal
¾ cup boiling water
½ cup yellow cornmeal
¼ cup molasses
3 tablespoons butter or
  margarine, softened
1½ teaspoons salt

1 package dry yeast
¼ cup warm water (105° to
  115°)
1 egg
2¾ cups all-purpose flour,
  divided

Grease a 9- x 5- x 3-inch loafpan. Sprinkle with 1 tablespoon cornmeal. Set aside. Combine boiling water and next 4 ingredients; stir well. Let cool. Dissolve yeast in warm water. Add yeast mixture, egg, and 1¼ cups flour to cornmeal mixture; beat at medium speed of an electric mixer 2 minutes. Stir in enough remaining flour to make a soft dough. Place in prepared pan. Cover and let rise in a warm place, free from drafts, 1 hour or until doubled in bulk. Bake at 375° for 50 to 55 minutes or until loaf sounds hollow when tapped. Remove bread from pan immediately, and let cool on a wire rack. Yield: 1 loaf.   Vivian Storey

Flavors of Cape Cod
The Thornton W. Burgess Society
East Sandwich, Massachusetts

Cream Cheese Braids

1 (8-ounce) carton
commercial sour cream,
scalded
½ cup sugar
½ cup butter or margarine
1 teaspoon salt
2 packages dry yeast

½ cup warm water (105° to
115°)
2 eggs, beaten
4 cups all-purpose flour
Filling (recipe follows)
Glaze (recipe follows)

Combine scalded sour cream, sugar, butter, and salt; mix well, and let cool to lukewarm. Dissolve yeast in warm water in a large mixing bowl; let stand 5 minutes. Stir in sour cream mixture and eggs. Gradually stir in flour (dough will be soft). Cover tightly, and chill 8 hours.

Divide dough into 4 equal portions. Working with one portion at a time, turn out onto a heavily floured surface, and knead 4 or 5 times. Roll to a 12- x 8-inch rectangle. Spread one-fourth of filling over rectangle, leaving a ½-inch margin around edges. Roll up jellyroll fashion, beginning at long side. Firmly pinch edge and ends to seal. Place roll, seam side down, on a greased baking sheet. Repeat procedure with remaining dough and filling.

Make 6 equally spaced x-shaped cuts across top of each loaf. Cover and let rise in a warm place (85°), free from drafts, 1 hour or until doubled in bulk. Bake at 375° for 15 to 20 minutes. Spread glaze over warm loaves. Yield: four 12-inch loaves.

Filling

2 (8-ounce) packages cream
cheese, softened
¾ cup sugar

1 egg, beaten
2 teaspoons vanilla extract
⅛ teaspoon salt

Combine all ingredients. Beat at high speed of an electric mixer until blended. Yield: about 2 cups.

Glaze

2 cups sifted powdered sugar
¼ cup milk

2 teaspoons vanilla extract

Combine all ingredients, stirring well. Yield: about ¾ cup.

According to Taste
The Service League of Lufkin, Texas

Philadelphia Sticky Buns

⅔ cup butter or margarine
½ cup sugar
½ cup milk
1 teaspoon salt
2 packages dry yeast
½ cup warm water (105° to 115°)
4 eggs, beaten
6 to 6½ cups all-purpose flour, divided
¼ cup butter or margarine, softened

⅔ cup sugar
1 teaspoon ground cinnamon
1 cup raisins
1½ cups firmly packed brown sugar
1 cup light corn syrup
½ cup butter or margarine
1 cup coarsely chopped pecans

Combine ⅔ cup butter, ½ cup sugar, milk, and salt in a saucepan. Cook over medium heat until butter melts. Let cool to lukewarm (105° to 115°). Dissolve yeast in warm water in a large bowl; let stand 5 minutes. Add butter mixture, eggs, and 2 cups flour. Beat mixture until smooth. Gradually stir in enough remaining flour to make a soft dough.

Turn dough out onto a lightly floured surface, and knead 5 minutes or until smooth and elastic. Place in a well-greased bowl, turning to grease top. Cover and let rise in a warm place (85°), free from drafts, 1 hour or until doubled in bulk.

Punch dough down; turn out onto a lightly floured surface, and knead 4 or 5 times. Let dough rest 5 minutes. Divide dough in half. Roll each half to a 15- x 8-inch rectangle on a lightly floured surface. Spread 2 tablespoons softened butter on each rectangle. Combine ⅔ cup sugar and cinnamon. Sprinkle half over dough. Sprinkle half of raisins over dough. Roll up dough, jellyroll fashion, starting with long side; pinch seam to seal. Cut roll into 12 equal slices. Repeat procedure with remaining half of dough.

Combine brown sugar, corn syrup, and ½ cup butter in a saucepan. Simmer 2 minutes. Spoon evenly into two 9-inch square baking pans. Sprinkle each with ½ cup pecans. Place 12 slices, cut side down, in each pan. Cover and let rise in a warm place 1 hour or until doubled in bulk. Bake at 375° for 25 minutes. Invert onto serving platters, and let stand 5 minutes. Remove pans. Yield: 2 dozen.

Philadelphia Homestyle
The Norwood-Fontbonne Academy Home and School
Philadelphia, Pennsylvania

Orange Rolls

1 package dry yeast
¼ cup warm water (105° to 115°)
½ cup commercial sour cream
¼ cup plus 2 tablespoons butter, melted
2 eggs
¼ cup sugar
1 teaspoon salt
3½ cups all-purpose flour, divided
2 tablespoons butter or margarine, melted
¾ cup sugar
2 tablespoons grated orange rind

Dissolve yeast in warm water in a large mixing bowl; let stand 5 minutes. Add sour cream, ¼ cup plus 2 tablespoons melted butter, eggs, ¼ cup sugar, and salt; mix well. Add 2 cups flour, mixing well. Gradually stir in enough remaining flour to make a soft dough.

Turn dough out onto a lightly floured surface, and knead 8 to 10 times or until smooth and elastic. Place in a well-greased bowl, turning to grease top. Cover and let rise in a warm place (85°), free from drafts, 2 hours or until doubled in bulk

Punch dough down; turn out onto a lightly floured surface, and knead 10 to 15 times. Divide dough in half; roll half of dough to a 12-inch circle. Brush circle with 2 tablespoons melted butter; cut into 12 wedges. Combine ¾ cup sugar and orange rind. Sprinkle half of sugar mixture over 12 wedges. Roll up each wedge, beginning at wide end. Place on a greased baking sheet, point side down. Repeat procedure with remaining half of dough, melted butter, and sugar mixture.

Cover and let rise in a warm place (85°), free from drafts, 1 hour or until rolls are doubled in bulk. Bake at 325° for 16 to 18 minutes. Yield: 2 dozen.   Anne Barrett

Acornucopia
The Valley Hospital Auxiliary
Ridgewood, New Jersey

Cakes

The Golden Gate Bridge, with its distinctive design and orange-red color, spans the gap in the hills where the ocean meets the bay. Extending almost two miles, the bridge forms a link between the west coast city of San Francisco and Marin County to the north.

☆☆☆

Hot Fudge Sundae Cake

1 cup all-purpose flour
¾ cup sugar
2 tablespoons cocoa
2 teaspoons baking powder
¼ teaspoon salt
½ cup milk
2 tablespoons vegetable oil

1 teaspoon vanilla extract
1 cup chopped pecans
1 cup firmly packed brown sugar
¼ cup cocoa
1¾ cups hot water
Ice cream

Combine first 5 ingredients in an ungreased 9-inch square pan. Add milk, oil, and vanilla; mix well. Stir in pecans. Sprinkle with brown sugar and ¼ cup cocoa. Pour hot water over batter. Bake at 350° for 40 minutes. Cool in pan 15 minutes. Spoon into dessert dishes, and top with ice cream. Yield: 9 servings.   Jo Anderson

Philadelphia Homestyle Cookbook
The Norwood-Fontbonne Academy Home and School
Philadelphia, Pennsylvania

Spiced Cake with Baked Icing

½ cup butter or margarine, softened
1 cup firmly packed brown sugar
1 egg
2 eggs, separated
1⅓ cups all-purpose flour
½ teaspoon baking powder

½ teaspoon baking soda
¼ teaspoon salt
½ teaspoon ground cinnamon
½ teaspoon ground cloves
½ cup buttermilk
½ cup firmly packed brown sugar
¼ cup chopped pecans

Cream butter and 1 cup sugar in a bowl. Add egg and 2 egg yolks; beat well. Sift together flour and next 5 ingredients. Add to creamed mixture alternately with buttermilk, mixing after each addition. Pour into a greased and floured 9-inch square baking pan.

Beat 2 egg whites (at room temperature) until stiff peaks form. Add brown sugar; beat well. Spread over batter. Bake at 350° for 25 minutes. Sprinkle with pecans; bake an additional 10 minutes. Cool. Cut into squares. Yield: 9 servings.   Gertrude B. Locke

Mountain Laurel Encore
The Bell County Extension Homemakers
Pineville, Kentucky

Oatmeal Cake

1 cup quick-cooking oats,
   uncooked
1⅓ cups boiling water
½ cup butter or margarine,
   softened
1 cup sugar
1 cup firmly packed brown
   sugar

2 eggs
1 teaspoon vanilla extract
1¾ cups all-purpose flour
1 teaspoon baking soda
½ teaspoon salt
1 teaspoon ground cinnamon
Dash of ground nutmeg
Topping (recipe follows)

Combine oats and water; let stand 20 minutes.

Cream butter and sugars. Add eggs, one at a time, beating well after each addition. Stir in vanilla.

Combine flour, soda, salt, cinnamon, and nutmeg. Add to creamed mixture, mixing well. Add oatmeal mixture, and beat well.

Pour batter into a greased 13- x 9- x 2-inch baking pan. Bake at 350° for 35 minutes. Remove from oven; spread topping over cake. Place under broiler, and broil until topping is browned. Yield: one 13- x 9- x 2-inch cake.

Topping

½ cup butter or margarine,
   softened
1 cup firmly packed brown
   sugar
¼ cup evaporated milk

1 teaspoon vanilla extract
1 cup chopped pecans
1 (3½-ounce) can flaked
   coconut

Cream butter and brown sugar. Add milk and vanilla, beating well. Stir in chopped pecans and coconut. Yield: enough for one 13- x 9- x 2-inch cake.

Ellie Gaver

Not By Bread Alone
Holy Trinity Episcopal Church
Charleston, South Carolina

Golden Raisin Carrot Cake

2 cups sugar
1 cup vegetable oil
4 eggs
1 teaspoon vanilla extract
2 cups all-purpose flour
1 teaspoon baking soda
1 teaspoon salt
2 teaspoons ground cinnamon
¼ teaspoon ground nutmeg
3 cups grated carrots
1 cup chopped pecans
1 cup golden raisins
Cream Cheese Frosting

Combine sugar and vegetable oil in a large mixing bowl; beat well at medium speed of an electric mixer. Add eggs, one at a time, beating well after each addition. Add vanilla; mix well.

Combine flour, soda, salt, cinnamon, and nutmeg. Add to creamed mixture, mixing well. Stir in grated carrots, chopped pecans, and raisins.

Pour batter into a greased and floured 13- x 9- x 2-inch baking pan. Bake at 350° for 45 to 50 minutes or until a wooden pick inserted in center comes out clean. Let cake cool completely. Spread Cream Cheese Frosting over cake. Yield: 15 servings.

Cream Cheese Frosting

¼ cup butter or margarine, softened
1 (8-ounce) package cream cheese, softened
1 teaspoon vanilla extract
1 (16-ounce) package powdered sugar, sifted
½ cup chopped pecans

Cream butter and cream cheese at medium speed of an electric mixer. Add vanilla; beat well. Gradually add sugar, beating until mixture is smooth and well blended. Stir in chopped pecans. Yield: enough for one 13- x 9- x 2-inch cake.

Putting on the Grits
The Junior League of Columbia, South Carolina

Black Forest Cake

1 (16½-ounce) can pitted dark sweet cherries
2 tablespoons cornstarch
¼ cup water
1 cup butter or margarine, softened
2 cups sugar
4 eggs
2 cups all-purpose flour, sifted
¼ teaspoon salt
1½ teaspoons baking soda
⅔ cup buttermilk
1 teaspoon vanilla extract

3 (1-ounce) squares unsweetened chocolate, grated
⅔ cup boiling water
Chocolate Butter Cream Frosting
1 tablespoon plus 1 teaspoon kirsch
Whipped Cream Frosting
1 (1-ounce) square semisweet chocolate, grated or shaved (optional)
Maraschino cherries (optional)

Drain liquid from pitted cherries into a small saucepan. Set cherries aside. Bring liquid to a boil over medium heat. Combine cornstarch and ¼ cup water, stirring until smooth. Pour cornstarch mixture slowly into boiling juice, stirring constantly until mixture is thickened and bubbly. Add pitted cherries. Cool. Set aside.

Cream butter and sugar, beating at medium speed of an electric mixer until light and fluffy. Add eggs, one at a time, beating well after each addition.

Combine flour and salt. Mix soda with buttermilk, and add to creamed mixture alternately with flour mixture, beginning and ending with flour mixture. Mix well after each addition. Stir in vanilla extract.

Melt unsweetened chocolate in boiling water, stirring until smooth. Blend melted chocolate into batter.

Pour batter into 3 greased and floured 9-inch round cakepans. Bake at 350° for 25 to 30 minutes or until a wooden pick inserted in center comes out clean. Cool in pans 10 minutes; remove layers from pans, and let cool completely on wire racks.

Spoon Chocolate Butter Cream Frosting into cookie press fitted with a plain ½-inch nozzle. Starting at outer edge of bottom cake layer, form 3 rings of frosting, working towards center, leaving 1½ inches between each ring. (Rings should be about 1-inch high.) Chill. Fill in between rings with reserved cherry mixture.

Place second layer gently on top of cherries, and punch holes in layer with a wooden pick. Sprinkle with kirsch. Spread one-third of Whipped Cream Frosting over second layer.

Place third layer gently on top of whipped cream. Spread top and sides with remaining Whipped Cream Frosting, reserving a small amount for garnish. Garnish with whipped cream rosettes and, if desired, grated chocolate and maraschino cherries. Refrigerate until ready to serve. Yield: one 3-layer cake.

Chocolate Butter Cream Frosting

¼ cup butter or margarine, softened
2 cups sifted powdered sugar
1 egg white
½ teaspoon vanilla extract
1½ ounces semisweet chocolate, melted

Cream butter at medium speed of an electric mixer; add sugar, egg white, vanilla, and chocolate, beating until fluffy. Yield: enough for one 3-layer cake.

Whipped Cream Frosting

3 cups whipping cream
½ cup sifted powdered sugar
¼ cup kirsch

Beat cream in a large mixing bowl at high speed of an electric mixer until foamy; gradually add powdered sugar and kirsch, beating until stiff peaks form. Yield: enough for one 3-layer cake.

Temptations
The Junior League of Lansing, Michigan

Snow White Coconut Cake

1 large fresh coconut	3 cups sifted cake flour
1 cup butter or margarine, softened	½ teaspoon baking powder
½ cup shortening	1 cup milk
3 cups sugar, sifted	½ teaspoon vanilla extract
5 eggs	½ teaspoon lemon extract
	Boiled Frosting

Using a strong ice pick, pierce the three shiny black dots that indicate the soft areas at the top of the coconut. Drain and set coconut milk aside.

Wrap the coconut in a heavy cloth. Give the coconut a few firm blows with a hammer until the shell cracks and falls apart. Remove meat from the coconut shell. Using a vegetable peeler, remove the brown skin of the coconut. Cut coconut meat into pieces.

Position shredding disc in food processor bowl; top with cover. Place coconut pieces in food chute and shred. Remove the shredded coconut, and store in refrigerator.

Cream butter and shortening; gradually add sugar, beating well at medium speed of an electric mixer. Add eggs, one at a time, beating well after each addition.

Combine flour and baking powder; add to creamed mixture alternately with milk, beginning and ending with flour mixture. Mix after each addition. Stir in vanilla and lemon flavorings.

Pour batter into 3 greased and floured 9-inch round cakepans. Bake at 375° for 30 minutes or until a wooden pick inserted in center comes out clean. Cool in pans 10 minutes; remove layers from pans, and let cool completely on wire racks.

Prick each layer at 1-inch intervals with a wooden pick; pour ¼ cup reserved coconut milk over each layer, reserving any remaining coconut milk for other uses. Stack layers with wax paper separating each layer; cover tightly. Store in refrigerator overnight. Spread Boiled Frosting between layers and on top and sides of chilled cake. Sprinkle with shredded coconut. Yield: one 3-layer cake.

Boiled Frosting

3 cups sugar	1 tablespoon light corn syrup
4 egg whites	¼ teaspoon salt
⅔ cup water	½ teaspoon vanilla extract

Combine first 5 ingredients in top of a large double boiler. Beat at low speed of an electric mixer 30 seconds or just until blended.

Place over boiling water; beat at high speed 10 minutes or until stiff peaks form. Remove from heat. Add vanilla; beat 2 minutes or until frosting is thick enough to spread. Yield: enough for one 3-layer cake.   Patti Jones Hall

Temptations
The Junior Service League of Rome, Georgia

Apple Cake

3 cups all-purpose flour
1¼ teaspoons baking soda
1 teaspoon salt
2 cups sugar
1½ cups vegetable oil
2 eggs, beaten
2 tablespoons vanilla extract

½ teaspoon lemon juice
3 cups peeled, chopped
  cooking apples
1½ cups chopped pecans,
  toasted
Glaze (recipe follows)

Combine flour, soda, and salt; mix well, and set aside.

Combine sugar, oil, eggs, vanilla, and lemon juice; beat 2 minutes at medium speed of an electric mixer. Add flour mixture; beat at low speed just until blended. Fold in apples and pecans.

Spoon batter into a greased and floured 10-inch tube pan. Bake at 325° for 1 hour and 20 minutes or until a wooden pick inserted in center comes out clean. Cool in pan 10 minutes. Remove from pan; immediately drizzle glaze over warm cake. Yield: one 10-inch cake.

Glaze

1 cup sugar
1 cup firmly packed light
  brown sugar
¼ cup butter or margarine

1 teaspoon cream of tartar
1 teaspoon ground cinnamon
1 teaspoon ground nutmeg
½ cup milk

Combine all ingredients, except milk, in a heavy saucepan. Stir in milk. Bring mixture to a full boil, and cook 2 minutes, stirring constantly. Let cool to lukewarm. Yield: 1½ cups.

According to Taste
The Junior Service League of Lufkin, Texas

L. S. Ayres Buttermilk Cake

1 cup shortening
3 cups sugar
1 tablespoon grated lemon
   rind
1 teaspoon salt
1 teaspoon vanilla extract
2 teaspoons lemon juice
6 eggs, separated
2½ cups plus 2 tablespoons
   all-purpose flour, sifted
¼ cup plus 2 tablespoons
   cornstarch

1 cup buttermilk
½ teaspoon baking soda
1 cup butter or margarine
1 cup sugar
¼ cup water
1 egg, beaten
1 tablespoon grated lemon
   rind
3 tablespoons lemon juice

Cream shortening; gradually add 3 cups sugar, beating at medium speed of an electric mixer. Add 1 tablespoon lemon rind, salt, vanilla, and 2 teaspoons lemon juice; beat at medium speed until well blended. Add egg yolks; beat well. Set aside

Combine flour and cornstarch; set aside. Combine buttermilk and soda; add to creamed mixture alternately with flour mixture.

Beat egg whites at high speed of an electric mixer until stiff peaks form. Gently fold into batter.

Pour batter into a greased and floured 10-inch tube pan. Bake at 350° for 1 hour and 15 minutes. Cool in pan 10 minutes; remove from pan, and let cool on a wire rack.

Combine butter and remaining ingredients in a saucepan. Cook over medium heat, stirring constantly, until mixtures comes to a boil. Pour over warm cake. Yield: one 10-inch cake.

Winners
The Junior League of Indianapolis, Indiana

Plantation Prune Cake

2½ cups all-purpose flour
1 teaspoon baking powder
1 teaspoon salt
1 teaspoon ground allspice
1 teaspoon ground cinnamon
1 teaspoon ground nutmeg
1 cup pecans, finely chopped
3 eggs
1 cup sugar

½ cup firmly packed brown
  sugar
1 cup vegetable oil
½ cup buttermilk
2 cups chopped cooked
  prunes
2 cups peeled, chopped
  cooking apples
Vanilla Glaze

Sift flour, baking powder, salt, allspice, cinnamon, and nutmeg in a medium bowl; stir in pecans. Set aside.

Beat eggs in a large bowl at high speed of an electric mixer. Gradually add sugars, beating until mixture is light and fluffy. Add vegetable oil and buttermilk, beating until well blended. Stir in chopped prunes and chopped apples. Add flour mixture, one-third at a time, beating well after each addition.

Pour batter into a greased and floured 10-inch tube pan. Bake at 350° for 1 hour and 15 minutes or until a wooden pick inserted in center comes out clean. Cool in pan 10 minutes.

Remove cake from pan, and place on a serving plate. Pour half of Vanilla Glaze over cake. Serve remaining glaze over individual slices of cake. Yield: one 10-inch cake.

Vanilla Glaze

1 cup sugar
½ teaspoon baking soda
½ cup buttermilk
1 tablespoon light corn syrup

½ cup butter or margarine
1 teaspoon vanilla extract
½ cup chopped pecans

Combine sugar, soda, buttermilk, corn syrup, and butter in a medium saucepan. Bring mixture to a boil over low heat, stirring constantly; cook 2 minutes. Remove from heat; stir in vanilla and chopped pecans. Yield: 2½ cups.

Upper Crust: A Slice of the South
The Junior League of Johnson City, Tennessee

Poppy Seed Cake

2½ cups all-purpose flour
2 teaspoons baking powder
1 teaspoon baking soda
½ teaspoon salt
1 cup butter or margarine,
 softened
1½ cups sugar

4 eggs, separated
1 cup buttermilk
⅓ cup poppy seeds
1 teaspoon almond extract
⅓ cup sugar
1 tablespoon ground
 cinnamon

Sift together flour, baking powder, soda, and salt; set aside. Cream butter and 1½ cups sugar. Add egg yolks, beating well. Combine buttermilk and poppy seeds. Add flour mixture to creamed mixture alternately with buttermilk mixture, beginning and ending with flour mixture. Stir in almond extract.

Beat egg whites (at room temperature) until stiff peaks form. Gently fold into batter. Pour one-third of batter into a greased and floured 10-inch tube pan. Combine remaining ⅓ cup sugar and cinnamon. Sprinkle half of sugar mixture over batter in pan. Repeat layers, ending with remaining one-third of batter. Bake at 350° for 1 hour or until wooden pick inserted in center comes out clean. Let cool in pan on a wire rack for 1 hour. Yield: one 10-inch cake.

Frances Nevin

The Little Red Cookbook
The Allen-Wells Chapter, American Red Cross
Fort Wayne, Indiana

Double-Frosted White Fruitcake

¾ cup butter or margarine,
 softened
1¼ cups sugar
1 tablespoon lemon juice
1 teaspoon vanilla extract
1 teaspoon almond extract
1 teaspoon orange extract
3 eggs, separated
⅔ cup milk
1¼ cups all-purpose flour,
 divided

1 cup golden raisins
¾ cup chopped walnuts
½ cup dried currants
½ cup candied citron
½ cup candied cherries,
 halved
White Buttercream Frosting
Bitter Chocolate Glaze
Red and green candied
 cherries (optional)

Cream butter; gradually add sugar, beating at medium speed of an electric mixer until light and fluffy. Stir in lemon juice and flavorings. Combine egg yolks and milk, stirring well. Add to creamed mixture alternately with 1 cup flour, beginning and ending with flour.

Dredge raisins, walnuts, currants, citron, and ½ cup cherries in remaining ¼ cup flour. Fold into batter. Beat egg whites (at room temperature) until stiff peaks form. Fold into batter.

Pour batter into a greased, wax paper-lined 9-inch square pan. Bake at 350° for 1 hour or until a wooden pick inserted in center comes out clean. Cool in pan 5 minutes. Remove from pan; peel off wax paper, and let cake cool on a wire rack. Spread frosting over top and sides of cake. Drizzle with Bitter Chocolate Glaze. Garnish with red and green candied cherries, if desired. Yield: one 9-inch cake.

White Buttercream Frosting

¼ **cup butter, softened**
2¼ **cups sifted powdered**
  sugar
1½ **tablespoons milk**

¼ **teaspoon vanilla extract**
¼ **teaspoon almond extract**
¼ **teaspoon orange flavoring**

Cream butter at medium speed of an electric mixer; gradually add sugar, beating until light and fluffy. Add milk; beat until spreading consistency. Stir in flavorings. Yield: enough frosting for one 9-inch cake.

Bitter Chocolate Glaze

1 **(1-ounce) square**
  unsweetened chocolate

1 **(1-ounce) square semisweet**
  chocolate

Melt chocolate together in top of a double boiler over simmering water, stirring until smooth. Remove from heat; let cool slightly. Yield: enough glaze for one 9-inch cake.

Christmas Memories Cookbook
Mystic Seaport Museum Stores
Mystic, Connecticut

Jamaican Mystery Cake

½ cup butter or margarine, softened

1¼ cups sugar

2 eggs

2 cups all-purpose flour

2 teaspoons baking powder

½ teaspoon salt

½ cup milk

3 ripe bananas, mashed

¾ cup chopped walnuts, toasted

1 medium banana, sliced

2 tablespoons Grand Marnier or other orange-flavored liqueur

Frosting (recipe follows)

½ cup chopped walnuts, toasted

Cream butter and sugar. Add eggs, one at a time, beating well after each addition. Combine flour, baking powder, and salt. Add to creamed mixture alternately with milk, beginning and ending with flour mixture. Fold in mashed bananas and ¾ cup chopped walnuts.

Pour batter into a greased 9- x 5- x 3-inch loafpan. Bake at 350° for 1 hour and 15 minutes or until a wooden pick inserted in center comes out clean. Cool in pan 5 minutes; remove from pan, and let cool completely on a wire rack.

Split cake horizontally into 2 layers. Place bottom layer, cut side up, on a cake plate. Arrange banana slices on cake layer. Sprinkle with liqueur. Spread with half of frosting. Top with remaining cake layer. Frost top and sides of cake with remaining frosting. Sprinkle with ½ cup chopped walnuts. Cover and chill 8 hours before serving. Yield: 8 servings.

Frosting

1 cup butter or margarine, softened

1 cup sugar

3 eggs

2 teaspoons instant coffee powder

¼ cup Kahlúa or other coffee-flavored liqueur

Cream butter and sugar at medium speed of an electric mixer until light and fluffy. Add eggs, one at a time, beating well after each addition. Dissolve coffee powder in Kahlúa. Add to creamed mixture, beating well. Yield: 3 cups.   Pam Levin

Some Enchanted Eating
Friends of the West Shore Symphony
Muskegon, Michigan

Frozen French Silk Cake

1 cup all-purpose flour
1 cup unsalted butter or margarine, divided
½ cup coarsely chopped pecans
¼ cup firmly packed dark brown sugar
¾ cup plus 2 tablespoons superfine sugar, divided

2 eggs
1 (1-ounce) square unsweetened chocolate, melted
1 cup whipping cream
2 teaspoons crème de cacao

Line a 9-inch square baking pan with aluminum foil, leaving an overhang to form handles. Grease foil.

Position knife blade in food processor bowl. Combine flour, ½ cup butter (cut into pieces), pecans, and brown sugar in food processor. Cover and pulse 4 or 5 times or until mixture resembles coarse meal. Press mixture into bottom of prepared pan. Bake at 350° for 18 to 20 minutes or until lightly browned. Let cool.

Cream remaining ½ cup butter in a large mixing bowl. Gradually add ¾ cup superfine sugar, beating until light and fluffy. Add eggs, one at a time, beating well after each addition. Add melted chocolate; beat 3 minutes at medium speed of an electric mixer. Spread mixture evenly over cooled crust. Cover; chill 2 hours.

Beat whipping cream in a medium mixing bowl at high speed of an electric mixer until soft peaks form. Gradually add remaining 2 tablespoons superfine sugar and crème de cacao, beating until stiff peaks form.

Remove chilled chocolate mixture from pan, using foil handles. Peel off foil. Cut chocolate-covered crust in half to form two 9- x 4½-inch rectangles. Place one rectangle, crust side down, on a serving plate; top with half of whipped cream mixture. Place remaining rectangle over whipped cream layer; spread half of remaining whipped cream mixture over top of cake. Garnish with remaining whipped cream mixture; freeze. Let cake stand 1 hour at room temperature before serving. Yield: 8 to 10 servings.

Noteworthy
The Ravinia Festival
Highland Park, Illinois

Chocolate Bavarian Cream Cake

¾ cup all-purpose flour
¼ cup sugar
¼ cup cocoa
12 egg whites
1 teaspoon cream of tartar

1 cup sifted sugar
1½ teaspoons vanilla extract
Bavarian Cream
Kahlúa Whipped Cream
Slivered almonds, toasted

Sift flour, ¼ cup sugar, and cocoa together 5 times; set aside.

Beat egg whites (at room temperature) until foamy. Add cream of tartar; beat until soft peaks form. Add 1 cup sugar, 1 tablespoon at a time, beating until stiff peaks form. Add vanilla, beating well. Sprinkle sifted flour mixture over egg white mixture, ¼ cup at a time; fold in carefully.

Pour batter into an ungreased 9-inch tube pan, spreading evenly. Bake at 350° for 40 to 45 minutes or until cake springs back when lightly touched. Invert pan; cool 1 hour and 30 minutes. Loosen cake from sides of pan, using a narrow metal spatula; remove from pan. Break cake into bite-size pieces. Set aside.

Lightly grease bottom and sides of 9-inch tube pan; line with wax paper. Alternately layer cake pieces and Bavarian Cream, beginning and ending with cake pieces. Chill 12 hours. Unmold onto a serving dish. Spread Kahlúa Whipped Cream on top and sides of cake. Sprinkle with almonds; chill thoroughly. Yield: one 9-inch cake.

Bavarian Cream

1 envelope unflavored gelatin
¼ cup cold water
4 eggs, separated
½ cup sugar
⅛ teaspoon salt
1 cup milk

2 (1-ounce) squares
   unsweetened chocolate,
   melted
1 cup whipping cream
1 teaspoon vanilla extract

Sprinkle gelatin over water in a bowl; set aside. Combine egg yolks, sugar, and salt in top of a double boiler. Add milk, stirring constantly, until thickened. Add gelatin mixture, stirring well. Remove from heat; stir in chocolate. Let mixture cool.

Beat egg whites (at room temperature) until stiff peaks form. Gently fold beaten egg whites into chocolate mixture.

Beat cream until soft peaks form. Add vanilla; beat until stiff peaks form. Gently fold whipped cream into chocolate mixture. Yield: enough for one 9-inch cake.

Kahlúa Whipped Cream

2 cups whipping cream	**¼ cup Kahlúa or other coffee-flavored liqueur**

Beat whipping cream until soft peaks form. Add Kahlúa; beat until stiff peaks form. Yield: enough for one 9-inch cake.

Even More Special
The Junior League of Durham and Orange Counties,
North Carolina

Almond Torte

½ teaspoon sugar	**1 tablespoon kirsch**
½ teaspoon all-purpose flour	**¼ teaspoon almond extract**
½ cup unsalted butter or margarine	**¼ cup all-purpose flour**
1 (7-ounce) tube almond paste	**¼ teaspoon baking powder**
¾ cup sugar	**1 cup fresh or frozen raspberries, thawed**
3 eggs	**Powdered sugar**

Grease an 8-inch round cakepan, and line with wax paper. Grease wax paper, and dust with ½ teaspoon sugar and ½ teaspoon flour. Set aside.

Cream butter and almond paste; gradually add ¾ cup sugar, beating well. Add eggs, one at a time, beating well after each addition. Add kirsch and almond extract, mixing well. Combine ¼ cup flour and baking powder; stir well. Add to batter, beating just until combined.

Pour batter into prepared cakepan. Bake at 325° for 40 to 50 minutes or until a wooden pick inserted in center comes out clean. Cool in pan 10 minutes; remove from pan, and let cool completely on a wire rack.

Press raspberries through a sieve; discard seeds. Transfer cake to a cake plate. Place paper doily on top of cake, and sift powdered sugar over top. Carefully remove doily. Serve with pureed raspberries. Yield: one 8-inch torte.   Narsai M. David

California Fresh
The Junior League of Oakland-East Bay, California

Blitz Torte

½ cup butter or margarine
½ cup sugar
4 eggs, separated
1 cup sifted cake flour
1 teaspoon baking powder
¼ cup plus 3 tablespoons
milk

1 cup sugar
1 cup slivered almonds
1 cup whipping cream,
whipped

Grease two 8-inch round cakepans, and line with wax paper. Grease wax paper. Set aside.

Cream butter in a large mixing bowl; gradually add ½ cup sugar, beating well at medium speed of an electric mixer. Add egg yolks, one at a time, beating well after each addition. Combine flour and baking powder; add to creamed mixture alternately with milk, beginning and ending with flour mixture. Mix well after each addition. Spread batter evenly into prepared pans. Set aside.

Beat egg whites (at room temperature). Gradually add 1 cup sugar, beating until stiff but not dry. Spread evenly over batter in pans. Sprinkle with almonds.

Bake at 350° for 25 minutes or until a wooden pick inserted in center comes out clean. Cool in pans 10 minutes; remove from pans, and let cool completely on wire racks.

Place 1 layer on cake platter. Spread evenly with whipped cream, reserving a small amount of whipped cream. Place remaining cake layer on top, and garnish with remaining whipped cream. Yield: one 2-layer torte.

Jane Prosser

Acornucopia
The Valley Hospital Auxiliary
Ridgewood, New Jersey

Lemon Macaroon Torte

1 (8-ounce) can almond paste
1 cup sugar
2 egg whites
3 egg yolks
½ cup sugar
⅓ cup all-purpose flour
1 cup warm milk
2 teaspoons butter or
   margarine
1 teaspoon vanilla extract
1 cup sugar

¼ cup cornstarch
1 cup water
3 egg yolks, beaten
2 tablespoons butter or
   margarine
2 tablespoons grated lemon
   rind
⅓ cup lemon juice
⅓ cup sliced almonds,
   toasted
Sifted powdered sugar

Combine first 3 ingredients; beat at medium speed of an electric mixer 3 to 5 minutes or until smooth. Set aside.

Trace two 8-inch circles on unglazed brown paper; place on separate baking sheets. Set aside.

Spoon three-fourths of almond paste mixture into a pastry bag fitted with star tip No. 7. Pipe a ring ½ inch from outer edge on one circle of paper. Bake at 325° for 20 to 25 minutes. Spoon remaining almond paste mixture onto remaining circle; spread to a thickness of ¼ inch. Bake at 325° for 18 to 20 minutes. Cool on racks for 30 minutes; invert and carefully remove paper.

Combine three egg yolks and ½ cup sugar in a medium saucepan; stir with a wire whisk 5 minutes or until mixture reaches ribbon stage. Stir in flour. Gradually add milk, stirring until well blended. Cook over medium heat, stirring constantly, until mixture thickens. Reduce heat, and cook 3 minutes. Remove from heat; stir in 2 teaspoons butter and vanilla. Cool.

Combine 1 cup sugar, cornstarch, and water in a saucepan. Cook over medium heat until mixture comes to a boil; remove from heat. Gradually stir about one-fourth of hot mixture into beaten egg yolks; add to remaining hot mixture. Cook 1 minute; remove from heat. Stir in 2 tablespoons butter, lemon rind, and juice.

Assemble torte by placing solid cooked shell on a serving platter. Spread milk mixture over top. Place cooked ring on milk mixture; fill ring with lemon mixture. Chill 2 hours. Garnish with sliced almonds and powdered sugar. Yield: 8 servings.

Taste the Seasons
Woodside-Atherton Auxiliary to Children's Hospital at Stanford
Menlo Park, California

Peppermint Angel Food

10 egg whites
¼ teaspoon salt
1½ teaspoons cream of tartar
1 cup sugar
1 cup sifted cake flour

1 cup sifted powdered sugar
1 teaspoon vanilla extract
1 teaspoon peppermint
  extract
Red food coloring

Beat egg whites (at room temperature) and salt until foamy. Add cream of tartar; beat until soft peaks form. Add 1 cup sugar, 2 tablespoons at a time, beating until stiff peaks form. Sift flour and powdered sugar together 4 times. Sprinkle over egg whites, ¼ cup at a time; fold in each addition carefully. Divide egg white mixture in half; fold vanilla into one half, and fold peppermint extract and a few drops of red food coloring into other half. Pour half of pink mixture into an ungreased 10-inch tube pan; add half of white mixture. Repeat layers, and swirl with a knife. Bake at 300° for 1 hour or until cake springs back when touched. Invert pan, and let cool. Yield: one 10-inch cake.   Lola Wollenweber

Between Greene Leaves
The Greene County Homemakers Extension Association
Carrollton, Illinois

Philadelphia Cream Cheese Pound Cake

1 cup butter or margarine,
  softened
1 (8-ounce) package cream
  cheese, softened
3 cups sugar

6 eggs
3 cups sifted cake flour
1 teaspoon vanilla extract
1 teaspoon lemon extract
Sifted powdered sugar

Cream butter and cream cheese. Add 3 cups sugar; beat until light and fluffy. Add eggs, one at a time; beat after each addition. Stir in flour; add flavorings. Pour batter into a greased and floured 10-inch Bundt pan. Bake at 325° for 1 hour and 15 minutes or until a wooden pick inserted in center comes out clean. Cool in pan 10 minutes; remove from pan, and let cool on a wire rack. Sprinkle with powdered sugar. Yield: one 10-inch cake. W. Wilson Goode

The Mayors' Cookbook
The United States Conference of Mayors
Washington, D.C.

Ginger and Cream Roll

⅔ cup sifted cake flour
2 teaspoons baking powder
¼ teaspoon salt
1 teaspoon ground cinnamon
1 teaspoon ground ginger
1 teaspoon ground allspice
3 eggs

½ cup sugar
¼ cup molasses
2 tablespoons sugar
1 cup whipping cream
2 tablespoons powdered sugar
½ teaspoon vanilla extract
Brandied Walnut Sauce

Grease bottom and sides of a 15- x 10- x 1-inch jellyroll pan with vegetable oil. Line pan with wax paper, and grease wax paper with oil. Set pan aside.

Sift together first 6 ingredients; set aside. Beat eggs until thick and lemon colored. Gradually add ½ cup sugar, beating until light and fluffy. Add molasses; beat well. Fold in flour mixture. Spread batter evenly in prepared pan. Bake at 375° for 10 to 12 minutes or until a wooden pick inserted in center comes out clean.

Sift 2 tablespoons sugar in a 15- x 10-inch rectangle on a towel. Loosen cake from sides of pan, and turn out onto sugared towel. Carefully peel off wax paper. Starting at long side, carefully roll up cake and towel together; chill.

Beat cream until foamy; gradually add powdered sugar and vanilla, beating until soft peaks form. Unroll cake; spread with whipped cream, and reroll cake, without towel. Place cake on a serving plate, seam side down; cover and refrigerate. Spoon Brandied Walnut Sauce over cake before serving. Yield: 8 to 10 servings.

Brandied Walnut Sauce

1 cup firmly packed brown
    sugar
¼ cup butter or margarine
¼ cup whipping cream

2 tablespoons light corn syrup
¼ cup brandy
½ cup chopped walnuts,
    toasted

Combine brown sugar, butter, whipping cream, and corn syrup in a saucepan over medium-low heat. Bring to a boil, stirring constantly. Reduce heat to low; cook 5 minutes. Stir in brandy and walnuts; simmer 1 minute. Yield: 1½ cups.   Trish Green

Bravo
The Greensboro Symphony Guild
Greensboro, North Carolina

Pumpkin Roll

3 eggs
1 cup sugar
⅔ cup mashed cooked
  pumpkin
¾ cup all-purpose flour
1 teaspoon baking soda
½ teaspoon ground cinnamon
3 to 4 tablespoons sifted
  powdered sugar

1 (8-ounce) package cream
  cheese, softened
1 cup sifted powdered sugar
2 tablespoons butter or
  margarine, softened
1 teaspoon vanilla extract
1 cup finely chopped pecans,
  divided

Grease a 15- x 10- x 1-inch jellyroll pan; line with wax paper.
Grease and flour wax paper.

Beat eggs and 1 cup sugar at medium speed of an electric mixer.
Add pumpkin, flour, soda, and cinnamon; mix well. Spread batter
into prepared pan. Bake at 375° for 15 minutes.

Sift 3 to 4 tablespoons powdered sugar in a 15- x 10-inch rectangle
on a towel. Loosen cake from pan, and turn out onto sugared towel.
Carefully peel off wax paper. Starting at narrow end, roll up cake
and towel together; place cake, seam side down, on a wire rack to
cool completely.

Beat cream cheese, 1 cup powdered sugar, butter, and vanilla at
medium speed of an electric mixer until well blended.

Unroll cake. Spread cake with cream cheese mixture; sprinkle
with ⅔ cup chopped pecans. Carefully reroll cake, without towel.
Place cake, seam side down, on a serving plate. Sprinkle remaining
pecans on cake. Yield: 10 servings.   Dorothy Resh

The Cove Cookery
St. John's Lutheran Church
Accident, Maryland

Chocolate Yogurt Cheesecake

1 cup chocolate wafer crumbs
¼ cup butter or margarine,
   melted
2 (8-ounce) packages cream
   cheese, softened
1 cup sugar
3 eggs
1½ teaspoons vanilla extract
6 (1-ounce) squares semisweet
   chocolate, melted and
   cooled

1 (8-ounce) carton plain
   yogurt
3 (1-ounce) squares semisweet
   chocolate
2 tablespoons butter or
   margarine
1 tablespoon light corn syrup
½ teaspoon vanilla extract

Combine crumbs and melted butter; press firmly into the bottom of an 8-inch springform pan. Chill.

Combine cream cheese and sugar in a medium bowl. Beat at medium speed of an electric mixer until mixture is smooth and well blended. Add eggs, one at a time, beating after each addition. Add 1½ teaspoons vanilla. Stir in melted chocolate and yogurt, blending well. Pour batter into prepared pan.

Place a 13- x 9- x 2-inch baking pan on lower rack of oven. Pour water into pan to a depth of 1 inch. Place cheesecake on middle rack of oven. Bake at 300° for 1 hour and 20 minutes or until cheesecake is set. Turn oven off, and partially open oven door; let cake cool in oven.

Combine chocolate, 2 tablespoons butter, corn syrup, and ½ teaspoon vanilla in a saucepan. Cook over medium heat until melted; cool slightly. Spoon glaze over cheesecake; chill at least 8 hours. Yield: 8 to 10 servings.

Unbearably Good!
The Junior Service League of Americus, Georgia

Crème de Cassis Cheesecake

2 cups vanilla wafer or butter
  cookie crumbs
¼ cup sugar
1 (1-ounce) square white
  chocolate, grated
¼ cup unsalted butter or
  margarine, melted
4 (8-ounce) packages cream
  cheese, softened
1¼ cups sugar
3 tablespoons crème de cassis

Dash of salt
4 eggs
3 (1-ounce) squares white
  chocolate, shaved
1 (16-ounce) carton
  commercial sour cream
¼ cup sugar
1 teaspoon almond extract
Additional white chocolate,
  shaved

Combine first 4 ingredients; press in bottom and up sides of a 10-inch springform pan. Chill.

Beat cream cheese and 1¼ cups sugar at high speed of an electric mixer until light and fluffy. Add crème de cassis and salt; mix well. Add eggs, one at a time, beating just until blended after each addition. Fold in shaved chocolate. Pour batter into prepared pan. Bake at 350° for 50 minutes. Let cool 10 minutes.

Combine sour cream, ¼ cup sugar, and almond extract. Spread over cheesecake. Bake at 350° for 10 minutes. Refrigerate cheesecake immediately for at least 8 hours. Garnish with additional shaved white chocolate. Yield: 12 to 14 servings.

Beyond Parsley
The Junior League of Kansas City, Missouri

Fudge-Almond Cheesecake

1½ cups gingersnap crumbs
¼ cup butter or margarine,
  melted
3 (8-ounce) packages cream
  cheese, softened
1 cup sugar
3 eggs

2 teaspoons almond extract
2 teaspoons vanilla extract
1 (6-ounce) package
  semisweet chocolate
  morsels
3 tablespoons butter or
  margarine

Combine crumbs and melted butter; press firmly into the bottom of a 9-inch springform pan. Set aside.

Beat cream cheese until light and fluffy. Gradually add sugar, beating well. Add eggs, one at a time, beating well after each addition. Add almond and vanilla flavorings; beat until smooth.

Pour batter into prepared pan. Bake at 350° for 45 minutes or until cheesecake is almost set. Turn oven off, and partially open oven door. Leave cake in oven to cool completely. Chill 8 hours.

Combine chocolate and butter in top of a double boiler; bring water to a boil. Reduce heat to low; cook until butter and chocolate melt. Let cool slightly. Remove from pan. Spread chocolate mixture over cheesecake. Yield: 10 to 12 servings.   Gary Sawyers

Cooking with Class
Frederick Community College
Frederick, Maryland

New York Cheesecake

1¼ cups graham cracker
  crumbs
¼ cup sugar
2 tablespoons butter or
  margarine, melted
5 (8-ounce) packages cream
  cheese, softened
1½ cups sugar
3 tablespoons all-purpose
  flour

Dash of salt
1½ teaspoons lemon juice
1 teaspoon vanilla extract
5 eggs
2 egg yolks
¼ cup whipping cream
Fresh fruit (optional)
Strawberry jelly, melted
  (optional)

Combine crumbs, ¼ cup sugar, and butter; press into the bottom of a buttered 10-inch springform pan. Chill.

Beat cream cheese at high speed of an electric mixer until light and fluffy. Add 1½ cups sugar, flour, salt, lemon juice, and vanilla; beat 5 minutes. Add eggs and yolks, one at a time, beating after each addition. Add cream; mix well. Pour batter into prepared pan. Bake at 425° for 10 minutes; reduce temperature to 250°, bake 1 hour and 15 minutes. Do not open oven door during baking time.

Cool 1 hour; cover and chill at least 8 hours. Garnish with fresh fruit glazed with melted jelly, if desired. Yield: 12 to 14 servings.

Cornsilk
The Junior League of Sioux City, Iowa

Praline Cheesecake

1 cup graham cracker crumbs
3 tablespoons sugar
3 tablespoons butter or
  margarine, melted
3 (8-ounce) packages cream
  cheese, softened
1¼ cups firmly packed dark
  brown sugar

2 tablespoons all-purpose
  flour
3 eggs
1½ teaspoons vanilla extract
½ cup finely chopped pecans
Pecan halves
Maple-flavored syrup

Combine graham cracker crumbs, 3 tablespoons sugar, and melted butter, stirring well. Firmly press crumb mixture evenly into the bottom of a 9-inch springform pan. Bake at 350° for 10 minutes. Let cool.

Beat cream cheese at high speed of an electric mixer until light and fluffy; gradually add brown sugar and flour, mixing well. Add eggs, one at a time, beating well after each addition. Stir in vanilla and chopped pecans.

Pour batter into prepared pan. Bake at 350° for 50 to 55 minutes. Let cool to room temperature on a wire rack; chill. Remove cheesecake from pan. Garnish with pecan halves, and brush with syrup. Yield: 10 to 12 servings.   Charlene Wilson

Bienvenue! La Cuisine de la Maison Destrehan
The River Road Historical Society
Destrehan, Louisiana

Cookies & Candies

New Orleans, Louisiana, is a diverse community held together by the Mississippi River. The French Quarter, or Vieux Carré (old square), with its narrow streets and balconied buildings, is the center of New Orleans. Jackson Square, surrounded by architectural treasures, including the Pontalba, is the heart of the French Quarter.

☆☆☆

Breakaway Cookie

1⅓ cups unbleached flour
½ cup sugar
½ cup finely ground almonds
1½ tablespoons grated lemon
  rind
1 tablespoon freshly squeezed
  lemon juice

⅛ teaspoon salt
½ cup plus 1 tablespoon
  unsalted butter or
  margarine
1½ tablespoons amaretto

Combine flour, sugar, almonds, lemon rind, lemon juice, and salt in a large bowl. Cut in butter with a pastry blender until mixture resembles coarse meal. Sprinkle amaretto evenly over surface of mixture; stir gently with a fork. (Mixture will be crumbly.)

Spread mixture evenly into a buttered and floured 11-inch round tart pan. (Do not press into pan.) Bake at 325° for 35 to 40 minutes or until lightly browned. Cool in pan on wire rack. Cover with aluminum foil; let stand overnight. Yield: one 11-inch cookie.

California Cooking
The Art Council, Los Angeles County Museum of Art
Los Angeles, California

White Chocolate and Almond Cookies

½ cup butter or margarine,
  softened
½ cup shortening
¾ cup firmly packed brown
  sugar
½ cup sugar
1 egg

1½ teaspoons vanilla extract
1¾ cups all-purpose flour
1 teaspoon baking soda
½ teaspoon salt
8 ounces white chocolate,
  chopped
¼ cup sliced almonds

Cream butter and shortening; gradually add sugars, beating at medium speed of an electric mixer until light and fluffy. Add egg and vanilla, beating well.

Combine flour, soda, and salt; add to creamed mixture, mixing well. Stir in white chocolate and almonds. Drop dough by teaspoonfuls onto ungreased cookie sheets. Bake at 375° for 8 to 10 minutes. Remove to wire racks to cool. Yield: 5 dozen.

Purple Sage and Other Pleasures
The Junior League of Tucson, Arizona

Cashew Cookies

½ cup butter or margarine, softened
1 cup firmly packed brown sugar
1 egg
½ teaspoon vanilla extract
2 cups all-purpose flour
¾ teaspoon baking powder
¾ teaspoon baking soda
¼ teaspoon salt
½ cup commercial sour cream
2 cups chopped cashews
Coffee Icing

Cream butter; gradually add brown sugar, beating well at medium speed of an electric mixer. Add egg and vanilla; beat well.

Combine flour, baking powder, soda, and salt. Gradually add to creamed mixture, mixing well. Add sour cream, mixing until smooth. Stir in cashews.

Drop by teaspoonfuls onto greased cookie sheets. Bake at 400° for 6 to 8 minutes or until golden brown. Cool on wire racks. Frost with Coffee Icing. Yield: 7 dozen.

Coffee Icing

¼ cup butter or margarine
3 tablespoons hot coffee
¼ teaspoon vanilla extract
2 cups sifted powdered sugar

Melt butter in a medium saucepan; add coffee and vanilla; stir well. Remove from heat; stir in powdered sugar until mixture is smooth. Yield: 1¼ cups.

Winning at the Table
The Junior League of Las Vegas, Nevada

Wasp Nests

½ cup sugar
¼ cup water
2 cups slivered almonds
8 (1-ounce) squares semisweet chocolate, grated
3 egg whites
2 cups sifted powdered sugar

Combine ½ cup sugar and water in a saucepan. Cook until mixture reaches thread stage (230°). Remove from heat. Stir in almonds and chocolate, using a wooden spoon.

Beat egg whites (at room temperature) until stiff peaks form. Gradually add powdered sugar, 1 tablespoon at a time, beating until well blended. Add chocolate-almond mixture; stir well.

Drop mixture by half teaspoonfuls onto greased and floured cookie sheets. Bake at 300° for 20 to 25 minutes or until cookies are very dry. Let stand 10 minutes. Transfer to wire racks to cool completely. Yield: 8 dozen. Jerry Ann Rader

Mountain Laurel Encore
The Bell County Extension Homemakers
Pineville, Kentucky

Swedish Oatmeal Cookies

⅓ cup sugar
¼ cup butter or margarine
1 tablespoon light corn syrup
½ cup chopped blanched
  almonds
⅛ teaspoon almond extract
½ cup shortening
½ cup sugar
½ cup firmly packed brown
  sugar

1 egg
½ teaspoon vanilla extract
¾ cup all-purpose flour
½ teaspoon baking soda
½ teaspoon salt
1½ cups quick-cooking oats,
  uncooked

Combine ⅓ cup sugar, butter, and corn syrup in a small saucepan; bring to a boil. Remove from heat; stir in almonds and almond extract. Set mixture aside.

Cream shortening; gradually add ½ cup sugar and brown sugar, beating well at medium speed of an electric mixer. Add egg and vanilla; beat well. Combine flour, soda, and salt; add to creamed mixture, beating well. Stir in oats.

Drop dough by rounded teaspoonfuls onto ungreased cookie sheets. Bake at 350° for 8 minutes. Remove from oven; place ½ teaspoon almond mixture in center of each cookie. Return to oven, and bake an additional 6 to 8 minutes or until browned. Cool slightly on cookie sheets; remove cookies to wire racks to cool completely. Yield: about 4 dozen. Louise Dillon

The Cove Cookery
The Ladies Aid Society, St. John's Lutheran Church
Accident, Maryland

Wasatch Mountain Ranger Cookies

1 cup butter or margarine, softened
1 cup sugar
1 cup firmly packed brown sugar
2 eggs
2 cups all-purpose flour
½ teaspoon baking powder
1 teaspoon baking soda
⅛ teaspoon salt
1 teaspoon vanilla extract
2 cups regular oats, uncooked
2 cups oven-toasted rice cereal, corn flakes, or ¾ cup shreds of wheat bran cereal
1 cup chopped pecans, walnuts, or unsalted peanuts
1 (6-ounce) package milk chocolate, peanut butter, or butterscotch morsels
1 cup flaked coconut (optional)
¾ cup raisins (optional)

Cream butter; gradually add sugars, beating well. Add eggs; mix well. Stir in flour and next 4 ingredients. Fold in oats, cereal, nuts, morsels, and, if desired, coconut and raisins. Drop dough by tablespoonfuls 2 inches apart onto ungreased cookie sheets. Bake at 350° for 10 minutes or until browned. Cool on wire racks. Yield: 5 dozen.

A Pinch of Salt Lake
The Junior League of Salt Lake City, Utah

Victorian Spice Cookies

½ cup shortening
1 cup sugar
1 cup applesauce
1 teaspoon baking soda
1 egg
2 cups all-purpose flour
½ teaspoon salt
½ teaspoon ground cinnamon
½ teaspoon ground nutmeg
½ teaspoon ground cloves

Cream shortening; gradually add sugar, beating well. Combine applesauce and soda; add to creamed mixture, stirring well. Add egg; stir well. Combine flour and remaining ingredients; add to creamed mixture, mixing well.

Drop dough by heaping teaspoonfuls onto ungreased cookie sheets. Bake at 375° for 15 minutes or until lightly browned. Cool on wire racks. Yield: about 3½ dozen.   Mary Ann Wyand

Recipes from Woodruff Place
The Woodruff Place Civic League
Indianapolis, Indiana

Brownies on Three Levels

1¼ cups flour, divided
1 cup quick-cooking oats, uncooked
½ cup firmly packed brown sugar
½ cup butter or margarine, melted
¼ teaspoon baking soda
¾ teaspoon salt, divided
⅓ cup butter or margarine
2 (1-ounce) squares unsweetened chocolate
2 eggs
1 cup sugar
1 teaspoon vanilla extract
½ cup chopped pecans
Frosting

Combine ½ cup flour, oats, brown sugar, ½ cup melted butter, soda, and ¼ teaspoon salt in a large mixing bowl. Stir until blended. Spoon mixture into a greased 9-inch square baking pan. Bake at 350° for 10 minutes.

Combine ⅓ cup butter and chocolate in a small saucepan; cook over low heat until melted. Set aside. Beat eggs at medium speed of an electric mixer until thick and lemon colored. Add 1 cup sugar, vanilla, and remaining ½ teaspoon salt; stir well. Stir in chocolate mixture, remaining ¾ cup flour, and pecans.

Spread evenly over crust. Bake at 350° for 25 minutes. Let cool in pan. Spread frosting over cooled brownies. Yield: 16 brownies.

Frosting

2 cups sifted powdered sugar
¼ cup butter or margarine, softened
2 tablespoons milk
1 teaspoon vanilla extract

Combine all ingredients in a large bowl; beat at high speed of an electric mixer until smooth. Yield: enough for 16 brownies.

Almost Heaven
The Junior League of Huntington, West Virginia

Butter Creme Brownies

1 (1-ounce) square semisweet
   chocolate
¼ cup butter
1 egg
½ cup sugar
¼ cup all-purpose flour

¼ cup finely chopped pecans
Butter Creme Filling
2 (1-ounce) squares semisweet
   chocolate
2 tablespoons butter

Melt 1 ounce chocolate and ¼ cup butter together in top of a double boiler. Remove from heat, and let cool slightly. Beat egg until foamy. Stir beaten egg into cooled chocolate mixture. Add sugar; beat well. Add flour and pecans, stirring until well blended.

Pour batter into a greased 8-inch square baking pan. Bake at 350° for 13 to 15 minutes. (Brownies will be thin in the pan.) Let cool completely. Top with Butter Creme Filling. Chill 10 minutes.

Melt remaining chocolate and butter in top of a double boiler. Remove from heat. Let cool slightly. Spread over Butter Creme Filling, and chill. Cut into thin bars to serve. Yield: 2 dozen.

Butter Creme Filling

1 cup sifted powdered sugar
2 tablespoons butter,
   softened

1 tablespoon evaporated milk
   or whipping cream
¼ teaspoon vanilla extract

Combine all ingredients. Beat at medium speed of an electric mixer until well blended. Yield: 1 cup. Edith McWilliams Lundy

Vintage Vicksburg
The Junior Auxiliary of Vicksburg, Mississippi

How-Now Brownies

1 (12-ounce) package
   semisweet chocolate
   morsels
¾ cup unsalted butter or
   margarine

4 eggs
¾ cup sugar
1 teaspoon vanilla extract
¾ cup whole wheat flour

Combine chocolate and butter in a saucepan. Cook over medium-low heat until melted, stirring constantly. Let cool slightly.

Beat eggs in a large mixing bowl, using a wire whisk. Add sugar and vanilla, beating well. Add cooled chocolate mixture and flour; stir just until blended. Pour batter into a greased 13- x 9- x 2-inch baking pan. Bake at 350° for 20 to 25 minutes. Cool and cut into bars. Yield: 4 dozen.

Look What's Cooking Now! Minnesota Heritage Cookbook Volume II
The American Cancer Society, Minnesota Division
Minneapolis, Minnesota

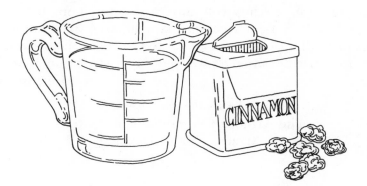

Deaconess Hermits

2½ cups all-purpose flour
1 teaspoon baking soda
½ teaspoon salt
1 teaspoon ground cinnamon
1 teaspoon ground cloves
1 cup sugar
1 cup raisins

½ cup chopped pecans
2 eggs
½ cup vegetable oil
¼ cup molasses
¼ cup strong coffee
1 teaspoon vanilla extract

Sift together flour, baking soda, salt, cinnamon, and cloves in a large mixing bowl. Add sugar and remaining ingredients, mixing well. Spread batter evenly in a lightly greased 15- x 10- x 1-inch jellyroll pan. Bake at 350° for 20 to 25 minutes. Cool; cut into squares. Yield: about 3 dozen.   Archie R. Taylor

The Maine Ingredient
Southern Coastal Family Planning, Inc.
Portland, Maine

Zucchini-Lemon Bars

1¼ cups sugar
1 cup vegetable oil
3 eggs
2 teaspoons grated lemon
  rind
¼ cup lemon juice
1¾ cups shredded zucchini

2 cups all-purpose flour
¼ teaspoon baking powder
2 teaspoons baking soda
1 teaspoon salt
1 cup chopped walnuts
Sifted powdered sugar

Combine 1¼ cups sugar, oil, eggs, lemon rind, and lemon juice in a large mixing bowl; mix well. Stir in zucchini.

Combine flour, baking powder, soda, and salt; gradually add to zucchini mixture, stirring well. Stir in walnuts. Pour batter into a greased 13- x 9- x 2-inch baking pan. Bake at 350° for 45 to 50 minutes or until a wooden pick inserted in center comes out clean. Cool; dust top with sifted powdered sugar. Cut into bars. Yield: 2 dozen.   Johanna Fuerst

Armour Centennial Cookbook
The Armour Centennial Committee
Armour, South Dakota

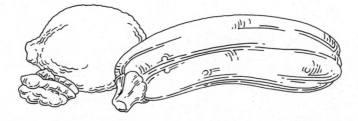

Gingerbread Cookies

¼ cup butter or margarine
½ cup firmly packed brown
  sugar
½ cup molasses
3½ cups all-purpose flour
1 teaspoon baking soda

½ teaspoon salt
1 teaspoon ground ginger
½ teaspoon ground cinnamon
¼ teaspoon ground cloves
¼ cup water

Cream butter and brown sugar; add molasses, beating well. Combine flour, baking soda, salt, ginger, cinnamon, and cloves. Add flour mixture to creamed mixture alternately with water, stirring well after each addition.

Working with one-fourth of dough at a time, shape dough into a ball; lightly knead until smooth. Roll dough to ¼-inch thickness on a floured surface. Cut dough with assorted 2- and 3-inch cutters, and place on lightly greased cookie sheets.

Bake at 350° for 8 minutes. Cool 2 minutes on cookie sheets; remove to wire racks to cool completely. Repeat procedure with remaining dough. Yield: 3½ dozen.

Steeped in Tradition
The Junior Service League of DeLand, Florida

Joe Froggers

1 cup shortening	2 teaspoons baking soda
2 cups sugar	7 cups all-purpose flour
¾ cup water	1 tablespoon ground ginger
1 tablespoon salt	1 teaspoon ground cloves
¼ cup dark rum	1 teaspoon ground nutmeg
2 cups dark molasses	½ teaspoon ground allspice

Cream shortening; gradually add sugar, beating at medium speed of an electric mixer until light and fluffy. Combine water and salt; let stand 1 minute. Add rum to water mixture; set aside. Combine molasses and soda; set aside.

Combine flour and spices; add to creamed mixture alternately with water mixture and molasses mixture, beginning and ending with flour mixture. Stir after each addition. Dough should be sticky. Chill 8 hours.

Divide dough in half; store one half in refrigerator. Roll half of dough to ½-inch thickness on a lightly floured surface. Cut with a 3-inch cutter, and place cookies 3 inches apart on ungreased cookie sheets. Bake at 375° for 15 minutes or until cookies are lightly browned (cookies will be soft, and tops will crack). Cool completely on wire racks. Repeat procedure with remaining dough. Yield: 2 dozen.   Nancy Titcomb

Flavors of Cape Cod
The Thornton W. Burgess Society
East Sandwich, Massachusetts

Ginger Puff Cookies

¾ cup shortening
1 cup sugar
1 egg
¼ cup molasses
1 tablespoon baking soda
½ teaspoon salt

1 teaspoon ground ginger
1 teaspoon ground cinnamon
¼ teaspoon ground cloves
2 cups all-purpose flour
Sugar

Cream shortening; gradually add 1 cup sugar, beating at medium speed of an electric mixer until light and fluffy. Add egg, and beat well. Add molasses and next 5 ingredients; mix well. Add flour to creamed mixture, beating well. Chill dough 8 hours.

Shape dough into 1-inch balls; roll in sugar. Place 3 inches apart on lightly greased cookie sheets. Bake at 350° for 12 minutes. (Tops of cookies will crack.) Cool on wire racks. Yield: 3½ dozen.

La Rue Meadows

What's Cooking at Woodlawn?
United Methodist Women, Woodlawn United Methodist Church
Birmingham, Alabama

Chocolate-Filled Snowballs

1 cup butter or margarine,
   softened
½ cup sugar
1 teaspoon vanilla extract
2 cups sifted all-purpose
   flour

1 cup finely chopped pecans
1 (6-ounce) package milk
   chocolate kisses, unwrapped
Sifted powdered sugar

Combine butter, ½ cup sugar, and vanilla in a medium bowl; beat until light and fluffy. Add flour and pecans, stirring until well blended. Cover and chill for 2 to 3 hours or until firm.

Shape 1 scant tablespoon dough around each chocolate kiss to make a ball; place on ungreased cookie sheets. Bake at 375° for 12 minutes or until set but not browned. Cool slightly on wire racks, then roll cookies in powdered sugar. Cool completely before storing. Roll again in powdered sugar, if desired. Yield: 3 dozen.

Sue Nelson

Bravo
The Greensboro Symphony Guild
Greensboro, North Carolina

Sesame Seed Twists

¾ cup butter or margarine	½ teaspoon salt
1 cup sugar	3 cups all-purpose flour,
2 eggs	divided
1 teaspoon vanilla extract	1 egg white, slightly beaten
1 tablespoon baking powder	3 tablespoons sesame seeds

Combine butter, sugar, eggs, vanilla, baking powder, salt, and 2 cups flour. Beat at low speed of an electric mixer until well blended, scraping bowl constantly with a rubber spatula. Stir in remaining 1 cup flour, using a wooden spoon; mix until smooth. Chill dough at least 3 hours.

Roll 1 tablespoon of dough into a 6-inch-long rope. Form a coil with rope; place on a buttered cookie sheet. Repeat procedure with remaining dough, placing coils 1 inch apart on cookie sheets. Brush with egg white; sprinkle with sesame seeds. Bake in a preheated 350° oven for 20 minutes or until lightly browned. Remove cookies to wire racks to cool. Yield: 3 dozen.   Jean L. Hait

From Palette to Palate
Cincinnati Art Museum
Cincinnati, Ohio

Chocolate Puffs

½ cup butter or margarine	2 teaspoons vanilla extract
¾ cup cocoa	1½ cups all-purpose flour
¼ cup vegetable oil	2 teaspoons baking powder
2 cups sugar	⅛ teaspoon ground cinnamon
4 eggs	Sifted powdered sugar

Melt butter in a small saucepan over medium heat. Add cocoa and oil, stirring until smooth. Pour into a large bowl; gradually add 2 cups sugar, 1 cup at a time, beating well after each addition at medium speed of an electric mixer. Beat in eggs; add vanilla.

Sift together flour, baking powder, and cinnamon. Add to chocolate mixture, and mix well. Cover and refrigerate 8 hours.

Shape dough into ¾-inch balls; roll in powdered sugar. Place on lightly greased cookie sheets, and bake at 375° for 8 to 10 minutes. Yield: 10 dozen.

Upper Crust: A Slice of the South
The Junior League of Johnson City, Tennessee

Toasted Nut Toffee

1 cup butter or margarine
1½ cups coarsely chopped
  pecans
1¼ cups sugar

2 tablespoons water
1 teaspoon vanilla extract
8 (1-ounce) squares semisweet
  chocolate

Melt butter in a heavy skillet; cook over medium heat until bubbly. Add pecans, and sauté for 30 seconds, stirring constantly. Stir in sugar and water; cook over low heat until sugar dissolves. Cover and cook over medium heat 2 to 3 minutes to wash down sugar crystals from sides of pan. Uncover and cook to hard crack stage (300°). Remove from heat, and stir in vanilla. Pour into a buttered 13- x 9- x 2-inch pan, spreading to edge of pan. Cool completely; loosen candy from sides of pan, and invert onto wax paper.

Melt chocolate in top of a double boiler; spread melted chocolate over toffee. Refrigerate until firm; break toffee into pieces. Yield: about 1 pound.

Dorothea Wright

A Book of Favorite Recipes
The Missionary Society of Victory Chapel
Dover, Delaware

Cheese Fudge

1 pound pasteurized process
  cheese
1 pound butter or margarine
4 (16-ounce) packages
  powdered sugar, sifted

1 cup cocoa
1 tablespoon vanilla extract
2 to 4 cups walnuts, chopped

Place cheese in top of a double boiler; bring water to a boil. Reduce heat to low; cook until cheese melts, stirring constantly.

Melt butter in a saucepan over medium heat.

Sift sugar and cocoa together in a large bowl. Add melted cheese and margarine to sugar mixture, stirring well with a wooden spoon. Add vanilla and nuts; knead until mixture is well blended. Spread in a 15- x 10- x 1-inch jellyroll pan. Cut into 1-inch squares. Yield: about 6½ pounds.

Billie Brocato

Simply Southern
The DeSoto School, Inc. Parents-Teachers Club
West Helena, Arkansas

Chocolate Truffles

1⅔ cups whipping cream
½ cup unsalted butter
1 pound semisweet chocolate, coarsely chopped

2 tablespoons Grand Marnier or other orange-flavored liqueur
Cocoa

Combine whipping cream and butter in a heavy saucepan; cook over low heat, stirring constantly, until butter melts. Bring mixture to a boil. Remove from heat; add chocolate, stirring until chocolate melts. Stir until mixture thickens. Stir in Grand Marnier. Cover and chill 3 to 4 hours, stirring frequently.

Shape mixture into 1-inch balls; roll lightly in cocoa. Yield: about 3½ dozen.

Uptown Down South
The Junior League of Greenville, South Carolina

Praline Nuggets

1 cup firmly packed light brown sugar
2 tablespoons ground pecans
1 tablespoon cornstarch
1 tablespoon bourbon

1 egg white
⅛ teaspoon cream of tartar
⅛ teaspoon salt
2 cups pecan halves

Combine brown sugar, ground pecans, and cornstarch in a large bowl. Add bourbon; stirring well. Set aside.

Beat egg white (at room temperature), cream of tartar, and salt at high speed of an electric mixer until stiff peaks form. Stir one-third of egg white mixture into sugar mixture. Fold in remaining egg white mixture. Add pecan halves, stirring to coat well.

Place pecan halves, flat side down, 2 inches apart on lightly greased cookie sheets. Bake at 300° for 12 minutes or until puffed and golden brown. Cool slightly before removing from cookie sheets. Cool on wire racks. Yield: about 9 dozen.   Betsy James

Angel Food
St. Anne's Church
Annapolis, Maryland

Christmas Caramels

1 cup sugar	1 cup half-and-half, divided
¾ cup dark corn syrup	1 teaspoon vanilla extract
½ cup butter or margarine	½ cup chopped walnuts

Combine sugar, corn syrup, butter, and ½ cup half-and-half in a large Dutch oven. Cook over low heat, stirring constantly, until sugar dissolves. Cover and cook over medium heat 2 to 3 minutes to wash down sugar crystals from sides of pan. Uncover and cook, stirring occasionally, until candy thermometer registers 224° (between soft ball and hard ball stage).

Stir in remaining ½ cup half-and-half. Continue to cook over medium heat until mixture reaches firm ball stage (244°). Remove from heat; stir in vanilla and walnuts. Spread mixture into a buttered 8-inch square pan. Mark top of warm candy in 1-inch squares, using a sharp knife. Let cool 5 hours. Cut into squares, and wrap individually in wax paper. Yield: 1½ pounds.   Jo Silman

Mountain Measures: A Second Serving
The Junior League of Charleston, West Virginia

Divinity Candy

2½ cups sugar	2 egg whites
½ cup water	½ teaspoon vanilla extract
½ cup light corn syrup	2 tablespoons ground pecans

Combine sugar, water, and syrup in a 3-quart saucepan; cook over low heat, stirring constantly, until sugar dissolves. Cover and cook over medium heat 2 to 3 minutes to wash down sugar crystals from sides of pan. Uncover and cook over high heat, without stirring, to hard ball stage (260°). Remove from heat.

Beat egg whites (at room temperature) in a large bowl until stiff peaks form. Pour hot mixture in a very thin stream over egg whites, beating at high speed of an electric mixer. Add vanilla; continue beating 5 to 10 minutes or until mixture holds its shape. Drop by teaspoonfuls onto wax paper. Sprinkle tops with ground pecans. Let cool. Yield: about 1¼ pounds.   Julia Hobby, Elaine Whisman

Temptations
Presbyterian Day School
Cleveland, Mississippi

Desserts

The Thomas Jefferson Memorial and blossoming cherry trees reflect in the Tidal Basin in Washington, D.C. Constructed on 18 acres of land in the East Potomac Park, the circular monument is made of white marble with a domed ceiling and is surrounded by 26 columns. Inside is a 19-foot statue of Thomas Jefferson.

☆☆☆

Grande Fruit Bowl

1 small cantaloupe, halved
and seeded
1 small honeydew, halved
and seeded
1 fresh pineapple, peeled,
cored, and cubed
2 cups watermelon balls
2 cups fresh strawberries,
hulled and quartered

1 (11-ounce) can mandarin
oranges, drained
½ cup Chablis or other dry
white wine
½ cup Grand Marnier or
other orange-flavored
liqueur
¼ cup sugar
6 kiwifruit, peeled and sliced

Scoop out melon balls from cantaloupe and honeydew; place in large bowl. Add pineapple, watermelon, strawberries, and mandarin oranges. Toss gently to mix. Combine wine, Grand Marnier, and sugar; stir until sugar dissolves. Pour over fruit mixture, and chill at least 3 hours. Add kiwifruit; toss gently. Yield: 12 servings.

Sounds Delicious!
The Volunteer Council of the Tulsa Philharmonic Society, Inc.
Tulsa, Oklahoma

Apple Crisp

3 or 4 cooking apples
1 cup all-purpose flour
1 cup sugar
1 teaspoon baking powder

½ teaspoon salt
1 egg
½ cup butter or margarine,
melted

Peel, core, and chop apples; place in a 12- x 8- x 2-inch baking dish. Sift together flour, sugar, baking powder, and salt. Cut egg into flour mixture with a pastry blender until mixture resembles coarse meal; sprinkle over apples. Pour butter over flour mixture, and bake at 350° for 40 minutes or until browned. Yield: 6 to 8 servings.   Estelle Wilkerson

What's Cooking at Woodlawn?
United Methodist Women, Woodlawn United Methodist Church
Birmingham, Alabama

Apples in Cider Sabayon Sauce

8 Golden Delicious apples,
  peeled, cored, and
  quartered (about 3½
  pounds)

3 tablespoons sugar
3 tablespoons butter or
  margarine
Cider Sabayon Sauce

Combine apples, sugar, and butter in a large Dutch oven; bring to a boil. Cover, reduce heat, and simmer 25 minutes or until apples are tender.

Place apples in a glass serving bowl, and top with chilled Cider Sabayon Sauce. Yield: 6 to 8 servings.

Cider Sabayon Sauce

4 egg yolks
½ cup sugar
¾ cup apple cider
1 teaspoon cornstarch

2 to 3 tablespoons Calvados
⅛ teaspoon ground cinnamon
⅛ teaspoon ground nutmeg

Combine egg yolks, sugar, cider, and cornstarch in top of a double boiler. Cook over boiling water, stirring constantly, until mixture coats a metal spoon. Remove from heat; add Calvados, cinnamon, and nutmeg. Mix well; chill. Yield: 1¾ cups.   Bobbi MacPhail

"delicious"
The Elisabeth Morrow School Parents Association
Englewood, New Jersey

Baked Spiced Apples

6 large baking apples, peeled
  and cored
⅓ cup butter or margarine,
  melted
⅓ cup fine, dry breadcrumbs
½ cup sugar
½ teaspoon ground cloves
1 teaspoon ground cinnamon

2 tablespoons sugar
½ cup ground almonds
1 egg white
3 tablespoons Chablis or
  other dry white wine
Commercial sour cream
  (optional)

Roll apples in butter. Combine breadcrumbs, ½ cup sugar, cloves, and cinnamon in a medium bowl. Roll buttered apples in crumb mixture; place apples in a greased 12- x 8- x 2-inch baking dish.

Combine 2 tablespoons sugar, almonds, and egg white, stirring well. Stuff each apple with about 1½ tablespoons nut mixture. Pour wine around apples in baking dish. Bake at 350° for 30 to 40 minutes or until apples are tender. Top each apple with a dollop of sour cream, if desired. Yield: 6 servings.   Sally Brown

From Palette to Palate
The Cincinnati Art Museum
Cincinnati, Ohio

Holiday Apple Dessert

¾ cup sugar
1 teaspoon ground cinnamon
6 large baking apples, peeled, cored, and thinly sliced
2 tablespoons butter or margarine
1 cup sugar

¾ cup all-purpose flour
½ teaspoon salt
1½ teaspoons ground cinnamon
½ cup butter or margarine, softened
Whipped cream

Combine ¾ cup sugar and 1 teaspoon cinnamon; mix well. Alternate layers of apples and sugar mixture in an 8-inch square baking dish, dotting each layer with 2 tablespoons butter.

Combine 1 cup sugar, flour, salt, and 1½ teaspoons cinnamon; add ½ cup butter, and stir with a fork until mixture is crumbly. Sprinkle flour mixture over apples. Bake, uncovered, at 350° for 50 minutes or until apples are tender. Spoon into serving bowls; top with whipped cream. Yield: 8 servings.   Phyllis McCormick

Home at the Range
Chapter EX-P.E.O.
Oakley, Kansas

Oriental Oranges

6 large navel oranges   ⅓ cup water
1 cup sugar   1 tablespoon grenadine

Remove rind from oranges with a citrus zester, being careful not to include the white pith. Peel and discard pith from oranges, using a sharp knife. Chill oranges until serving time.

Blanch orange rind in boiling water for 2 minutes. Rinse in cold water. Repeat blanching process three times, using fresh water each time to remove the bitterness.

Combine sugar, ⅓ cup water, and grenadine in a saucepan; bring to a boil over medium heat, stirring until sugar dissolves. Add orange rind, and return to a boil. Reduce heat to low; cook 5 minutes without stirring. Transfer rind to wax paper, using a slotted spoon; reserve syrup. Cover rind, and set aside.

Slice oranges, and place on a serving dish with slices overlapping. Spoon syrup over orange slices; arrange candied rind on top. Yield: 6 servings.

California Cooking
The Art Council, Los Angeles County Museum of Art
Los Angeles, California

Rhubarb Dessert

2 cups all-purpose flour   5 cups sliced rhubarb
2 teaspoons sugar   ½ cup milk
1 cup butter or margarine   ¼ cup fresh orange juice
1½ cups sugar   3 eggs, separated
2 tablespoons all-purpose   ¼ cup plus 2 tablespoons
  flour   sugar

Combine 2 cups flour and 2 teaspoons sugar; cut in butter with a pastry blender until mixture resembles coarse meal. Press crumb mixture evenly in bottom of a 13- x 9- x 2-inch baking pan. Bake at 375° for 15 to 20 minutes or until crust is browned. Set aside.

Combine 1½ cups sugar and 2 tablespoons flour in a heavy 5-quart saucepan. Add rhubarb, milk, and orange juice. Cook over medium heat, stirring constantly, until thickened.

Beat egg yolks at high speed of an electric mixer until thick and lemon colored. Gradually stir about one-fourth of hot mixture into yolks; add to remaining hot mixture, stirring constantly. Cook over medium heat 2 to 3 minutes, stirring constantly. Pour mixture over crust. Cool.

Beat egg whites (at room temperature) until foamy; gradually add ¼ cup plus 2 tablespoons sugar, 1 tablespoon at a time, beating 2 to 4 minutes or until stiff peaks form and sugar dissolves. Spread meringue over filling. Bake at 350° for 12 to 15 minutes or until browned. Yield: 12 servings.

Brunch Basket
The Junior League of Rockford, Illinois

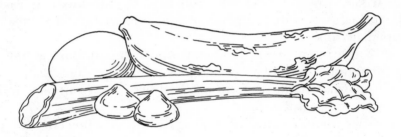

Adult Banana Split

1 cup butter or margarine
1 cup plus 2 tablespoons firmly packed brown sugar
4 medium bananas, peeled and sliced
¼ cup orange juice, strained
3 tablespoons fresh lemon juice, strained

2 tablespoons Grand Marnier or other orange-flavored liqueur
1 tablespoon banana-flavored liqueur
Vanilla ice cream
Unsweetened whipped cream
Macadamia nuts, chopped and toasted

Melt butter in a medium saucepan; add brown sugar, and stir until smooth. Stir in bananas; coat well. Add juices and liqueurs; simmer 2 minutes. Serve immediately over ice cream. Top with whipped cream and nuts. Yield: 8 servings.   Darlene Young

Bravo
The Greensboro Symphony Guild
Greensboro, North Carolina

Brownie Baked Alaska

1 quart vanilla ice cream	½ teaspoon salt
½ cup butter or margarine	2 eggs, beaten
2 (1-ounce) squares	2 cups sugar, divided
unsweetened chocolate	1 teaspoon vanilla extract
¾ cup all-purpose flour	1 cup chopped pecans
½ teaspoon baking powder	5 egg whites

Line a 1-quart freezer-proof bowl (about 7 inches in diameter) with wax paper, leaving an overhang around the edges. Pack ice cream into bowl, and freeze until very firm.

Combine butter and chocolate in a heavy saucepan. Cook over low heat, stirring frequently, until melted. Remove from heat. Combine flour, baking powder, and salt; add to chocolate mixture, mixing well. Add eggs; stir in 1 cup sugar, and mix well. Add vanilla and chopped pecans.

Pour batter into a greased 8-inch round cakepan. Bake at 350° for 30 to 35 minutes or until a wooden pick inserted in center comes out clean. Cool cake in pan 10 minutes. Remove cake from pan, and let cool completely on a wire rack.

Place cake on an ovenproof serving dish. Invert bowl of ice cream onto cake layer, leaving wax paper intact; remove bowl. Place ice cream-topped cake in freezer.

Beat egg whites (at room temperature) at high speed of an electric mixer until foamy; gradually add remaining 1 cup sugar, 1 tablespoon at a time, beating at high speed until stiff peaks form and sugar dissolves. Remove ice cream-topped cake from freezer, and peel off wax paper. Quickly spread meringue over entire surface, making sure edges are sealed.

Bake at 500° for 3 to 4 minutes or until meringue is lightly browned. Cut into wedges, using a sharp knife, and serve immediately. Yield: 10 to 12 servings.

Note: After meringue is sealed, the dessert can be returned to the freezer for up to one week and baked just before serving.

Clock Wise Cuisine
The Junior League of Detroit, Michigan

Grapefruit Sorbet

¾ cup sugar
2 large grapefruit, peeled and
   sectioned
1 cup freshly squeezed
   grapefruit juice or
   unsweetened grapefruit
   juice

2 tablespoons kirsch
1 egg white

Position knife blade in food processor bowl; add sugar, and top with cover. Process for 30 seconds. Set aside.

Position knife blade in food processor bowl; add grapefruit sections, and top with cover. Process until smooth. Pour pureed grapefruit into a bowl, and set aside.

Combine sugar, grapefruit juice, and kirsch in a saucepan; bring mixture to a boil, stirring constantly. Reduce heat, and simmer 5 minutes. Let cool. Stir in pureed grapefruit.

Pour mixture into a 12- x 8- x 2-inch baking dish, and freeze until almost firm. Spoon mixture into food processor bowl, and process until smooth. Add egg white, and process until well blended. Spoon mixture into eight 6-ounce custard cups. Freeze until firm. Let stand at room temperature 5 minutes before serving. Yield: 8 servings.

Gulfshore Delights
The Junior League of Fort Myers, Florida

San Francisco Bread Pudding

2 cups broken French bread
  slices
1 cup milk
1 cup whipping cream
1 cup sugar
½ cup raisins
½ cup shredded coconut
½ cup chopped pecans

¼ cup unsalted butter or
  margarine, melted
1 egg
1 egg yolk
1 tablespoon vanilla extract
½ teaspoon ground cinnamon
¼ teaspoon ground nutmeg
Lemon Rum Sauce

Combine first 13 ingredients in a large mixing bowl; mix well. Spoon pudding into a buttered 12- x 8- x 2-inch baking dish. Bake at 350° for 40 to 45 minutes or until pudding is firm. Let cool. Cut into squares, and spoon Lemon Rum Sauce over each serving. Yield: 8 servings.

Lemon Rum Sauce

¼ cup plus 2 tablespoons
  unsalted butter or
  margarine
3 tablespoons sugar

¼ cup lemon juice
1 teaspoon grated lemon rind
2 egg yolks, beaten
3 to 6 tablespoons rum

Combine butter and sugar in a saucepan; cook over low heat until sugar dissolves. Add lemon juice and rind. Gradually stir about one-fourth of hot mixture into egg yolks; add to remaining hot mixture, stirring constantly. Cook over low heat, stirring constantly, until slightly thickened. Stir in rum to taste. Yield: 1 cup.

San Francisco Encore
The Junior League of San Francisco, California

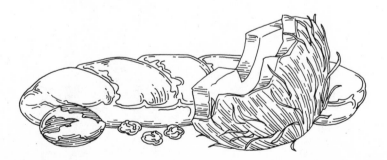

Bread Pudding with Whiskey Sauce

4 cups broken bread slices
2 cups sugar
4 eggs
2 cups milk
1½ teaspoons ground
  cinnamon
1 tablespoon vanilla extract
½ teaspoon salt
¾ cup butter or margarine,
  melted
½ cup raisins
Whiskey Sauce

Combine bread and sugar in a large mixing bowl.

Combine eggs, milk, cinnamon, vanilla, and salt in container of an electric blender; process until foamy. Pour over bread and sugar mixture; set aside at room temperature for 2 hours.

Add melted butter and raisins to bread mixture; mix well. Pour mixture into a 13- x 9- x 2-inch baking pan. Bake at 350° for 25 to 30 minutes or until pudding is very firm. Let pudding cool; cut into squares. Place in dessert dishes, and spoon Whiskey Sauce over each serving. Yield: 12 servings.

Whiskey Sauce

½ cup butter or margarine
1 cup sugar
1 egg, beaten
2 to 4 tablespoons bourbon

Place butter and sugar in top of a double boiler; bring water to a boil. Reduce heat to low; cook, stirring constantly, until butter melts and sugar dissolves. Gradually stir in egg, using a wire whisk. Cool slightly; stir in bourbon to taste. Yield: 1½ cups.

Artist's Palate Cookbook
Women's Volunteer Committee, New Orleans Museum of Art
New Orleans, Louisiana

Old-Fashioned Syrup Bread with Lemon Sauce

2 cups pure sugar cane syrup	1 teaspoon baking powder
¼ cup butter or margarine, softened	1 teaspoon baking soda
2 eggs	1 teaspoon salt
2½ cups all-purpose flour	Lemon Sauce

Combine syrup, butter, and eggs in a large bowl; mix well. Combine flour, baking powder, soda, and salt; gradually add to syrup mixture, mixing well. Pour batter into a greased 13- x 9- x 2-inch baking pan. Bake at 350° for 30 to 40 minutes or until a wooden pick inserted in center comes out clean. Cool in pan 10 minutes; remove from pan, and cut into squares. Serve with warm Lemon Sauce. Yield: 12 servings.

Lemon Sauce

½ cup sugar	2 tablespoons butter or margarine
1 tablespoon cornstarch	
1 cup boiling water	2 tablespoons lemon juice
1 tablespoon grated lemon rind	

Combine first 4 ingredients in a saucepan, stirring well. Cook over medium heat, stirring constantly, until clear and thickened. Remove from heat; stir in butter and lemon juice. Yield: about 1½ cups.

Unbearably Good!
The Junior Service League of Americus, Georgia

El Radiante Pumpkin Flan

1¼ cups sugar, divided	1½ cups evaporated milk
½ teaspoon salt	⅓ cup water
1 teaspoon ground cinnamon	1½ teaspoons vanilla extract
1 cup cooked, mashed pumpkin	½ cup whipping cream
5 eggs, slightly beaten	1 tablespoon sugar
	¼ teaspoon ground ginger

Place ½ cup sugar in a heavy saucepan over medium heat. Using oven mitts, caramelize sugar by shaking pan occasionally until sugar melts and turns a light golden brown. Remove from heat. Pour hot caramel mixture into an 8-inch square pan; turning the pan to coat evenly. Cool. (Mixture may crack slightly as it cools.)

Combine ¾ cup sugar, salt, and cinnamon in a large bowl. Add pumpkin and eggs; mix well. Stir in evaporated milk, water, and vanilla. Mix well. Pour over caramelized sugar; place in a large shallow pan. Pour hot water to a depth of 1 inch into large pan. Bake at 350° for 1 hour and 20 minutes or until a knife inserted near the center comes out clean. Remove pan from water, and let cool to room temperature. Chill.

Beat whipping cream, 1 tablespoon sugar, and ginger until stiff peaks form.

Loosen edges of custard with a spatula, and invert onto a serving plate. Cut into squares, and top each serving with whipped cream mixture. Yield: 9 servings.

Note: Stirring may be necessary when caramelizing the sugar if a gas burner is used.   Dick Landis

Angel Food
St. Anne's Church
Annapolis, Maryland

Mrs. Whitney's Bavarian Cream

4 cups milk
4 eggs
½ cup sugar
⅛ teaspoon salt
2 envelopes unflavored
   gelatin

½ cup Chablis or other dry
   white wine
2 cups whipping cream,
   whipped
Sauce (recipe follows)

Place milk in top of a double boiler; bring water to a boil. Cook until milk is thoroughly heated. Set aside.

Beat eggs until foamy. Add sugar and salt, beating until thickened. Gradually stir 1 cup of hot milk into egg mixture; add to remaining milk, stirring constantly. Cook custard in double boiler over low heat, stirring occasionally, 30 minutes or until thickened. Sprinkle gelatin over wine; add to custard. Chill until slightly thickened. Fold whipped cream into custard. Spoon custard into a 10-cup mold. Chill 8 hours. Unmold onto a serving plate, and serve with sauce. Yield: 10 servings.

Sauce

2 egg yolks
½ cup milk, scalded
1 cup sugar

¼ cup butter or margarine
¾ cup Chablis or other dry
   white wine

Place egg yolks in top of a double boiler. Beat until thick and lemon colored. Gradually add milk, mixing well. Add sugar; bring water to a boil. Add butter, and cook, stirring constantly, until thickened. Stir in wine. Yield: 2 cups.   Margaret Whitney

Not By Bread Alone
Holy Trinity Episcopal Church
Charleston, South Carolina

Ricotta Mousse

1 (16-ounce) carton ricotta
   cheese
¼ cup plus 1 tablespoon
   sugar, divided
¾ cup plus 2 tablespoons
   whipping cream, divided

2 tablespoons rum
2 tablespoons amaretto
1 teaspoon vanilla extract
Chopped pecans (optional)
Shaved chocolate (optional)

Combine cheese, 3 tablespoons sugar, and 2 tablespoons cream in a small bowl. Beat at medium speed of an electric mixer 5 minutes or until smooth. Add rum and amaretto. Mix well. Combine remaining 2 tablespoons sugar, ¾ cup cream, and vanilla in a medium bowl. Beat at high speed of an electric mixer until soft peaks form. Fold into cheese mixture. Serve in ice cream or sherbet dishes. Garnish with chopped nuts and shaved chocolate, if desired. Yield: 4 to 6 servings.   Monica Sinker

Philadelphia Homestyle Cookbook
The Norwood-Fontbonne Academy Home and School
Philadelphia, Pennsylvania

Chocolate Crown Mousse

20 ladyfingers, split
  lengthwise
½ cup dry sherry
1 (12-ounce) package
  semisweet chocolate morsels
2 (8-ounce) packages cream
  cheese, softened

1½ cups firmly packed brown
  sugar, divided
4 eggs, separated
¼ teaspoon salt
2 teaspoons vanilla extract
2 cups whipping cream

Place ladyfingers, cut side down, on an ungreased baking sheet; bake at 375° for 5 minutes. Cool 10 minutes. Brush cut side of ladyfingers with sherry. Line the sides of a 10-inch springform pan with ladyfingers; arrange remaining ladyfingers on bottom of pan.

Place chocolate morsels in top of a double boiler; bring water to a boil. Reduce heat to low; cook, stirring occasionally, until chocolate melts. Cool 10 minutes.

Beat cream cheese and ¾ cup brown sugar at high speed of an electric mixer until light and fluffy. Add egg yolks, one at a time, beating well after each addition. Stir in cooled chocolate.

Beat egg whites (at room temperature) and salt at high speed of an electric mixer until stiff peaks form. Add vanilla and remaining ¾ cup brown sugar; beat until stiff.

Beat whipping cream until soft peaks form. Fold beaten egg whites and whipped cream into cream cheese mixture; pour into prepared pan. Chill 8 hours. Yield: 20 servings.   Janie Altmeyer

Treat Yourself to the Best
The Junior League of Wheeling, West Virginia

Lemon Mousse
with Fresh Raspberry Sauce

1 envelope unflavored gelatin	3 eggs, separated
2 tablespoons Chablis or other dry white wine	½ cup sugar, divided
⅓ cup fresh lemon juice	1 cup whipping cream, whipped
1½ tablespoons grated lemon rind	Raspberry Sauce
	Fresh mint sprigs (optional)

Sprinkle gelatin over wine in top of a double boiler; let stand 1 minute. Bring water to a boil. Cook, stirring constantly, until gelatin dissolves. Add lemon juice and lemon rind, stirring well.

Beat egg yolks at medium speed of an electric mixer until thick and lemon colored. Gradually add 3 tablespoons sugar; beating well. Add gelatin mixture, stirring well.

Beat egg whites (at room temperature) until foamy; gradually add remaining 5 tablespoons sugar, beating until soft peaks form. Gently fold whipped cream and half of beaten egg whites into lemon mixture. Gently fold lemon mixture into remaining beaten egg whites. Spoon into a 1-quart soufflé dish, and chill 8 hours or until mousse is firm. Spoon Lemon Mousse onto individual dessert plates, and spoon Raspberry Sauce over each serving. Garnish with fresh mint sprigs, if desired. Yield: 6 servings.

Raspberry Sauce

1 (10-ounce) package frozen raspberries, thawed and drained	1 tablespoon Grand Marnier or other orange-flavored liqueur
2 tablespoons sugar	
1 tablespoon fresh lemon juice	

Position knife blade in food processor bowl; place all ingredients in processor bowl, and top with cover. Process until mixture is smooth. Press pureed raspberry mixture through a sieve; discard seeds. Yield: ⅓ cup.

Bluegrass Winners
The Garden Club of Lexington, Kentucky

Strawberry Cloud Soufflé with Chocolate Berry Garnish

2 pints fresh strawberries, washed and hulled
2 envelopes unflavored gelatin
¾ cup cold water
¼ cup kirsch
2 tablespoons sugar
1 tablespoon lemon juice
4 egg whites
¼ teaspoon salt
¼ cup sugar
1 cup whipping cream, whipped
1 pint fresh strawberries
1 (6-ounce) package semisweet chocolate morsels

Cut a piece of aluminum foil or wax paper long enough to fit around a 1½-quart soufflé dish, allowing a 1-inch overlap; fold lengthwise into thirds. Lightly oil one side of foil; wrap around outside of soufflé dish, oiled side against dish, allowing foil to extend 3 inches above rim to form a collar. Secure foil with freezer tape.

Place 2 pints strawberries in container of an electric blender or food processor; top with cover and process until smooth. Set aside.

Sprinkle gelatin over cold water in a small saucepan; let stand 1 minute. Cook over low heat until gelatin dissolves; cool slightly. Add to pureed strawberries, stirring well. Stir in kirsch, 2 tablespoons sugar, and lemon juice. Chill until slightly thickened.

Beat egg whites (at room temperature) and salt until soft peaks form. Gradually add ¼ cup sugar, 1 tablespoon at a time, beating until stiff peaks form. Fold egg whites into strawberry mixture. Gently fold whipped cream into strawberry mixture. Spoon into prepared soufflé dish, and chill until firm.

Rinse 1 pint strawberries, and dry thoroughly on paper towels (chocolate will not stick to wet strawberries). Set aside.

Place chocolate morsels in top of a double boiler; bring water to a boil. Reduce heat to low, and cook until chocolate melts. Cool chocolate to lukewarm (110°).

Insert bamboo skewers into stem end of strawberries. Dip in chocolate to cover two-thirds of each strawberry. Stand skewers in a drinking glass until chocolate has hardened. Remove collar from soufflé. Garnish soufflé with chocolate-covered strawberries. Yield: 6 to 8 servings.

Tidewater on the Half Shell
The Junior League of Norfolk-Virginia Beach, Virginia

Tropical Trifle

2 (10¾-ounce) commercial
  pound cakes
24 coconut cookies, crumbled
1 to 1½ cups cream sherry,
  divided
¼ cup plus 2 tablespoons
  brandy, divided
2 cups plus 2 tablespoons
  guava jelly
2 tablespoons finely chopped
  crystallized ginger

Pastry Cream
2½ cups plus 2 tablespoons
  pineapple preserves
1 cup whipping cream
1 tablespoon sifted powdered
  sugar
1 teaspoon cream sherry
½ cup chopped macadamia
  nuts (optional)

Slice pound cake into ¼-inch slices; trim and discard crust. Line bottom of a 16-cup trifle bowl with half of cake slices and half of crumbled cookies. Sprinkle with ½ to ¾ cup cream sherry and 3 tablespoons brandy. Spread with guava jelly.

Fold ginger into Pastry Cream, and spread half over guava jelly. Repeat layers, using remaining cake slices, cookie crumbs, cream sherry, and brandy. Top with pineapple preserves and remaining Pastry Cream. Cover and chill.

Beat whipping cream until foamy; gradually add powdered sugar and 1 teaspoon sherry, beating until soft peaks form. Spread whipped cream over trifle; garnish with macadamia nuts, if desired. Yield: 16 servings.

Pastry Cream

6 egg yolks
½ cup sugar
½ cup all-purpose flour

2 cups hot milk
2 tablespoons butter
1 tablespoon vanilla extract

Combine egg yolks and sugar in top of a double boiler. Beat until mixture thickens and forms ribbons. Add flour; stir well. Gradually add hot milk, beating constantly.

Cook over boiling water, stirring constantly, until thickened and smooth. Remove from heat; add butter and vanilla, stirring until butter melts. Cover with plastic wrap, pressing directly onto pudding; chill thoroughly. Yield: 2½ cups.

Maui Cooks: A Collection of Island Recipes
Kokua Services
Pukalani, Maui, Hawaii

Double Chocolate Terrine with Chocolate Rum Sauce

1 cup finely chopped walnuts
12 (1-ounce) squares
  semisweet chocolate
¾ cup unsalted butter or
  margarine

3 tablespoons cocoa
⅓ cup sugar
4 eggs, separated
1 egg white
Chocolate Rum Sauce

Grease a 9- x 5- x 3-inch loafpan. Line the bottom with greased unglazed brown paper. Cover bottom of pan with walnuts, and press firmly ½ inch up sides of pan. Set aside.

Combine chocolate, butter, and cocoa in a medium saucepan. Cook over low heat until butter and chocolate melt. Remove from heat, and let cool slightly. Transfer to a large mixing bowl. Add sugar; beat well. Add egg yolks, one at a time, beating well after each addition. Beat 5 egg whites (at room temperature) until stiff peaks form. Stir about one-fourth of egg whites into chocolate mixture. Fold in remaining egg whites. Pour mixture into prepared pan. Cover and chill at least 8 hours.

Invert terrine onto a serving platter, and remove pan. Spoon about ⅓ cup Chocolate Rum Sauce onto each serving plate. Top with a slice of terrine. Yield: 10 servings.

Chocolate Rum Sauce

1¼ cups sugar
½ cup unsalted butter or
  margarine
½ cup cocoa
3 (1-ounce) squares
  unsweetened chocolate

⅛ teaspoon salt
1 cup whipping cream
1 tablespoon dark rum

Combine sugar, butter, cocoa, chocolate, and salt in a heavy saucepan. Cook over low heat until butter and chocolate melt. Remove from heat. Gradually add cream, beating until smooth. Stir in rum. Yield: 3 cups.

Beyond Parsley
The Junior League of Kansas City, Missouri

Strawberry Cheesecake Trifle

2 (8-ounce) packages cream
  cheese, softened
2 cups sifted powdered sugar
1 (8-ounce) carton
  commercial sour cream
2 teaspoons vanilla extract
¼ teaspoon almond extract
1 cup whipping cream
1 teaspoon vanilla extract
1 tablespoon sugar

1 commercial angel food
  cake, cut into 1-inch cubes
2 quarts fresh strawberries,
  hulled and sliced
3 tablespoons sugar
3 tablespoons amaretto
Fresh whole strawberries
Fresh mint leaves

Combine cream cheese and powdered sugar in a large mixing bowl. Beat at high speed of an electric mixer until well blended. Stir in sour cream, 2 teaspoons vanilla, and almond extract.

Beat whipping cream until foamy; add 1 teaspoon vanilla and 1 tablespoon sugar; beat until stiff peaks form. Fold whipped cream into cream cheese mixture. Add cake, and stir gently to coat well.

Combine sliced strawberries, 3 tablespoons sugar, and amaretto. Layer strawberries and cream cheese mixture in a trifle bowl, beginning and ending with strawberries. Chill. Garnish with whole strawberries and mint leaves. Yield: 12 to 14 servings.

A Pinch of Salt Lake
The Junior League of Salt Lake City, Utah

Almond-Pumpkin Charlotte

10 ladyfingers
2 envelopes unflavored
  gelatin
⅔ cup milk
⅓ cup dark rum
4 eggs, separated
⅔ cup firmly packed brown
  sugar, divided
2 cups cooked, mashed
  pumpkin
1 teaspoon grated orange rind

1 teaspoon ground cinnamon
½ teaspoon ground nutmeg
½ teaspoon ground ginger
¼ teaspoon ground cloves
1 cup whipping cream
3 tablespoons sugar
½ cup chopped, blanched
  almonds, toasted
Whipped cream

Split ladyfingers in half lengthwise. Trim one end of ladyfingers to fit an 8-inch springform pan; line with ladyfingers, cut side down.

Combine gelatin, milk, rum, egg yolks, and ⅓ cup brown sugar in a large saucepan; cook over low heat 5 to 10 minutes or until thickened. Remove from heat; add pumpkin, orange rind, cinnamon, nutmeg, ginger, and cloves, stirring well. Set mixture aside.

Beat egg whites (at room temperature) in a large bowl until soft peaks form. Gradually add remaining ⅓ cup brown sugar, beating until stiff peaks form. Set aside.

Beat whipping cream until foamy; gradually add 3 tablespoons sugar, beating until soft peaks form. Gently fold egg white mixture alternately with whipped cream mixture into pumpkin mixture; fold in almonds. Pour into prepared pan.

Cover and chill 8 hours. Pipe rosettes of whipped cream around edges of charlotte. Yield: 10 servings.   Janet Joyce

Suncoast Seasons
The Dunedin Youth Guild, Inc.
Dunedin, Florida

Mini Blinis

2 (1-pound) loaves sandwich bread	2 egg yolks
2 (8-ounce) packages cream cheese, softened	1 cup sugar
½ cup sugar	1 teaspoon ground cinnamon
	½ cup butter or margarine, melted

Trim crust from bread slices. Roll each slice with a rolling pin to flatten. Combine cream cheese, ½ cup sugar, and egg yolks in a medium bowl. Beat at medium speed of an electric mixer until well blended. Spread one side of each slice of bread with 1 heaping teaspoonful of cream cheese mixture. Roll up tightly, jellyroll fashion, beginning at short end.

Combine 1 cup sugar and cinnamon, stirring well. Dip each roll in melted butter; roll in sugar mixture. Place on cookie sheets, and freeze 2 hours.

Remove from freezer. Cut each roll in half crosswise. Bake at 400° for 10 to 12 minutes. Yield: 6 dozen.   Mavis Bevitz

Culinary Arts & Crafts
The Park Maitland School
Maitland, Florida

Chocolate-Dipped Fruit

1 pint fresh strawberries	¼ cup light corn syrup
4 (1-ounce) squares semisweet chocolate	1 (6-ounce) package dried apricots
4 ounces bittersweet chocolate	½ pound candied pineapple
¼ cup butter or margarine	Chopped pecans (optional)

Rinse strawberries, and dry thoroughly with paper towels (chocolate will not stick to wet strawberries). Set aside.

Combine chocolate, butter, and corn syrup in a heavy saucepan. Cook over low heat, stirring frequently, until melted. Remove from heat, and stir until mixture is partially cool.

Dip fruit halfway into chocolate; roll in pecans, if desired. Place on wax paper to cool. Store in refrigerator. Yield: 12 servings.

Carolyn Collins

Santa Barbara: 200 Years of Good Taste
The Santa Barbara Historical Society—Docent Council
Santa Barbara, California

Sweet Cheese Fondue

¼ cup butter or margarine	¼ to ½ cup sugar
¼ cup all-purpose flour	⅓ cup Grand Marnier or other orange-flavored liqueur
2 cups half-and-half	
8 ounces French triple cream cheese	1 teaspoon grated orange rind

Melt butter in a saucepan over medium heat; stir in flour. Gradually add half-and-half, and cook, stirring constantly, until thickened. Add cheese; cook, stirring constantly, until melted and smooth. Stir in sugar, Grand Marnier, and orange rind. Pour mixture into a fondue pot. Serve fondue with pound cake cubes and assorted fresh fruit. Yield: about 3½ cups.

Bytes: Colorado's Family-Friendly Cookbook
Graland Country Day School
Denver, Colorado

Eggs & Cheese

America's Dairyland, the gently rolling hills of Wisconsin, contains 40,000 dairy farms and 2 million dairy cows. With each cow producing 1500 gallons of milk a year, it's no wonder that Wisconsin produces nearly forty percent of America's cheese. Marketing over 200 varieties, Wisconsin produces more cheese than any other state.

☆☆☆

Shrimp Eggs

¼ cup butter or margarine
3 tablespoons all-purpose
  flour
¾ cup chicken broth
¾ cup half-and-half
2 egg yolks, beaten
⅓ cup grated Parmesan
  cheese

6 hard-cooked eggs
1 teaspoon lemon juice
½ teaspoon finely chopped
  onion
⅛ teaspoon salt
1 cup chopped cooked
  shrimp
2 tablespoons dried parsley

Melt butter in a medium saucepan over low heat; add flour, stirring until smooth. Cook 1 minute, stirring constantly. Gradually stir in chicken broth; cook over medium heat, stirring constantly, until thickened and bubbly.

Combine half-and-half and 2 beaten egg yolks in a medium bowl; mix well. Gradually stir about one-fourth of hot mixture into yolk mixture; add to remaining hot mixture. Cook, stirring constantly, 2 to 3 minutes or until thickened. Add cheese; stir until cheese melts. Remove from heat.

Slice hard-cooked eggs in half lengthwise, and carefully remove yolks. Mash yolks, and stir in lemon juice, onion, and salt. Add shrimp and 1 tablespoon cheese sauce; mix well. Spoon shrimp mixture into egg whites.

Arrange eggs in a chafing dish; pour remaining sauce over eggs. Sprinkle with parsley. Yield: 4 to 6 servings.

Peachtree Bouquet
The Junior League of DeKalb County, Georgia

Creole Eggs

1 large onion, chopped
2 medium-size green peppers,
  chopped
½ cup chopped celery
1 green onion, chopped
¼ cup plus 2 tablespoons
  butter or margarine,
  divided
1 (16-ounce) can whole
  tomatoes, undrained
1½ teaspoons chili powder

¼ teaspoon salt
¼ teaspoon pepper
2 tablespoons all-purpose
  flour
1 cup milk
12 hard-cooked eggs, thinly
  sliced
½ cup buttered, soft
  breadcrumbs
¼ cup grated Parmesan
  cheese

Sauté first 4 ingredients in ¼ cup butter in a skillet until tender. Stir in tomatoes, chili powder, salt, and pepper. Cook over medium heat, stirring occasionally, until thickened.

Melt remaining 2 tablespoons butter in a heavy saucepan over low heat; add flour, stirring until smooth. Cook 1 minute, stirring constantly. Gradually add milk; cook over medium heat, stirring constantly, until thickened and bubbly.

Combine tomato mixture and white sauce; stir well. Spread ½ cup tomato mixture in a greased 13- x 9- x 2-inch baking dish. Layer half of the eggs and half of the remaining tomato mixture. Repeat layers. Combine breadcrumbs and Parmesan cheese; sprinkle evenly over casserole. Bake at 350° for 30 minutes or until hot and bubbly. Yield: 12 servings.   Mrs. Reeves Carter

Vintage Vicksburg
The Junior Auxiliary of Vicksburg, Mississippi

Fancy Egg Scramble

¼ cup plus 2 tablespoons
  butter or margarine,
  divided
2 tablespoons all-purpose
  flour
½ teaspoon salt
⅛ teaspoon pepper
2 cups milk
1 cup (4 ounces) shredded
  process American cheese

1 cup (6 ounces) chopped
  Canadian bacon
¼ cup chopped green onions
12 eggs, beaten
1 (4-ounce) can mushroom
  stems and pieces, drained
2¼ cups soft breadcrumbs
⅛ teaspoon paprika

Melt 2 tablespoons butter in a heavy saucepan over low heat; add flour, salt, and pepper, stirring until smooth. Gradually add milk; cook over medium heat, stirring constantly, until mixture is thickened and bubbly. Add shredded cheese; stir until melted. Remove from heat, and set aside.

Sauté Canadian bacon and onions in 3 tablespoons butter in a large skillet until onions are tender. Add eggs; cook over medium heat, stirring constantly, until set. Remove from heat; stir in cheese sauce and mushrooms. Spoon into a lightly greased 12- x 8- x 2-inch baking dish.

Melt remaining 1 tablespoon butter; stir in breadcrumbs; mix well, and sprinkle over egg mixture. Sprinkle casserole with paprika. Bake, uncovered, at 350° for 30 minutes. Yield: 8 servings.

Sassafras!
The Junior League of Springfield, Missouri

Chili Rellenos Casserole

4 slices bread	2 cups milk
Butter or margarine, softened	2 teaspoons paprika
2 cups (8 ounces) shredded Cheddar cheese	1 teaspoon salt
2 cups (8 ounces) shredded Monterey Jack cheese	½ teaspoon dried whole oregano
1 (4-ounce) can green chiles, diced	½ teaspoon garlic powder
6 eggs, beaten	½ teaspoon dry mustard
	½ teaspoon pepper

Trim crust from bread. Spread each bread slice with butter; place bread, buttered side down, in an 11- x 7- x 2-inch baking dish. Top with cheeses; sprinkle with chiles.

Combine eggs and remaining ingredients in a large bowl, mixing well. Pour over cheese. Cover and chill at least 4 hours.

Uncover and bake at 325° for 50 minutes to 1 hour or until lightly browned. Let casserole stand 10 minutes before serving. Yield: 6 to 8 servings.

Cooking with the Santa Fe Opera
The Santa Fe Opera Guild
Santa Fe, New Mexico

South-of-the-Border Egg Casserole

10 eggs
½ cup all-purpose flour
1 teaspoon baking powder
½ cup butter or margarine,
  melted
4 cups (16 ounces) shredded
  Monterey Jack cheese

1 (24-ounce) carton
  large-curd cottage cheese
1 (4-ounce) can chopped
  green chiles, drained
Picante sauce (optional)

Beat eggs. Stir in flour, baking powder, and butter. Add cheese and remaining ingredients, except picante sauce; stir well. Pour mixture into a greased 13- x 9- x 2-inch baking dish. Bake, uncovered, at 400° for 15 minutes. Reduce heat to 350°, and bake for 30 minutes or until mixture is bubbly and golden brown. Serve with picante sauce, if desired. Yield: 10 to 12 servings.

Rare Collection
The Junior League of Galveston County, Texas

Rancher's Omelet

6 slices bacon, diced
2 tablespoons chopped onion
1 cup diced potatoes
6 eggs, beaten
2 tablespoons chopped, fresh
  parsley

¼ to ½ teaspoon salt
Dash of hot sauce
2 tablespoons milk

Cook bacon in a 10-inch omelet pan or heavy skillet until crisp; drain, reserving 2 tablespoons drippings in skillet. Set bacon aside.

Sauté onion in drippings over medium heat until tender. Add potatoes, and cook until browned. Combine eggs, parsley, salt, and hot sauce; stir just until blended.

Pour egg mixture into skillet; add bacon and milk. As mixture starts to cook, gently lift edges of omelet with a spatula and tilt pan so that uncooked portion flows underneath. Loosen omelet with a spatula, and fold in half. Gently slide omelet onto a serving plate. Yield: 2 servings.

Marlene Raasch

The Great Entertainer Cookbook
The Buffalo Bill Historical Center
Cody, Wyoming

Orange Omelet

6 eggs, separated
2 tablespoons plus 1½
 teaspoons sifted powdered
 sugar
⅓ cup orange juice
1 tablespoon grated orange
 rind

⅛ teaspoon salt
2 tablespoons unsalted butter
 or margarine
1½ teaspoons sugar
Fresh mint sprigs (optional)
Orange slices (optional)

Beat egg yolks until thick and lemon colored. Add powdered sugar, orange juice, and orange rind; beat well.

Beat egg whites (at room temperature) and salt until stiff peaks form. Gently fold egg whites into yolk mixture.

Melt butter in a 10-inch ovenproof skillet over medium-high heat, tilting to coat surface. Pour in egg mixture. Reduce heat to medium. Cook, uncovered, 4 to 5 minutes or just until set. Transfer omelet to oven. Broil 6 to 8 inches from heat for 1 minute or until lightly browned. Turn oven off. Leave omelet in oven 5 minutes.

Slide omelet onto a serving plate. Sprinkle with sugar, and garnish with fresh mint sprigs and orange slices, if desired. Serve immediately. Yield: 6 servings.

Private Collection 2
The Junior League of Palo Alto, California

Onion Frittata

2 tablespoons butter or
  margarine
2 cups chopped onion
½ cup sliced fresh
  mushrooms
⅓ cup sliced celery
⅓ cup chopped green pepper
½ cup diced cooked ham
¼ cup diced pimiento,
  drained
2 cups soft bread cubes,
  toasted

1½ cups (6 ounces) shredded
  Swiss cheese
6 eggs
2 tablespoons all-purpose
  flour
¼ teaspoon salt
⅛ teaspoon pepper
1½ cups half-and-half
Dash of hot sauce

Melt 2 tablespoons butter in a 12-inch ovenproof skillet. Sauté
onion, mushrooms, celery, and green pepper in butter until tender.
Add ham and pimiento; cook 3 minutes, and remove from heat.
Layer bread cubes and cheese over onion mixture in skillet. Combine eggs, and remaining ingredients; beat just until blended. Pour
egg mixture into skillet. Bake at 350° for 25 minutes or until eggs
are set and frittata is golden brown. Yield: 10 servings.

The Market Place
The Augusta Junior Woman's Club, Inc.
Augusta, Georgia

California Frittata

3 tablespoons butter or
  margarine
6 fresh mushrooms, sliced
2 medium zucchini, diced
2 green onions, sliced
1 medium avocado, sliced
  lengthwise

½ teaspoon salt
½ teaspoon dried whole basil
¼ teaspoon pepper
4 eggs, beaten
1 cup (4 ounces) shredded
  Monterey Jack or Swiss
  cheese

Melt butter in a 10-inch nonstick skillet. Add mushrooms, zucchini, and onions; sauté 4 minutes over medium heat. Remove from
heat. Arrange avocado over mushroom mixture; sprinkle with salt,
basil, and pepper. Add beaten eggs, and cook over medium heat
until eggs are set. Lift edges with a spatula, and tilt pan so that

uncooked portion flows underneath. Sprinkle with cheese; cover and cook 2 to 3 minutes or until cheese melts. Yield: 4 servings.

A Taste of California
San Francisco Home Economists in Business
San Francisco, California

Spinach and Sausage Frittata

½ pound Italian sausage
½ pound fresh mushrooms, sliced
½ cup minced onion
2 tablespoons olive oil
1 (10-ounce) package frozen chopped spinach, thawed and drained
6 eggs, slightly beaten

1 cup (4 ounces) grated Romano cheese, divided
1 cup (4 ounces) shredded provolone cheese, divided
2 cloves garlic, minced
1 teaspoon dried whole basil
½ teaspoon dried whole marjoram
¼ teaspoon pepper

Remove casings from sausage. Brown sausage in a large skillet, stirring to crumble. Drain well, and set sausage aside.

Sauté mushrooms and onion in olive oil until lightly browned. Stir in spinach, and cook 3 minutes. Set aside.

Combine eggs, ⅔ cup Romano cheese, ⅓ cup provolone cheese, garlic, basil, marjoram, and pepper. Add sausage mixture; mix well. Pour into a greased 10-inch pieplate. Sprinkle with remaining ⅓ cup Romano cheese and ⅔ cup provolone cheese. Bake at 350° for 30 to 40 minutes or until set. Yield: one 10-inch pie.

Bytes: Colorado's Family-Friendly Cookbook
The Graland Country Day School
Denver, Colorado

Zucchini-Mushroom Frittata

2 medium zucchini, chopped
½ pound fresh mushrooms,
  chopped
1 medium-size green pepper,
  chopped
1 medium onion, chopped
1 clove garlic, minced
3 tablespoons vegetable oil
6 eggs
¼ cup half-and-half

2 (8-ounce) packages cream
  cheese, cut into small
  pieces
2 cups cubed day-old white
  bread, crust removed
1½ cups (6 ounces) grated
  Cheddar cheese
½ teaspoon salt
⅛ teaspoon pepper

Sauté zucchini, mushrooms, green pepper, onion, and garlic in oil in a skillet 5 minutes or until tender. Set aside.

Beat eggs and half-and-half in a bowl. Add cream cheese, bread, Cheddar cheese, salt, pepper, and vegetable mixture. Mix well.

Pour mixture into a greased 10-inch springform pan; bake at 350° for 55 minutes or until browned and set. Let stand 10 minutes. Carefully remove sides of pan, and transfer frittata to a warm serving plate. Serve immediately. Yield: 8 servings.

Purple Sage and Other Pleasures
The Junior League of Tucson, Arizona

Broccoli Cheese Pie

1 cup (4 ounces) shredded
  Cheddar cheese
¾ cup all-purpose flour
½ teaspoon salt
¼ teaspoon dry mustard
¼ cup butter or margarine,
  melted
1 medium onion, chopped
¼ pound fresh mushrooms,
  sliced
1 tablespoon butter or
  margarine

2 tablespoons all-purpose
  flour
1 cup half-and-half
1 teaspoon salt
¼ teaspoon ground nutmeg
⅛ teaspoon pepper
2 cups chopped cooked
  broccoli
3 eggs, slightly beaten.

Combine first 5 ingredients, using a pastry blender. Press evenly into bottom and up sides of a 10-inch pieplate.

Sauté onion and mushrooms in 1 tablespoon butter in a medium skillet until tender. Stir in 2 tablespoons flour; add half-and-half, 1 teaspoon salt, nutmeg, and pepper. Simmer 1 minute. Add broccoli and eggs; blend well. Pour mixture into prepared pieplate. Bake at 400° for 15 minutes; reduce heat to 375°, and bake 20 minutes or until set. Yield: one 10-inch pie.

The Steinbeck House Cookbook
The Valley Guild
Salinas, California

Sausage-Grits Soufflé

1 pound bulk pork sausage	⅛ teaspoon pepper
1 cup quick-cooking grits	¼ cup butter or margarine
8 eggs, beaten	2 cups (8 ounces) shredded
1½ cups milk	sharp Cheddar cheese,
¼ teaspoon salt	divided

Cook sausage over medium heat until browned, stirring to crumble. Drain well, and set aside.

Cook grits according to package directions. Combine eggs, milk, salt, and pepper in a large bowl. Stir in grits. Add butter and 1½ cups cheese, stirring until cheese melts. Stir in sausage. Spoon into a greased 3-quart casserole. Bake, uncovered, at 350° for 1 to 1½ hours. Sprinkle with remaining ½ cup cheese. Bake an additional 2 minutes or until cheese melts. Yield: 8 to 10 servings.

Joanne Moore Frierson

Perennials
The Junior Service League of Gainesville, Georgia

Swiss Cheese-Mushroom Soufflé

3½ tablespoons butter or
  margarine
½ cup all-purpose flour
2 cups milk
½ teaspoon salt
⅛ teaspoon pepper
Dash of ground nutmeg

4 eggs
1⅓ cups shredded Swiss
  cheese, divided
Mushroom Filling
1 tablespoon butter or
  margarine

Melt 3½ tablespoons butter in a heavy saucepan over low heat; add flour, stirring until smooth. Cook 1 minute, stirring constantly. Gradually add milk; cook over medium heat, stirring constantly, until mixture is thickened and bubbly. Remove from heat; stir in salt, pepper, and nutmeg. Add eggs, one at a time, beating well with a wire whisk after each addition. Beat in 1 cup Swiss cheese.

Pour half of cheese mixture into a lightly buttered 9-inch square baking dish. Spread Mushroom Filling over cheese mixture. Cover with remaining cheese mixture. Sprinkle top with remaining ⅓ cup Swiss cheese. Dot with butter. Bake at 400° for 25 minutes or until soufflé is puffed and golden brown. Serve soufflé immediately. Yield: 8 servings.

Mushroom Filling

1 tablespoon butter or
  margarine
1 teaspoon vegetable oil
2 cups minced fresh
  mushrooms

1 tablespoon minced shallots
1 tablespoon all-purpose flour
⅛ teaspoon salt
⅛ teaspoon pepper
¼ cup whipping cream

Melt butter in a large skillet over medium heat; add vegetable oil. Sauté mushrooms and shallots 5 minutes or until brown. Add flour, salt, and pepper, stirring until mixture is smooth. Cook 1 minute, stirring constantly. Reduce heat, and stir in whipping cream. Cook, stirring constantly, until mixture is thickened and bubbly. Yield: about 1 cup.
                                          Linda Gates Sahn

The Pride of Peoria: Recipes and Reminiscences
The Junior League of Peoria, Illinois

Orange Daydreamer

4 (1-inch-thick) slices
   raisin-cinnamon bread
1 (8-ounce) package cream
   cheese, softened
½ cup chopped pecans
1 teaspoon orange juice
½ teaspoon grated orange
   rind

1 cup all-purpose flour
2 teaspoons sugar
2 teaspoons baking powder
½ teaspoon salt
1 cup half-and-half
2 eggs, beaten
Vegetable oil
Orange Syrup

Make a deep slit in each bread slice to form a pocket. Set aside.

Combine cream cheese, pecans, orange juice, and orange rind in a small bowl; mix well. Spoon cream cheese mixture evenly into each bread slice. Set aside.

Combine flour, sugar, baking powder, and salt in a large bowl. Add half-and-half and eggs; beat until mixture is smooth. Dip bread slices into egg mixture, coating well.

Carefully lower filled bread, one slice at a time, into deep hot oil (375°); fry until lightly browned, turning once. Drain on paper towels. Serve with Orange Syrup. Yield: 4 servings.

Orange Syrup

2 cups orange juice
2 cups sugar
2 teaspoons grated orange
   rind

½ to 1 teaspoon ground
   cinnamon
4 oranges, peeled and
   sectioned

Combine orange juice, sugar, orange rind, and cinnamon in a saucepan. Cook over low heat, stirring frequently, until sugar dissolves. Add oranges. Yield: about 3 cups.   Judy Helman

There Once Was a Cook . . .
The Wesley Institute, Inc.
Pittsburgh, Pennsylvania

Welsh Rarebit

1 tablespoon butter or
  margarine
4 cups (16 ounces) shredded
  process American cheese
⅔ cup beer or milk
1 egg yolk

1 teaspoon dry mustard
1 teaspoon Worcestershire
  sauce
¼ teaspoon hot sauce
⅛ teaspoon salt
⅛ teaspoon pepper

Melt butter in a large saucepan. Stir in cheese. Gradually add beer, stirring until cheese begins to melt. Combine egg yolk and remaining ingredients. Add to cheese mixture. Cook over medium heat until cheese melts and mixture is thoroughly heated. Serve over hot toast. Yield: 4 servings.   Mrs. Charles Price

Offerings Past and Present
St. Luke's Episcopal Church Women
Salisbury, North Carolina

Macaroni and Cheese

½ (8-ounce) package elbow
  macaroni
3 tablespoons butter or
  margarine
¼ cup all-purpose flour
¾ teaspoon salt
¼ teaspoon dry mustard

⅛ teaspoon pepper
2 cups milk
½ teaspoon steak sauce
1 tablespoon minced onion
1 cup (4 ounces) shredded
  Cheddar cheese

Cook macaroni according to package directions; drain.

Melt butter in top of a double boiler over simmering water. Stir in flour, salt, mustard, and pepper. Cook 1 minute, stirring constantly. Gradually add milk, steak sauce, and onion. Cook until thickened, stirring constantly. Stir in cheese.

Combine cheese mixture and macaroni in a greased 1½-quart casserole, tossing gently. Bake, uncovered, at 400° for 20 minutes. Yield: 6 servings.   Jerri Jones

Kitchen Sampler
The Junior Service League of Bessemer, Alabama

Never-Fail Macaroni and Cheese

1 (8-ounce) package elbow
    macaroni
2 tablespoons butter or
    margarine, cut into small
    pieces
½ teaspoon salt
3 cups (12 ounces) shredded
    Cheddar cheese
2½ cups milk
3 eggs, beaten

Cook macaroni according to package directions; drain. Layer half each of macaroni, butter, salt, and cheese in a 2½-quart casserole. Repeat layers, ending with cheese.

Combine milk and beaten eggs, and pour over mixture in casserole. Bake, uncovered, at 350° for 1 hour. Yield: 8 servings.

Susie Wilson

Kitchen Sampler
The Junior Service League of Bessemer, Alabama

Hot Cheese Sandwiches

2 (5-ounce) jars process
    cheese spread
1 (3-ounce) can grated
    Parmesan cheese
½ cup butter or margarine,
    softened
1 egg
1 pound bacon, cooked and
    crumbled
1 (1½-pound) loaf day-old
    sandwich bread

Beat cheese spread, Parmesan cheese, butter, and egg at medium speed of an electric mixer until light and fluffy. Stir in crumbled bacon, blending well.

Trim crust from bread; cut slices into quarters. Spread 1 piece of bread with cheese mixture. Top with second piece of bread; spread top of sandwich with cheese mixture. Repeat procedure with remaining cheese mixture and bread slices. Bake at 350° for 10 minutes. Serve immediately. Yield: 12 servings.   Mary Till

What's Cooking at Woodlawn?
United Methodist Women, Woodlawn United Methodist Church
Birmingham, Alabama

Panzarotti

2 cups all-purpose flour
½ teaspoon salt
1 teaspoon pepper, divided
2 tablespoons shortening
1 egg, beaten
2 tablespoons plus 1½
   teaspoons cold water

1 (12-ounce) package
   mozzarella cheese, cubed
½ pound prosciutto, diced
½ cup chopped fresh parsley
1 egg, beaten
Vegetable oil

Combine flour, salt, and ½ teaspoon pepper in a medium mixing bowl; cut in shortening with a pastry blender until mixture resembles coarse meal.

Combine 1 beaten egg and cold water; sprinkle over flour mixture. Stir with a fork just until dry ingredients are moistened. Shape dough into a ball. Roll dough to ⅛-inch thickness on a lightly floured surface. Cut into six 6-inch circles. Cover and set aside.

Combine mozzarella cheese, remaining ½ teaspoon pepper, prosciutto, parsley, and 1 beaten egg. Stir well. Spoon mixture evenly onto half of each pastry circle. Dip fingers in water, and moisten edges of pastry circles; fold circles in half, making sure edges are even. Press edges of each filled pastry firmly together to seal, using a fork dipped in flour.

Heat 1½ inches of oil to 375° in a large skillet. Fry pies until golden brown on both sides, turning once. Drain well on paper towels. Serve warm. Yield: 6 servings.   Florence Massey

Our Special Blend
The Rehabilitation Center of Eastern Fairfield County
Bridgeport, Connecticut

Fish & Shellfish

From Pensacola to St. George Island, fishing is an integral and traditional part of life. A shrimp boat, resting dockside in the Florida Panhandle, reflects a quiet moment in an otherwise rigorous and physically demanding profession.

☆☆☆

Kentucky Fried Catfish

2 pounds catfish, cleaned and dressed	1 cup buttermilk
	2 cups yellow cornmeal
1 teaspoon salt	1 pound shortening

Cut catfish into serving-size pieces. Sprinkle with salt; dip in buttermilk, and dredge in cornmeal. Fry fish in hot shortening (360°) in a heavy skillet over medium heat until golden brown, turning to brown both sides. Drain on paper towels. Remove to a serving platter. Yield: 4 to 6 servings.

To Market, To Market
The Junior League of Owensboro, Kentucky

Mushroom-Stuffed Flounder Roll-Ups

½ cup chopped green onions	2 (5-ounce) flounder fillets
1 clove garlic, minced	1 teaspoon lemon juice
1 teaspoon olive oil	¼ teaspoon salt
1 cup chopped fresh mushrooms	1 teaspoon chopped fresh parsley
¼ teaspoon salt	½ teaspoon grated lemon rind
⅛ teaspoon pepper	1 teaspoon olive oil
⅛ teaspoon dried whole thyme	

Sauté green onions and garlic in 1 teaspoon oil in a small skillet. Add mushrooms, ¼ teaspoon salt, pepper, and thyme. Sauté for 5 minutes or until vegetables are tender.

Sprinkle fillets with lemon juice and ¼ teaspoon salt. Spoon half of mushroom mixture into center of each fillet, and roll up to enclose filling; secure with wooden picks.

Place rolls, seam side down, in a 1-quart casserole; sprinkle rolls with parsley, lemon rind, and remaining 1 tcaspoon oil. Bake at 400° for 15 minutes or until fish flakes easily when tested with a fork. Yield: 2 servings.   Dr. John C. Sheldon

Cooking with Class
Frederick Community College
Frederick, Maryland

Kedgeree

3 tablespoons butter or
  margarine
1 teaspoon finely minced
  onion
¼ teaspoon turmeric
¼ teaspoon red pepper
¼ teaspoon salt
½ cup whipping cream

2 cups cooked long-grain rice
2 cups cooked, flaked cod
  (about 1¼ pounds)
2 hard-cooked eggs, sliced
Fresh parsley sprigs
  (optional)
Paprika (optional)

Melt butter in a saucepan over medium heat. Sauté onion in melted butter 3 minutes or until tender. Stir in turmeric, red pepper, and salt. Add cream; fold in rice, fish, and sliced eggs. Cook, stirring occasionally, 2 to 3 minutes or until thoroughly heated. Transfer to a serving bowl. Garnish with parsley sprigs and paprika, if desired. Yield: 4 servings.   Laura Maleady

Flavors of Cape Cod
The Thornton W. Burgess Society
East Sandwich, Massachusetts

Fish Chinese Style

1 (8-ounce) ono fillet
2 tablespoons butter or
  margarine
1 tablespoon grated fresh
  gingerroot
1 teaspoon minced garlic

1 teaspoon sugar
2 tablespoons soy sauce
⅓ cup chopped green onions
3 tablespoons vegetable oil
Fresh cilantro sprigs

Sauté fillet in butter 5 minutes, turning once. Transfer to a serving platter. Sprinkle fillet with gingerroot, garlic, sugar, soy sauce, and green onions. Heat oil in a skillet over high heat 1 minute or until very hot (almost smoking). Drizzle hot oil over fish. Garnish with cilantro, and serve immediately. Yield: one serving.
Note: Other mild fish, such as grouper or sole, may be substituted for ono.

Maui Cooks: A Collection of Island Recipes
Kokua Services
Pukalani, Maui, Hawaii

Grouper Kiev

½ cup butter or margarine, softened
2 tablespoons chopped fresh parsley
1 tablespoon lemon juice
¾ teaspoon Worcestershire sauce
½ teaspoon salt
¼ teaspoon hot sauce
⅛ teaspoon pepper
1 clove garlic, finely chopped
1 (2-pound) grouper fillet
2 eggs, beaten
2 tablespoons water
½ cup all-purpose flour
1½ cups soft breadcrumbs
Vegetable oil

Combine first 8 ingredients; mix well, and shape into a stick. Cover and freeze until firm.

Cut grouper into 6 equal pieces. Place between 2 sheets of wax paper; flatten to ½-inch thickness, using a meat mallet or rolling pin. Cut a 2-inch strip along one side of each fillet forming a pocket.

Cut butter mixture into 12 pats; place 2 pats in center of each fillet. Secure each opening with a wooden pick. Combine eggs and water; beat well. Dredge each fillet in flour, dip in egg mixture, and coat with breadcrumbs. Fry in deep hot oil (375°) until fillets are golden brown; drain well. Remove wooden pick before serving. Yield: 6 servings.   Liz Cavanah

Sugar Beach
The Junior League of Ft. Walton Beach, Florida

Salmon with Avocado Butter

¼ cup butter or margarine,
softened
⅓ cup mashed ripe avocado
1 tablespoon lemon juice
1 tablespoon mayonnaise
½ teaspoon Worcestershire
sauce
⅛ teaspoon salt

1 small clove garlic, minced
3 drops hot sauce
2 tablespoons chopped fresh
parsley
4 (6- to 8-ounce) salmon
steaks, 1-inch thick
1 lime, quartered

Cream butter until smooth in a small bowl. Add avocado, lemon
juice, mayonnaise, Worcestershire sauce, salt, garlic, and hot sauce;
beat at medium speed of an electric mixer until smooth. Stir in
parsley. Cover and chill 1 hour. Let stand at room temperature 10
minutes before serving.

Place salmon steaks on a lightly greased rack in broiler pan. Broil
4 to 5 inches from heat 5 to 7 minutes on each side or until fish
flakes easily when tested with a fork. Serve steaks with lime wedges
and Avocado Butter. Yield: 4 servings.

Note: Avocado Butter may be prepared 1 or 2 days ahead.

Clock Wise Cuisine
The Junior League of Detroit, Michigan

Saumon en Papillote

3 tablespoons butter or
margarine, melted
½ pound fresh mushrooms,
sliced
1 tablespoon lemon juice
2 tablespoons butter or
margarine
¾ pound carrots, scraped and
cut into julienne strips
½ cup green onions, cut into
2-inch pieces
¼ teaspoon salt

1 tablespoon finely chopped
fresh tarragon
4 skinless salmon fillets
(about 1½ pounds)
2 tablespoons plus 2
teaspoons finely chopped
shallots
1 tablespoon plus 1 teaspoon
Chablis or other dry white
wine
Salt and freshly ground
pepper to taste

Cut four 12-inch rounds of parchment paper or aluminum foil;
place rounds on 2 large baking sheets. Brush top side of rounds

lightly with 3 tablespoons melted butter, leaving edges ungreased. Set aside.

Sprinkle mushrooms with lemon juice. Sauté mushrooms in 2 tablespoons butter in a large heavy skillet over medium heat for 1 minute. Add carrots, green onions, and ¼ teaspoon salt; stir well. Cover and cook 8 minutes or until vegetables are crisp-tender; stir in tarragon. Cover; set aside.

Spoon vegetable mixture evenly onto half of each prepared parchment round near the center. Cover vegetable mixture with salmon fillets. Sprinkle each serving with 2 teaspoons shallots and 1 teaspoon wine. Sprinkle with salt and pepper to taste.

Fold over remaining halves of parchment rounds; pleat and crimp edges together to seal securely. Place packages on a large baking sheet. Bake at 525° for 7 minutes. Transfer immediately to individual serving plates. To serve, cut a cross in the top of each package with scissors, and fold edges back. Yield: 4 servings.

Robert B. Blackwell

The Mayors' Cookbook
The United States Conference of Mayors
Washington, D.C.

Barbecued Swordfish

½ cup soy sauce
½ cup orange juice
¼ cup catsup
¼ cup chopped fresh parsley
2 tablespoons lemon juice
1 teaspoon pepper
2 cloves garlic, minced
6 (1-inch-thick) swordfish
   steaks (about 2 pounds)

Combine soy sauce, orange juice, catsup, chopped parsley, lemon juice, pepper, and minced garlic. Add swordfish; cover and marinate in refrigerator for 1 hour.

Remove swordfish from marinade, reserving marinade. Grill swordfish over hot coals 6 minutes on each side or until fish flakes easily when tested with a fork, basting frequently with marinade. Yield: 6 servings.   Mrs. Fred I. Sharp

Carnegie Treasures Cookbook
Women's Committee, The Carnegie Museum of Art
Pittsburgh, Pennsylvania

Red Snapper, Veracruz Style

3 pounds red snapper fillets, skinned

2 tablespoons lime juice

1 teaspoon salt

1 medium onion, thinly sliced

2 large cloves garlic, sliced

¼ cup olive oil

2 pounds fresh tomatoes, peeled, seeded, and chopped

1 large bay leaf

¼ teaspoon dried whole oregano

12 pitted green olives, halved

2 tablespoons capers

2 pickled jalapeño peppers, seeded and cut into strips

½ teaspoon salt

1 cup all-purpose flour

1 teaspoon salt

¼ teaspoon pepper

Vegetable oil

3 tablespoons olive oil

Sprinkle fillets evenly with lime juice and 1 teaspoon salt. Cover and refrigerate for 2 hours.

Sauté onion and garlic in ¼ cup hot olive oil in a large skillet until tender, but not brown. Add tomatoes, bay leaf, oregano, olives, capers, peppers, and ½ teaspon salt; mix well. Simmer, uncovered, for 30 minutes. Remove and discard bay leaf.

Combine flour, 1 teaspoon salt, and pepper in a plastic bag; drop in fish fillets, one at a time, and shake until completely coated. Fry in hot vegetable oil (360°) over medium heat until golden brown, turning to brown both sides. Drain on paper towels. Transfer fillets to a large baking dish; top with sauce. Sprinkle 3 tablespoons olive oil over sauce; bake, uncovered, at 325° for 20 minutes or until fish flakes easily when tested with a fork. Yield: 6 to 8 servings.

Some Like It South!
The Junior League of Pensacola, Florida

Grilled Tuna with Lemon-Tarragon Sauce

½ cup olive oil

2 tablespoons Chablis or other dry white wine

2 tablespoons finely chopped fresh parsley

¼ teaspoon dried whole tarragon

6 (1-inch-thick) tuna fillets

Lemon-Tarragon Sauce

Lemon slices (optional)

Combine oil, wine, parsley, and tarragon; stir well. Pat fillets dry with paper towels. Brush each side of fillets with oil mixture.

Grill 5 inches over low coals 8 to 10 minutes on each side or until fish flakes easily when tested with a fork, basting often with oil mixture. Top each fillet with Lemon-Tarragon Sauce. Garnish with lemon, if desired. Yield: 6 servings.

Lemon-Tarragon Sauce

⅓ cup tarragon vinegar
¼ cup minced shallots
2 tablespoons fresh lemon
  juice

¼ teaspoon dried whole
  tarragon
1 cup butter or margarine,
  softened

Combine first 4 ingredients in a saucepan. Cook over medium heat, stirring occasionally, until mixture reduces to 2 tablespoons. Add butter, 1 tablespoon at a time, stirring constantly with a wire whisk. Cook until mixture thickens slightly. Yield: 1 cup.

Taste the Seasons
Woodside-Atherton Auxiliary to Children's Hospital at Stanford
Menlo Park, California

Galveston Crab Cakes

1 pound fresh lump
  crabmeat, drained and
  flaked
¾ cup seasoned, dry
  breadcrumbs
1 egg, beaten
¼ cup mayonnaise
1 teaspoon Worcestershire
  sauce

1 teaspoon dry mustard
½ teaspoon salt
¼ teaspoon pepper
½ teaspoon dried parsley
  flakes
Vegetable oil
Lemon wedges (optional)

Combine crabmeat and breadcrumbs in a large bowl; set aside. Combine egg and next 6 ingredients. Add egg mixture to crabmeat mixture, stirring gently to combine; shape into 6 patties. Fry patties in hot oil (360°) until golden brown, turning once. Drain on paper towels. Garnish with lemon wedges, if desired. Yield: 6 servings.

Rare Collection
The Junior League of Galveston County, Texas

Oyster Casserole

2 (12-ounce) containers fresh
  Standard oysters, drained
⅓ cup chopped fresh parsley
¼ cup chopped green onions
2 cups cracker crumbs
½ cup butter or margarine,
  melted
2 tablespoons fresh lemon
  juice
2 teaspoons Worcestershire
  sauce
½ teaspoon dry mustard

Place oysters in a 10- x 6- x 2-inch baking dish or a 9-inch pieplate. Sprinkle with parsley and green onions. Combine crumbs and remaining ingredients, stirring well. Sprinkle over casserole. Bake, uncovered, at 450° for 10 to 15 minutes or until oysters are golden and edges begin to curl. Serve immediately. Yield: 6 servings.

Stir Crazy!
The Junior Welfare League of Florence, South Carolina

Scallops and Shrimp with Saffron Fettuccine in Cream Sauce

3 quarts water
1½ pounds fresh saffron
  fettuccine or plain fresh
  fettuccine
¾ cup vegetable oil, divided
4 cloves garlic
1 pound medium-size fresh
  shrimp, peeled and
  deveined
1 pound bay scallops, rinsed
  and drained
2 large sweet red peppers,
  cut into julienne strips
½ cup dry sherry
1½ cups whipping cream
½ teaspoon ground saffron
¼ teaspoon ground cumin
¼ cup minced fresh cilantro
¼ cup chopped green onions
Salt and pepper to taste

Bring water to a boil in a large Dutch oven. Add fettuccine; return to a boil. Boil for 3 minutes or until cooked, but still firm. Drain; rinse with cold water, and drain again. Transfer fettuccine to a large serving bowl. Add ¼ cup oil, tossing gently. Cover and set aside.

Pour remaining ½ cup oil in a large skillet. Place over medium heat until hot. Peel and crush garlic, and add to hot oil. Sauté 1 minute or until lightly browned. Remove garlic, using a slotted spoon; discard.

Add shrimp to oil in skillet. Sauté 1 minute or until shrimp turn pink. Remove shrimp with a slotted spoon, and transfer to a large bowl. Add scallops to oil. Sauté 1 to 2 minutes or until scallops are done. Remove scallops with a slotted spoon, and add to shrimp.

Sauté red pepper strips in hot oil 1 minute over medium heat. Add sherry, and continue sautéing 2 to 3 minutes. Remove red pepper strips with a slotted spoon, and add to shrimp and scallops. Add cream, saffron, and cumin to oil in skillet, stirring well. Simmer, uncovered, for 5 minutes. Remove from heat, and pour over shrimp mixture in bowl. Let mixture cool for 30 minutes. Add to cooked fettuccine. Sprinkle with cilantro and green onions. Add salt and pepper to taste. Toss well. Yield: 8 servings.

The Gardner Museum Café Cookbook
The Isabella Stewart Gardner Museum
Boston, Massachusetts

Shellfish Casserole

1 cup peeled and deveined
  chopped cooked shrimp
1 cup fresh lump crabmeat,
  drained and flaked
1 cup chopped celery
¼ cup chopped green pepper
¼ cup chopped green onions

½ teaspoon salt
¼ teaspoon pepper
1 cup mayonnaise
1 teaspoon Worcestershire
  sauce
1 cup buttered breadcrumbs

Combine all ingredients, except breadcrumbs. Spoon into a 1-quart casserole. Sprinkle with breadcrumbs. Bake at 350° for 30 minutes or until casserole is golden brown. Serve immediately. Yield: 4 servings.

Rockport Collection
The Rockport Art Association
Rockport, Texas

Barbecued Shrimp

5 pounds unpeeled fresh
  shrimp, with heads
2 cups butter or margarine
2 (6-ounce) cans frozen
  orange juice concentrate,
  thawed

⅔ cup Worcestershire sauce
1 tablespoon plus 1 teaspoon
  garlic powder
2 tablespoons whole
  peppercorns, crushed
3 loaves French bread, sliced

Wash shrimp thoroughly; drain well. Place 2½ pounds shrimp in a 13- x 9- x 2-inch baking pan; dot with 1 cup butter. Pour 1 can orange juice concentrate over shrimp; sprinkle with ⅓ cup Worcestershire sauce, 2 teaspoons garlic powder, and 1 tablespoon peppercorns. Repeat procedure with remaining ingredients, except bread. Bake at 350° for 30 minutes or until shrimp turn pink and shells start to pull away, basting frequently with pan juices. Serve with French bread. Yield: 12 servings.   M. T. Melvin

Down the Bayou
The Bayou Civic Club
Larose, Louisiana

Barbecued Shrimp

1 cup butter or margarine
¾ cup Worcestershire
  sauce
¾ cup lemon juice
2 to 4 cloves garlic
1 tablespoon pepper
1 tablespoon plus 1 teaspoon
  salt

1 teaspoon dried whole
  rosemary
2 teaspoons hot sauce
2½ pounds unpeeled large
  fresh shrimp
1 medium onion, sliced
1 lemon, sliced and seeded
French bread

Melt butter in a medium saucepan; add Worcestershire sauce and next 6 ingredients, stirring well. Set aside. Wash shrimp thoroughly; drain well. Place shrimp in a 13- x 9- x 2-inch baking dish. Pour sauce over shrimp. Separate onion into rings; arrange onion rings and lemon slices over shrimp mixture. Bake at 400°, uncovered, for 20 minutes or until shrimp turn pink and shells start to pull away. Serve with French bread. Yield: 6 servings.   Jennifer Duet

Down the Bayou
The Bayou Civic Club
Larose, Louisiana

Shrimp à la Creole

4 pounds unpeeled fresh
    shrimp
2 cups water
1 tablespoon liqud crab boil
¾ cup vegetable oil
¾ cup all-purpose flour
8 green onions, chopped or 1
    large onion, chopped
2 to 3 cloves garlic, minced
1 teaspoon salt
¼ teaspoon pepper

Red pepper to taste
1 (6-ounce) can tomato paste
4 green peppers, finely
    chopped
3 bay leaves
⅛ teaspoon dried whole
    thyme
¼ teaspoon sugar
1 tablespoon dry sherry
    (optional)
3 cups hot cooked rice

Peel and devein shrimp; set shrimp aside. Boil shrimp peelings in water with crab boil for 5 minutes. Strain and reserve liquid.

Combine oil and flour in a large Dutch oven; cook over medium heat, stirring constantly, 15 to 20 minutes or until caramel colored. Stir in onions and garlic; cook until slightly brown. Add shrimp, salt, ¼ teaspoon pepper, red pepper, tomato paste, and green peppers; cook over medium heat 5 minutes, stirring constantly. Add 1 cup shrimp stock, bay leaves, thyme, and sugar. Reduce heat to low; cook 15 minutes, stirring frequently. Stir in sherry, if desired. Remove and discard bay leaves; serve over hot cooked rice. Yield: 6 to 8 servings.

Artist's Palate Cookbook
Women's Volunteer Committee, New Orleans Museum of Art
New Orleans, Louisiana

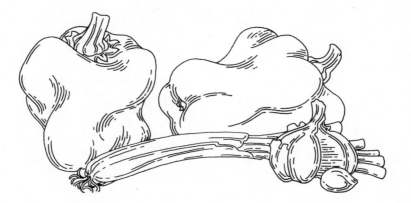

Palmito con Arroz y Camarão
(Palm Hearts with Rice and Shrimp)

1 pound unpeeled fresh
  shrimp
1 clove garlic, crushed
1 tablespoon minced green
  pepper
1 tablespoon minced onion
1 tablespoon minced fresh
  parsley
2 tablespoons olive oil
2 tablespoons tomato sauce
½ teaspoon salt
⅛ teaspoon pepper

2 cups cooked rice
1 (14-ounce) can palm hearts,
  drained and cut into ½-inch
  pieces
1 green pepper, cut into
  strips
2 tablespoons chopped
  pimiento
2 tablespoons sliced black
  olives
2 tablespoons chopped green
  olives

Peel and devein shrimp; set shrimp aside.

Sauté garlic, minced green pepper, onion, and parsley in olive oil in a large skillet until vegetables are tender. Add shrimp, and cook over medium heat 5 minutes or until shrimp turn pink, stirring occasionally.

Stir in tomato sauce, salt, pepper, and cooked rice; cook over medium heat 2 to 3 minutes or just until mixture is thoroughly heated. Add palm hearts, stirring gently. Transfer shrimp mixture to a serving platter, and garnish with green pepper strips, chopped pimiento, sliced black olives, and chopped green olives. Yield: 4 servings.   Maria Azevedo

"delicious"
The Elisabeth Morrow School Parents Association
Englewood, New Jersey

Meats

The Indian Scout statue stands on a hill in Penn Valley Park with an excellent vantage point for viewing the downtown district of Kansas City, Missouri. Geographically located in the heart of America, Kansas City has experienced many changes in the years since the railroad connected the city to Chicago, and it became a major livestock-distribution center.

☆☆☆

Delicious Mushroom Pot Roast

1 (4-pound) chuck or rump
  roast
1 teaspoon salt
¼ teaspoon pepper
2 tablespoons all-purpose
  flour
2 tablespoons vegetable oil
1 large onion, thinly sliced
¼ cup water
¼ cup catsup
½ teaspoon dried whole
  marjoram

½ teaspoon dried whole
  rosemary
½ teaspoon dried whole
  thyme
¼ teaspoon dry mustard
2 cloves garlic, minced
⅓ cup sherry
1 bay leaf
Mushroom Gravy

Sprinkle roast with salt and pepper. Dredge in flour, and brown on all sides in hot oil in a Dutch oven. Add sliced onion.

Combine water, catsup, marjoram, rosemary, thyme, mustard, garlic, and sherry. Pour over roast; add bay leaf. Cover and cook over low heat 3 hours or until roast is tender. Remove and discard bay leaf.

Remove roast to a serving platter, reserving drippings in Dutch oven for gravy. Serve roast with Mushroom Gravy. Yield: 6 servings.

Mushroom Gravy

Pan drippings
1 (6-ounce) jar sliced
  mushrooms

¼ cup cold water
2 tablespoons all-purpose
  flour

Skim off and discard fat from drippings in which roast was cooked. Add mushrooms and liquid to pan drippings. Blend water and flour together, and gradually add to mixture in skillet. Cook over medium heat, stirring until gravy thickens. Yield: 4 cups.

Billie Koon Brady

Prescriptions for Good Eating
The Greenville County Medical Society Auxiliary
Greenville, South Carolina

Smoked Eye of the Round

½ cup Worcestershire sauce
½ cup teriyaki sauce
¼ cup plus 2 tablespoons
  lemon juice
¼ cup white wine vinegar
2 tablespoons seasoned salt
1 (4- to 5-pound) eye of
  round roast

Combine first 5 ingredients in a small bowl; mix well. Place roast in a large shallow dish; pour marinade over top, and cover tightly. Marinate in refrigerator 12 to 24 hours, turning occasionally. Remove roast from marinade, and set aside.

Prepare charcoal fire in smoker, and let burn 10 to 15 minutes. Place water pan in smoker, and fill with water. Place roast on food rack. Cover with smoker lid, and cook 6 to 7 hours, refilling water pan and adding charcoal as needed.

Remove roast from food rack. Let stand 10 minutes. Slice roast thinly to serve. Yield: 12 servings.

Taste of the South
The Symphony League of Jackson, Mississippi

Sauerbraten

1 (3½-pound) eye of round
  roast
1 teaspoon salt
½ teaspoon pepper
2 medium onions, sliced
1 small carrot, scraped and
  minced
1 stalk celery, chopped
8 whole cloves
4 bay leaves
½ teaspoon whole
  peppercorns
1½ cups red wine vinegar
2½ cups water
¼ cup butter or margarine
Gingersnap Gravy

Rub roast with salt and pepper. Place in a large deep ovenproof dish. Add onions and next 5 ingredients. Combine vinegar and water in a saucepan; bring to a boil. Pour over roast; cover and marinate in refrigerator at least 48 hours, turning roast occasionally.

Remove roast from marinade, reserving marinade. Pat roast dry with paper towels. Melt butter in a large Dutch oven. Add roast; brown on all sides. Strain marinade, and pour over roast. Cover and simmer 2½ to 3 hours or until tender, turning once. Remove roast to a serving platter, reserving 1½ cups marinade for gravy. Serve roast with Gingersnap Gravy. Yield: 6 servings.

Gingersnap Gravy

2 tablespoons sugar
1½ cups marinade
½ cup water

8 gingersnaps, crushed
½ cup commercial sour
cream

Melt sugar in a medium skillet. Stir in 1½ cups marinade and ½ cup water. Add gingersnap crumbs. Cook, stirring frequently, until mixture is slightly thickened. Stir in sour cream. Cook just until thoroughly heated. Yield: 2½ cups.   Fredericka Miller

Appetizers, Entrées 'n More
The Winona Memorial Foundation Auxiliary
Indianapolis, Indiana

Fileto Saltedo

½ cup olive oil
2 medium baking potatoes,
peeled and cubed
1 small onion, chopped
1 small green pepper,
chopped
1 clove garlic, minced
1 medium-size tomato, seeded
and diced
¼ pound diced cooked ham

4½ ounces chorizo, sliced
2 pounds top sirloin beef, cut
into ¾-inch cubes
3 tablespoons tomato sauce
½ teaspoon salt
¼ cup frozen green peas,
thawed
1 tablespoon sliced pimiento
¼ cup dry sherry
3 cups hot cooked yellow rice

Place olive oil in a large nonstick skillet over medium heat. Add potatoes, and cook 3 to 4 minutes or until browned. Remove potatoes with a slotted spoon, and set aside. Combine onion, green pepper, and garlic in skillet. Sauté until vegetables are tender. Add tomato; sauté 1 minute. Remove vegetable mixture from skillet with a slotted spoon. Set aside.

Combine ham and chorizo in skillet. Sauté over medium heat 5 minutes. Add beef to meat in skillet, and sauté over medium-high heat 3 to 4 minutes. Add potatoes and vegetable mixture, and stir in tomato sauce and salt. Cook, stirring gently, until beef reaches desired degree of doneness. Stir in peas, pimiento, and sherry. Serve over hot cooked rice. Yield: 6 servings.

Gulfshore Delights
The Junior League of Fort Myers, Florida

BBQ Beef Sandwiches

1 (3-pound) boneless chuck
  roast
½ teaspoon salt
⅛ teaspoon pepper
3 tablespoons vegetable oil
1 cup water
1 medium onion, chopped
½ cup chopped celery
2 tablespoons firmly packed
  brown sugar

2 teaspoons dry mustard
2 tablespoons Worcestershire
  sauce
2 tablespoons vinegar
1 teaspoon liquid smoke
1 (14-ounce) bottle catsup
2 tablespoons fresh lemon
  juice
1 cup water
12 hamburger buns

Sprinkle roast with salt and pepper. Brown on all sides in hot oil in
a Dutch oven. Add 1 cup water; cover and bake at 350° for 2 hours
or until tender. Shred when cool. Combine onion and next 9
ingredients in a saucepan, and simmer 10 minutes. Add beef, and
mix well. Serve on buns. Yield: 12 servings.   Vicki Barnes

Our Country Cookin'
The Junior Social Workers of Chickasha, Oklahoma

Beef, Villa Cancello

¼ cup vegetable oil
2 pounds lean boneless
  sirloin, cut into 1-inch
  cubes
½ cup all-purpose flour
2 medium onions, chopped
1 clove garlic, minced
2 cups diluted canned beef
  broth
1 cup Burgundy or other dry
  red wine
2 tablespoons olive oil
1 bay leaf
¼ cup pearl onions
½ cup chopped fresh parsley,
  divided

½ teaspoon salt
½ teaspoon sugar
¼ teaspoon dried whole
  oregano
¼ teaspoon pepper
6 carrots, scraped and cut
  into 1-inch pieces
3 stalks celery, cut into
  1-inch pieces
½ cup fresh green peas
⅓ cup sliced fresh
  mushrooms
1 teaspoon cornstarch
1 tablespoon water

Heat vegetable oil in a Dutch oven. Dredge beef in flour. Add beef
to oil, browning on all sides. Remove meat, and set aside.

Add onion and garlic to oil in Dutch oven. Cook over medium heat until tender. Add beef, broth, and next 9 ingredients. Bring to a boil. Cover, reduce heat, and simmer 1 hour. Add carrots, celery, and peas. Cover and simmer 1 hour. Add mushrooms, and cook 5 minutes. Combine cornstarch and water. Stir into beef mixture. Cook until mixture is thickened and meat is tender. Remove and discard bay leaf. Yield: 6 servings.   Paul Strauss

Chord en Bleu
The Orchestra of Illinois Guild
Glenview, Illinois

Beef Marengo

1 (2½-pound) boneless top round roast	2 tablespoons tomato paste
2 tablespoons vegetable oil	3 celery tops
2 tablespoons olive oil	2 sprigs fresh parsley
2 tablespoons all-purpose flour	1 bay leaf
1 teaspoon salt	1 teaspoon dried whole thyme
½ teaspoon freshly ground pepper	24 boiling onions
1 cup Burgundy or other dry red wine	2 tablespoons butter or margarine
1 cup diluted canned beef broth	½ pound fresh mushrooms, sliced
	1 large tomato, peeled, seeded, and chopped

Trim excess fat from roast; cut into 1-inch cubes.

Brown meat in oils in a Dutch oven. Remove meat. Stir in flour, salt, and pepper; cook 1 minute, stirring constantly. Return meat to Dutch oven; add wine, broth, tomato paste, celery, parsley, bay leaf, and thyme. Cover and simmer 2 hours. Remove and discard celery and bay leaf.

Cut ends from onions. Blanch onions in boiling water 2 minutes; drain well. Remove paper skin from onions, and sauté onions in butter in a skillet until lightly browned; add mushrooms, and cook until tender. Add onion mixture to meat mixture in Dutch oven; simmer 20 minutes. Stir in tomato; cook 10 minutes. Serve immediately. Yield: 6 servings.

California Fresh
The Junior League of Oakland-East Bay, California

Boeuf Bourguignon

1 (4-pound) boneless chuck
  roast, cut into 2-inch cubes
2½ cups Burgundy or other
  dry red wine
8 ounces salt pork, cut into
  ¼-inch cubes
1 tablespoon butter or
  margarine
30 boiling onions
1 pound fresh mushrooms
3 tablespoons butter or
  margarine
Bouquet garni
2 tablespoons chopped green
  onions

¼ cup finely chopped carrot
3 tablespoons all-purpose
  flour
1 cup canned beef broth,
  diluted and heated
1 tablespoon tomato paste
1 teaspoon salt
1 teaspoon dried whole
  thyme
1 clove garlic, minced
⅛ teaspoon freshly ground
  pepper
2 tablespoons finely chopped
  fresh parsley
Hot cooked rice

Combine beef cubes and wine in a large shallow container. Cover and marinate in refrigerator 2 to 3 hours.

Cook salt pork in 1 quart boiling water for 5 minutes. Drain on paper towels; pat dry. Heat 1 tablespoon butter in a skillet. Add salt pork, and fry over medium-high heat until pork is crisp and all fat is rendered. Remove and discard pork, reserving pan drippings in skillet. Brown onions in pan drippings in skillet over medium heat. Transfer onions and 3 tablespoons pan drippings to a shallow baking dish. Bake at 350° for 30 minutes or until tender. Set aside.

Sauté mushrooms in 3 tablespoons butter in a large skillet for 2 to 3 minutes. Remove from heat, and set aside.

Remove beef cubes from wine, reserving wine. Pat beef cubes dry with paper towels. Brown beef in several batches in 3 tablespoons pan drippings, adding more drippings as needed. Transfer browned beef to a 5-quart casserole. Add bouquet garni. Set aside.

Sauté green onions and carrot in a large skillet until tender. Add flour. Cook 1 minute, stirring constantly. Gradually stir in beef broth. Add wine and tomato paste. Bring to a boil, stirring until thickened. Stir in salt, thyme, garlic, pepper, and parsley. Pour over beef in casserole. Bake at 325° for 2½ hours or until meat is tender. Remove from oven; add mushroom and onion mixtures. Bake an additional 15 minutes. Serve over rice. Yield: 10 servings.

Some Like It South!
The Junior League of Pensacola, Florida

Sirloin Sesame Steak

½ cup vegetable oil
⅓ cup sesame seeds
4 medium onions, sliced
½ cup soy sauce
¼ cup lemon juice
1 tablespoon sugar

¼ teaspoon cracked pepper
2 cloves garlic, crushed
1 (2½- to 3-pound) boneless top sirloin steak, 1 to 1½ inches thick

Combine oil and sesame seeds in a skillet. Cook over medium-high heat until sesame seeds are golden. Combine sesame seeds, onion, soy sauce, lemon juice, sugar, pepper, and garlic in a 13- x 9-x 2-inch baking dish. Stir well. Add steak, basting with marinade. Cover and marinate in refrigerator at least 5 hours. Remove steak from marinade, reserving marinade. Grill steak over hot coals 12 minutes on each side or to desired degree of doneness, basting with marinade. Yield: 6 servings. Happy Waller

Bravo
The Greensboro Symphony Guild
Greensboro, North Carolina

Flank Steak with Mustard Caper Sauce

1 tablespoon butter or margarine
1 tablespoon vegetable oil
1 (1½-pound) flank steak
3 tablespoons butter or margarine
3 tablespoons dry vermouth

1 tablespoon Dijon mustard
¼ teaspoon Worcestershire sauce
1½ tablespoons capers
Fresh watercress sprigs (optional)

Melt 1 tablespoon butter and oil in a skillet. Add steak, and cook over medium heat 5 minutes on each side or to desired degree of doneness. Remove steak to a serving platter, reserving drippings in skillet. Add 3 tablespoons butter to drippings in skillet, and melt over medium heat. Combine vermouth, mustard, Worcestershire sauce, and capers; gradually add to melted butter, stirring with a wire whisk until smooth. Slice steak diagonally across the grain into thin slices; pour sauce over steak. Garnish with watercress, if desired. Yield: 4 to 6 servings.

Private Collection 2
The Junior League of Palo Alto, California

Steak au Poivre

3 tablespoons cracked black
pepper
4 (8-ounce) rib-eye steaks
2 tablespoons butter or
margarine
2 tablespoons vegetable oil
2 tablespoons finely chopped
shallots

¼ cup Cognac
¾ teaspoon cornstarch
¾ cup undiluted canned beef
broth, divided
3½ tablespoons whipping
cream
1½ tablespoons butter or
margarine

Press cracked pepper into both sides of each steak. Cover and refrigerate 1 hour. Heat 2 tablespoons butter and oil in a skillet over medium heat. Cook steaks 3 minutes on each side, or until browned. Remove steaks from skillet, cover, and keep warm.

Sauté shallots in skillet over medium heat until tender. Wipe out excess oil from skillet with paper towels. Pour Cognac into skillet, and ignite, using a long match.

After flames die, dissolve cornstarch in 2 tablespoons beef broth, and add to Cognac with remaining beef broth, stirring until thickened. Stir in cream. Add 1½ tablespoons butter, and swirl to blend. Serve over steaks. Yield: 4 servings.   Sara Scott

Down Home in High Style
The Houston Academy
Dothan, Alabama

Chinese Green Pepper Steak

1½ pounds sirloin steak,
1-inch thick
¼ cup vegetable oil
1 clove garlic, minced
1 teaspoon salt
1 teaspoon ground ginger
½ teaspoon pepper
2 large onions, thinly sliced
1 tablespoon cornstarch
¼ cup water

1 (8-ounce) can sliced water
chestnuts, drained
½ cup canned beef broth,
diluted
¼ cup soy sauce
½ teaspoon sugar
3 large green peppers, sliced
4 green onions, chopped
(optional)
Hot cooked rice

Partially freeze steak; slice diagonally across the grain into 3- x ⅛-inch strips. Heat oil in a large skillet; sauté garlic, salt, ginger, and pepper until garlic is golden. Add steak, and cook 5 minutes or until browned. Remove meat. Add sliced onion, and cook 5 minutes.

Combine cornstarch and water; mix well. Return meat to skillet, add cornstarch mixture, water chestnuts, broth, soy sauce, and sugar. Simmer until sauce thickens. Stir in green peppers; cook 5 minutes. Add green onions, if desired. Serve over hot cooked rice. Yield: 6 to 8 servings.   Dorothy J. Beermann

Nebraska Feeders Auxiliary Cookbook
Madison, Nebraska

Beef Brisket in Beer

1 (3- to 4-pound) beef brisket
¼ teaspoon salt
¼ teaspoon pepper
1 medium onion, sliced
1 (12-ounce) can beer
¼ cup chili sauce

2 tablespoons firmly packed
    brown sugar
1 clove garlic, minced
½ cup water
2 tablespoons all-purpose
    flour

Trim excess fat from brisket. Place brisket in a 13- x 9- x 2-inch baking dish; sprinkle with salt and pepper. Cover with onion slices. Combine beer, chili sauce, brown sugar, and garlic; pour over meat. Cover with aluminum foil, and bake at 350° for 3½ hours. Remove foil; bake an additional 30 minutes, basting occasionally with pan juices. Remove meat to a platter; keep warm.

Skim fat from pan juices. Pour off liquid, reserving 1 cup. Combine water and flour in a saucepan. Add 1 cup liquid; cook over medium heat until thickened and bubbly. Slice meat across grain into thin slices, and serve with gravy. Yield: 8 to 10 servings.
                                                            Anne Austen

There Once Was a Cook . . .
The Wesley Institute, Inc.
Pittsburgh, Pennsylvania

Best-Ever Brisket Barbecue

1 (4-pound) beef brisket
2 tablespoons chili powder
1½ teaspoons salt
1½ teaspoons pepper
1 teaspoon crushed bay
  leaves
1 cup catsup
1 cup water
½ cup cider vinegar
¼ cup Worcestershire sauce

3 stalks celery, chopped
2 tablespoons chopped onion
1 clove garlic, minced
3 bay leaves
1 teaspoon sugar
1 teaspoon paprika
1 teaspoon chili powder
⅛ teaspoon salt
Dash of pepper

Trim excess fat from brisket. Place brisket, fat side up, in a roasting pan. Combine 2 tablespoons chili powder, 1½ teaspoons salt, 1½ teaspoons pepper, and 1 teaspoon crushed bay leaves; sprinkle over brisket. Cover and bake at 275° for 4 hours.

Combine catsup and remaining ingredients in a large saucepan. Bring to a boil; reduce heat and simmer 15 minutes. Strain.

Scrape seasonings off brisket; cut meat into thin slices. Pour sauce over sliced meat, and serve immediately. Yield: 8 servings.

A Pinch of Salt Lake
The Junior League of Salt Lake City, Utah

Irish Corned Beef and Cabbage with Mustard Sauce

1 (4-pound) corned beef
  brisket
2 medium onions, sliced
1 medium onion, studded
  with 3 whole cloves
1 large carrot, scraped and
  sliced
1 bunch fresh parsley

1 bay leaf
¼ teaspoon pepper
2 pounds small new potatoes,
  peeled
1 (2-pound) cabbage, cut into
  wedges
Irish Mustard Sauce

Combine corned beef and water to cover in a large Dutch oven; bring to a boil. Remove from heat. Drain. Add fresh water to cover. Add onion, carrot, parsley, bay leaf, and pepper. Bring to a boil. Skim off foam, if necessary. Reduce heat, cover, and simmer 4 hours or until tender. Remove onion and parsley. Add potatoes to Dutch oven. Simmer 10 minutes. Add cabbage wedges, and simmer 20 minutes or until vegetables are tender. Remove and discard bay leaf.

Transfer corned beef and vegetables to a serving platter. Serve with Irish Mustard Sauce. Yield: 6 to 8 servings.

Irish Mustard Sauce

1 tablespoon cornstarch
2 teaspoons sugar
1 teaspoon dry mustard
½ teaspoon salt
1 cup water
¼ cup cider vinegar

1 tablespoon butter or
  margarine, melted
1 teaspoon grated fresh
  horseradish
2 egg yolks, beaten

Combine first 4 ingredients in a medium saucepan; stir well. Add water. Cook over low heat, stirring constantly, until thickened. Remove from heat. Stir in vinegar, butter, and horseradish. Gradually stir about one-fourth of hot mixture into yolks; add to remaining hot mixture, stirring constantly. Cook over low heat, stirring constantly, until thickened. Yield: 1½ cups.   Grace E. Easley

McComb's International Cuisine Affair
McComb Interdenominational Care Association
McComb, Mississippi

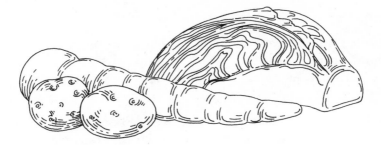

"Connecticut" Spaghetti Sauce

1 large onion, chopped
1 clove garlic, crushed
2 tablespoons butter or margarine
2 tablespoons vegetable oil
1 (6-ounce) can tomato paste
2 cups water
1 teaspoon sugar
1 teaspoon salt
½ teaspoon pepper
1 (35-ounce) can Italian plum tomatoes, undrained

1 (28-ounce) can whole tomatoes, undrained
1 whole chicken breast, skinned and cut into 4 pieces
4 country-style ribs, cut into serving-size pieces
8 sausage links
½ cup hot water
Meatballs (recipe follows)
1 (1-pound) package spaghetti

Sauté onion and garlic in butter and oil in a large Dutch oven for 1 minute. Stir in tomato paste. Cook 2 minutes, stirring constantly. Add 2 cups water, sugar, salt, and pepper; stir well.

Place plum tomatoes in container of an electric blender. Cover and process until pureed. Add to mixture in Dutch oven. Repeat procedure with whole tomatoes, and add to mixture in Dutch oven. Simmer, uncovered, 2 hours, stirring occasionally.

Place chicken, ribs, and sausage in a roasting pan. Bake at 350° for 35 to 45 minutes or until done. Add meat to sauce in Dutch oven, reserving pan juices. Pour ½ cup hot water into roasting pan with pan juices; stir well. Add to sauce, and simmer, uncovered, 1 hour. Add meatballs, and simmer 1 additional hour.

Cook spaghetti according to package directions. Drain. Serve sauce over hot cooked spaghetti. Yield: 10 to 12 servings.

Meatballs

½ pound ground beef
½ pound ground pork
½ cup soft breadcrumbs
1 small onion, chopped

2 eggs, beaten
¼ cup milk
¼ teaspoon salt
¼ teaspoon pepper

Combine all ingredients, mixing well. Shape into 1-inch balls. Brown meatballs, in 2 batches, in a large nonstick skillet over medium-high heat. Yield: 3 dozen meatballs.   Louise Thoman

Our Special Blend
The Rehabilitation Center of Eastern Fairfield County
Bridgeport, Connecticut

Tamale Pie

½ pound bulk pork sausage
1 pound ground chuck
2 cups sliced celery
1 cup chopped onion
1 clove garlic, minced
2 cups fresh corn
1 (16-ounce) can tomatoes
2 teaspoons chili powder

1½ teaspoons salt
½ cup yellow cornmeal
1 (6-ounce) can pitted ripe
  olives
1½ cups (6 ounces) shredded
  Cheddar cheese
Paprika

Cook sausage and ground chuck in a skillet until browned, stirring to crumble. Drain. Stir in celery, onion, and garlic; cook until tender. Stir in corn and next 3 ingredients; simmer 15 minutes. Slowly stir in cornmeal, cooking until thickened. Remove from heat; stir in olives. Pour into a greased 2-quart casserole; sprinkle with cheese and paprika. Bake, uncovered, at 350° for 35 minutes or until set. Yield: 6 to 8 servings.   Stephen Birmingham

From Palette to Palate
The Cincinnati Art Museum
Cincinnati, Ohio

Picadillo

2 medium onions, finely
  chopped
2 large green peppers,
  chopped
2 cloves garlic, minced
2 tablespoons olive oil
1½ pounds lean ground beef
½ teaspoon salt
½ teaspoon celery salt
¼ teaspoon dried whole
  oregano

¼ teaspoon pepper
2 tablespoons Worcestershire
  sauce
1 (8-ounce) can tomato sauce
1 (16-ounce) can whole
  tomatoes, undrained and
  chopped
1 (3-ounce) jar pimiento-
  stuffed olives, drained
½ cup raisins
Hot cooked yellow rice

Sauté onion, pepper, and garlic in hot oil in a skillet until tender. Add beef. Cook until browned; stir to crumble. Drain. Add salt and next 8 ingredients; stir well. Cover. Simmer 30 minutes; stir occasionally. Serve over rice. Yield: 6 to 8 servings.   Karon Wakstein

Beyond the Bay
The Junior Service League of Panama City, Florida

Greek Green Bean and Beef Bake

1 large onion, chopped
1 teaspoon minced garlic
1 tablespoon butter or
   margarine
1½ pounds ground beef
½ cup dry sherry
1 (8-ounce) can tomato sauce
1 teaspoon salt
1 teaspoon pepper
½ teaspoon ground cinnamon
¼ teaspoon ground nutmeg

2 eggs
1½ cups small-curd cottage
   cheese
1 tablespoon finely chopped
   fresh parsley
2 cups cooked green beans
¼ cup grated Parmesan
   cheese
2 tablespoons fine, dry
   breadcrumbs

Sauté onion and garlic in butter in a large skillet. Add ground beef; cook until meat is browned, stirring to crumble. Drain. Add sherry, tomato sauce, salt, pepper, cinnamon, and nutmeg; set aside. Combine eggs, cottage cheese, and parsley; set aside.

Layer green beans, meat mixture, and cottage cheese mixture in a 12- x 8- x 2-inch baking dish. Sprinkle with Parmesan cheese and breadcrumbs. Bake at 350° for 40 minutes. Yield: 8 servings.

Kathryn Greene

The Grace Cathedral Cookbook
The Women's Evening Organization
San Francisco, California

Hazel's Goulash

2 pounds ground beef
2 tablespoons vegetable oil
5 small onions, finely
   chopped
4 green peppers, finely
   chopped
2 cloves garlic, minced
¼ teaspoon salt
¼ teaspoon pepper
2 (8-ounce) cans tomato sauce
2 (6-ounce) cans tomato paste

1 (14½-ounce) can stewed
   tomatoes, undrained
1 (12-ounce) can whole kernel
   corn, drained
1 (6-ounce) can pitted ripe
   olives, drained
1 (12-ounce) package egg
   noodles, cooked and
   drained
4 cups (16 ounces) shredded
   Cheddar cheese

Brown ground beef in oil in a large Dutch oven, stirring to crumble. Add onion, green pepper, garlic, salt, and pepper; cook over medium heat 10 minutes, stirring frequently. Stir in tomato sauce, tomato paste, and stewed tomatoes; cook 15 minutes. Add corn and olives; stirring well.

Remove from heat; gently stir in noodles. Spoon mixture into two 12- x 8- x 2-inch baking dishes. Sprinkle evenly with cheese, and bake, uncovered, at 350° for 45 minutes or until hot and bubbly. Yield: 16 servings.   Hazel G. Peré

Down the Bayou
The Bayou Civic Club
Larose, Louisiana

Meat Roll

2 **pounds ground beef**
¾ **cup soft breadcrumbs**
½ **cup tomato juice**
2 **eggs, beaten**
2 **tablespoons chopped fresh parsley**
½ **teaspoon dried whole oregano**

¼ **teaspoon salt**
¼ **teaspoon pepper**
1 **small clove garlic, minced**
8 **thin slices ham**
1½ **cups (6 ounces) shredded mozzarella cheese**
3 **(1-ounce) slices mozzarella cheese**

Combine ground beef, breadcrumbs, tomato juice, eggs, parsley, oregano, salt, pepper, and garlic, mixing well; shape into a 12- x 10-inch rectangle on a sheet of wax paper. Arrange ham slices over meat mixture, leaving a 1-inch margin around edges. Top with shredded mozzarella cheese. Beginning at short end, roll up, jellyroll fashion, lifting wax paper to help in rolling. Press edges and ends together to seal.

Place roll, seam side down, in a lightly greased 13- x 9- x 2-inch baking pan. Bake at 350° for 1 hour and 15 minutes; remove from oven. Cut each cheese slice into 2 triangles, and arrange on top of roll with edges slightly overlapping. Let stand 5 minutes before serving. Yield: 6 to 8 servings.   Janet Palmer

Colorado WIFE
Women Involved in Farm Economics
Kiowa County, Colorado

Veal in Vermouth

1 (1½-pound) veal steak
(½-inch thick)
¼ cup all-purpose flour
¼ cup butter or margarine
½ pound fresh mushrooms,
sliced
1 clove garlic, minced

1 tablespoon lemon juice
½ teaspoon salt
Dash of pepper
⅓ cup dry vermouth
2 tablespoons finely chopped
fresh parsley

Place veal between 2 sheets of wax paper, and flatten to ¼-inch thickness, using a meat mallet or rolling pin. Cut veal into 2-inch squares, and dredge in flour.

Melt butter in a large skillet. Add veal, several pieces at a time, cooking until browned on both sides. Return all veal to skillet. Add mushrooms, garlic, lemon juice, salt, pepper, and vermouth. Cover and simmer 20 minutes or until veal is tender. Garnish with parsley. Yield: 4 to 6 servings.   Mary Lou DeFillippo

Treat Yourself to the Best
The Junior League of Wheeling, West Virginia

Veal and Artichoke Moussaka

4 (9-ounce) packages frozen
artichoke hearts
¼ cup butter or margarine
1 large onion, chopped
2 pounds ground veal
2 large tomatoes, seeded and
chopped
½ cup Burgundy or other dry
red wine
⅓ cup chopped fresh parsley
1 teaspoon salt

1 teaspoon garlic powder
¼ teaspoon ground cinnamon
¼ teaspoon ground nutmeg
¼ teaspoon pepper
Sauce (recipe follows)
3 eggs, beaten
1 cup seasoned, dry
breadcrumbs
1 cup grated Parmesan
cheese

Cook artichoke hearts according to package directions. Drain well, and set aside.

Melt butter in a large skillet over medium heat. Add onion, and sauté until tender. Add veal; cook until lightly browned, stirring to crumble. Combine tomatoes and wine in a medium saucepan. Cook over medium heat 1 to 2 minutes or until thoroughly heated. Add to veal mixture. Stir in parsley, salt, garlic powder, cinnamon, nutmeg, and pepper. Simmer, uncovered, 30 minutes. Stir in 3 tablespoons sauce; set aside. Whisk eggs into remaining sauce; set aside.

Sprinkle ½ cup breadcrumbs evenly in bottom of a greased 3-quart shallow baking dish. Arrange half of artichoke hearts over breadcrumbs. Top with half of veal mixture. Sprinkle with ½ cup Parmesan cheese. Repeat layers, beginning with remaining ½ cup breadcrumbs. Top with sauce. Bake, uncovered, at 300° for 30 minutes. Yield: 8 servings.

Sauce

¼ cup butter or margarine
¼ cup all-purpose flour
3 cups milk, scalded

1 teaspoon salt
¼ teaspoon pepper

Melt butter over low heat in a saucepan; add flour, stirring until smooth. Cook 1 minute, stirring constantly. Gradually add milk; cook over medium heat, stirring constantly, until mixture is thickened and bubbly. Stir in salt and pepper. Yield: about 3 cups.

Deborah L. Sutton

Mountain Measures: A Second Serving
The Junior League of Charleston, West Virginia

Sherry-Glazed Roast Leg of Lamb

1 (5- to 6-pound) leg of lamb
1 clove garlic, slivered
3 to 4 fresh mint sprigs,
   finely chopped
½ teaspoon salt
½ teaspoon pepper

½ teaspoon ground thyme
1 medium onion, cut into
   eighths
⅓ cup dry sherry
⅓ cup mint or currant jelly

Make several slits on outside of lamb, and insert garlic slivers. Combine mint, salt, pepper, and thyme; rub on roast. Layer onion in a roasting pan; place roast on onions. Insert meat thermometer, making sure it does not touch fat or bone. Bake at 325° for 2 to 2½ hours. Combine sherry and jelly. Glaze roast with sherry mixture; bake an additional 30 minutes or until thermometer registers 160°. Let stand 10 minutes before carving. Yield: 6 to 8 servings.

Oregon Sampler: Resorts & Recipes
The Assistance League of Corvallis, Oregon

Marinated Broiled Lamb

1 (5- to 7-pound) leg of lamb, boned
½ cup vegetable oil
¼ cup lemon juice
1 teaspoon salt
1 teaspoon dried whole oregano
½ teaspoon dried whole rosemary
½ teaspoon dried whole basil
¼ teaspoon pepper
2 bay leaves
2 cloves garlic, minced

Place lamb in a large shallow dish. Combine oil and remaining ingredients; pour over meat, turning to coat with marinade. Cover and marinate in refrigerator at least 12 hours, turning occasionally. Remove and discard bay leaves. Place lamb, fat side down, on rack in a roasting pan. Broil 4 inches from heat for 20 minutes; turn meat, and brush with marinade. Lower broiler rack one notch; broil an additional 20 minutes. Yield: 8 to 10 servings.   Louise Szymanski

Not by Bread Alone
Holy Trinity Episcopal Church
Charleston, South Carolina

Lamb Pilaf with Apricots

2 pounds boneless leg of lamb, cubed
¼ cup plus 2 tablespoons butter or margarine
2 onions, chopped
2 tablespoons raisins
1 clove garlic, minced
½ teaspoon ground cinnamon
¼ teaspoon ground allspice
¼ teaspoon ground nutmeg
1 (6-ounce) package dried apricots
¼ teaspoon salt
⅛ teaspoon pepper
Hot cooked rice

Brown lamb in butter in a Dutch oven over medium heat. Add onion, raisins, garlic, cinnamon, allspice, and nutmeg. Cover with water 1 inch above meat. Bring to a boil. Reduce heat, and simmer, uncovered, 1½ hours. Stir in apricots, salt, and pepper. Simmer 30 minutes or until lamb is tender. Serve over rice. Yield: 6 servings.

Savoring the Southwest
Roswell Symphony Guild Publications
Roswell, New Mexico

Turkish Pilaf

2 pounds boneless lamb, cut
  into 1-inch cubes
¼ cup butter or margarine,
  melted
3 medium onions, chopped
¼ teaspoon ground cinnamon
¼ teaspoon pepper
1 teaspoon salt
1 cup uncooked long-grain
  rice

¾ cup pitted prunes,
  chopped
½ cup raisins
2 tablespoons water
3 tablespoons lemon juice
1 tablespoon minced fresh
  parsley
½ cup slivered almonds,
  toasted

Sauté lamb in butter in a skillet over medium heat until lightly browned. Add onion, cinnamon, and pepper. Reduce heat, and simmer 2½ hours. Stir in 1 teaspoon salt; remove from heat.

Prepare rice according to package directions. Combine prunes and raisins; add boiling water to cover. Let stand 5 minutes; drain.

Remove meat from skillet, reserving pan drippings. Place meat and fruit in a buttered 3-quart casserole; toss gently. Spoon rice over meat. Add 2 tablespoons water to pan drippings; pour over rice. Cover and bake at 350° for 45 minutes; adding more water, if necessary. Add lemon juice and remaining ingredients; toss gently. Yield: 8 servings.

Even More Special
The Junior League of Durham and Orange Counties,
North Carolina

Celebration Lamb Chops

6 (1½-inch-thick) loin lamb
  chops
¼ cup fresh lemon juice
2 tablespoons minced garlic

1 tablespoon dried whole
  oregano
1½ teaspoons pepper

Place chops on rack of a broiler pan. Sprinkle both sides of each chop with 1 teaspoon lemon juice, ½ teaspoon garlic, ¼ teaspoon oregano, and ⅛ teaspoon pepper. Broil chops 8 minutes on each side or to desired degree of doneness. Yield: 6 servings.

Rare Collection
The Junior League of Galveston County, Texas

Stuffed Crown Roast of Pork with Mustard Sauce

1 (16-rib) crown roast of pork
½ teaspoon salt
½ teaspoon pepper
½ teaspoon dried whole
   thyme
4 cups breadcrumbs
⅔ cup milk
1 pound bulk pork sausage
1 cup minced onion
¼ cup butter or margarine
1½ cups chopped celery
½ cup raisins
½ cup fresh cranberries
4 cooking apples, peeled and
   diced
¼ cup all-purpose flour
1 cup Chablis or other dry
   white wine
2 cups whipping cream
¾ cup chicken broth
¾ cup water
3 tablespoons Dijon mustard

Season roast with salt, pepper, and thyme. Place roast, bone ends up, on rack in a shallow roasting pan. Cover exposed ends of ribs with aluminum foil. Insert meat thermometer into roast, making sure it does not touch fat or bone. Bake at 400° for 20 minutes. Reduce heat to 325°, and bake for 40 minutes. Reserve drippings. Combine breadcrumbs and milk; set aside. Cook sausage in a large skillet until browned, stirring to crumble. Drain. Sauté onion in butter until tender. Add celery, raisins, cranberries, and apples; sauté 5 minutes. Spoon stuffing into center of roast. Place remaining stuffing in a 9-inch square pan. Bake roast and pan of stuffing at 325° for 1 hour or until thermometer registers 160°.

Heat ¼ cup pan drippings in a medium saucepan; stir in flour. Cook, stirring constantly, until thickened. Add wine, and cook until mixture is reduced to ¼ cup. Add whipping cream, broth, and water; cook until thickened. Stir in mustard; serve warm with roast. Yield: 8 servings.   Beverley Rowland

"delicious"
The Elisabeth Morrow School Parents Association
Englewood, New Jersey

Pork Roast with Mustard Sauce and Honey Apples

1 tablespoon rubbed sage
¼ teaspoon dried whole marjoram
2 tablespoons soy sauce
2 cloves garlic, minced

½ cup Dijon mustard
1 (5-pound) rolled boneless pork loin roast
Honey Apples

Combine sage, marjoram, soy sauce, garlic, and mustard in a small bowl. Mix well.

Place roast, fat side up, in a shallow roasting pan; spread with mustard mixture. Insert meat thermometer, making sure it does not touch fat. Bake, uncovered, at 325° for 2 to 2½ hours or until thermometer registers 160°. Serve roast with Honey Apples. Yield: 10 to 12 servings.

Honey Apples

4 Granny Smith Apples
½ cup honey
¼ teaspoon salt

¼ teaspoon ground cinnamon
2 tablespoons cider vinegar

Peel, core, and slice apples into ½-inch-thick slices. Set aside.

Combine honey, salt, cinnamon, and vinegar in a large saucepan; bring to a boil. Add apples; reduce heat, and simmer 10 minutes. Yield: about 2 cups.

Winning at the Table
The Junior League of Las Vegas, Nevada

Grilled Pork with Cilantro Butter

½ cup butter or margarine, softened
3 tablespoons fresh lime juice
3 tablespoons finely chopped fresh cilantro
3 tablespoons finely chopped fresh parsley
⅛ teaspoon white pepper
½ cup olive oil

¼ cup fresh lime juice
¼ cup finely chopped fresh cilantro
1 tablespoon minced fresh gingerroot
1½ teaspoons grated lime rind
1 (2- to 3-pound) boneless pork loin roast, butterflied

Combine butter, 3 tablespoons lime juice, 3 tablespoons cilantro, parsley, and white pepper. Place butter mixture on wax paper, and shape into a log 1 inch in diameter. Chill 8 hours.

Combine oil, ¼ cup lime juice, ¼ cup cilantro, gingerroot, and lime rind in a small bowl, blending well. Set aside.

Place pork between 2 sheets of wax paper; flatten until even, using a meat mallet or rolling pin. Cut small slits on both sides of pork. Place in a 13- x 9- x 2-inch baking dish. Pour marinade over pork. Cover and marinate in refrigerator 8 hours.

Grill pork 5 inches from medium coals 10 to 15 minutes on each side or to desired degree of doneness, basting frequently with marinade. Transfer meat to a cutting board. Cover and let stand 5 minutes before slicing. Serve with Cilantro Butter. Yield: 4 to 6 servings.

Taste the Seasons
Woodside-Atherton Auxiliary to Children's Hospital at Stanford
Menlo Park, California

Pork Tenderloin Javanese

1 cup minced onion
6 Brazil nuts, grated
2 cloves garlic, minced
¼ cup olive oil
¼ cup lemon juice
¼ cup soy sauce
2 tablespoons brown sugar

2 tablespoons ground coriander
¼ teaspoon crushed red pepper
1 (2-pound) pork tenderloin, cut into 1-inch cubes
Hot cooked rice

Combine first 9 ingredients; mix well. Add pork, and stir to coat; cover and marinate in refrigerator 45 minutes.

Thread pork onto metal skewers. Grill over medium coals 25 to 30 minutes or to desired degree of doneness, turning and basting kabobs frequently with marinade. Serve pork kabobs over hot cooked rice. Yield: 6 servings.   Edwin Anderson

Centennial Cookbook: 100 Years of Free Masonry in North Dakota
The Grand Masonic Lodge
Fargo, North Dakota

Stir-Fried Wild Rice

⅔ cup uncooked wild rice
1 (8-ounce) lean pork
   tenderloin
3 tablespoons vegetable oil
1 cup sliced celery
1 cup sliced green onions
1 cup sliced fresh
   mushrooms
1 (8-ounce) can sliced water
   chestnuts, drained
8 ounces fresh snow pea
   pods, trimmed
1 tablespoon grated fresh
   gingerroot
1 tablespoon cornstarch
1 tablespoon dry sherry
3 tablespoons soy sauce
½ teaspoon salt
½ cup cashews

Wash wild rice in 3 changes of hot water; drain. Cook wild rice according to package directions, omitting salt.

Partially freeze pork tenderloin; slice diagonally across the grain into ¼-inch strips. Place oil in a heavy saucepan over medium-high heat for 1 minute. Add pork and stir-fry 3 to 5 minutes or until pork is no longer pink. Add celery, green onions, mushrooms, water chestnuts, snow peas, and gingerroot; stir-fry 3 to 5 minutes or until vegetables are crisp-tender. Stir in wild rice.

Combine cornstarch, sherry, soy sauce, and salt in a small bowl; stir well. Pour over pork mixture; cook over low heat, stirring constantly, 1 minute or until sauce is thickened. Sprinkle with cashews. Yield: 4 servings.

Wild Rice, Star of the North
The 1006 Summit Avenue Society
St. Paul, Minnesota

Pork Kabobs

1 (12-ounce) can beer
½ cup orange marmalade
¼ cup sugar
½ cup soy sauce
1 clove garlic, minced
1½ pounds lean, boneless
   pork, cut into 1-inch cubes

16 large fresh mushrooms
8 pearl onions, peeled and
   blanched
1 large green pepper, cut into
   1-inch pieces

Combine first 5 ingredients. Add pork, and stir to coat; cover and marinate in refrigerator overnight. Add vegetables to marinade one hour before cooking. Stir to coat. Alternate meat and vegetables on metal skewers. Grill kabobs about 6 inches from medium-hot coals for 20 minutes or until well done, turning and basting often with marinade. Yield: 6 servings.   Linda Johnston Rust

Pig Out
The Junior League of Waterloo-Cedar Falls, Iowa

Orange Pork Chops

6 (1-inch-thick) pork chops
1 (11-ounce) can mandarin
   oranges, undrained
¼ cup firmly packed brown
   sugar
3 whole cloves

½ teaspoon salt
½ teaspoon ground cinnamon
¼ cup catsup
1 tablespoon vinegar
1 teaspoon prepared mustard

Brown pork chops on both sides in a skillet; drain. Drain oranges, reserving ½ cup juice. Combine juice with remaining ingredients. Add oranges and juice mixture to pork chops. Cover and simmer 45 minutes or until pork chops are tender. Yield: 6 servings.

To Market, To Market
The Junior League of Owensboro, Kentucky

Oriental Barbecue

1 (10-ounce) jar plum jam
⅓ cup dark corn syrup
⅓ cup soy sauce
¼ cup chopped green onions

2 cloves garlic, minced
2 teaspoons ground ginger
2 pounds country-style
   spareribs

Combine all ingredients, except spareribs, in a medium saucepan. Cook over medium heat until jam melts. Place ribs in a 13- x 9- x 2-inch baking pan; pour jam mixture over ribs. Bake at 350° for 1 hour, basting and turning ribs every 15 minutes. Yield: 2 to 4 servings. Gwen T. Coe

The Great Entertainer Cookbook
The Buffalo Bill Historical Center
Cody, Wyoming

Szechuan Sausage in Pita Pockets

1½ pounds hot link sausage
1½ pounds lean ground pork
1 medium eggplant, unpeeled and cubed (about 1 pound)
3 tablespoons peanut oil
2 pints cherry tomatoes, halved
2 large sweet red peppers, chopped
1 (8-ounce) package mozzarella cheese, cubed
1 large onion, finely chopped
¾ cup chopped green onions
¼ cup minced garlic
2 tablespoons minced fresh gingerroot
2 tablespoons soy sauce
1 to 2 tablespoons chili paste with garlic
2 teaspoons sugar
½ cup chopped fresh cilantro
8 (6-inch) pita bread rounds, cut in half
Red leaf lettuce

Sauté sausage until thoroughly heated. Drain on paper towels. Let cool, and slice thinly; set aside. Place ground pork in skillet over medium heat. Cook until browned, stirring to crumble. Drain well, and set aside. Sauté eggplant in oil in a large skillet until tender. Drain well, and set aside.

Combine tomato halves, red pepper, cheese, and onions in a large bowl. Add sausage, pork, and eggplant. Toss gently. Combine garlic, gingerroot, soy sauce, chili paste, and sugar in a small bowl. Add to sausage mixture, tossing gently to coat well. Cover and chill.

Just before serving, add cilantro to chilled sausage mixture. Place pita bread on baking sheets. Bake at 350° for 2 minutes or until thoroughly heated. Fill each pita half with about 1 cup mixture. Arrange pita halves on lettuce-lined platter. Yield: 16 servings.

San Francisco Encore
The Junior League of San Francisco, California

Glazed Ham Loaf

2 pounds ground cooked ham
2 pounds ground fresh pork
1½ cups cracker crumbs
⅓ cup chopped onion
4 eggs, well beaten
1¼ teaspoons salt

2 cups milk
2 tablespoons chopped fresh
parsley
Glaze (recipe follows)
Mustard sauce (recipe
follows)

Combine ground ham and ground pork with cracker crumbs in a large mixing bowl. Add onion, eggs, salt, milk, and parsley; mix well. Shape into 2 loaves, and place on a 15- x 10- x 1-inch jellyroll pan; bake at 350° for 30 minutes. Baste with glaze, and continue baking for 1 hour, basting occasionally with glaze. Serve with mustard sauce. Yield: 12 servings.

Glaze

1 cup plus 3 tablespoons
firmly packed brown sugar
1 tablespoon plus 1½
teaspoons dry mustard

½ cup cider vinegar

Combine all ingredients in small saucepan. Bring to a boil over medium heat; boil for 1 minute. Yield: 1 cup plus 2 tablespoons.

Mustard Sauce

½ cup mayonnaise
½ cup commercial sour
cream
¼ cup prepared mustard
1 tablespoon minced fresh
chives

2 tablespoons prepared
horseradish
1 teaspoon lemon juice
⅛ teaspoon salt

Blend all ingredients together in a small bowl. Yield: 1⅓ cups.

Dixie Sayre Miller

America Discovers Columbus
The Junior League of Columbus, Ohio

Pasta, Grains, & Rice

Windmills, used for grinding grain into flour, dot the landscape near Cape Cod, Massachusetts. Generally a flat peninsula with sand dunes, low hills, and numerous lakes, Cape Cod is bounded by Cape Cod Bay to the north, Buzzards Bay to the west, Vineyard and Nantucket sounds to the south and the Atlantic Ocean to the east.

☆☆☆

Tortellini

2 (8-ounce) packages tortellini
with Parmesan cheese
¾ cup olive oil, divided
1 cup frozen green peas,
thawed and drained
1 green pepper, chopped
2 medium carrots, scraped
and cut into julienne strips

½ cup chopped fresh parsley
¼ cup red wine vinegar
2 cloves garlic, minced
1 teaspoon dried whole basil
¼ teaspoon salt
¼ teaspoon pepper

Cook tortellini according to package directions; drain well. Combine tortellini and ¼ cup oil in a bowl; toss gently. Cover and chill 30 minutes. Add peas, pepper, and carrots; cover and chill.

Combine ½ cup oil, parsley, and remaining ingredients in a jar. Cover tightly, and shake vigorously. Pour over salad, and toss gently. Yield: 12 servings.

Silver Soirees
The Service Guild of Birmingham, Alabama

Cold Tortellini Salad

1 (8-ounce) package spinach
tortellini
2 cups broccoli flowerets
1 Bermuda onion, sliced
1 cup garbanzo beans, rinsed
and drained
1 cup kidney beans, rinsed
and drained
1 cup lima beans, rinsed and
drained
1 (6-ounce) jar marinated
artichoke hearts, drained

1 (6-ounce) can pitted ripe
olives, drained
1 (16-ounce) bottle
commercial creamy Italian
salad dressing
24 cherry tomatoes, halved
1 medium-size ripe avocado,
peeled and sliced
¼ pound salami, sliced and
quartered
1 cup (4 ounces) freshly
grated Parmesan cheese

Cook tortellini according to package directions, omitting salt; drain. Rinse with cold water; drain. Combine tortellini and next 7 ingredients. Add creamy Italian dressing; toss gently. Cover and chill at least 8 hours. Stir in tomatoes, avocado, and salami; sprinkle with cheese. Yield: 8 to 10 servings.

A Pinch of Salt Lake
The Junior League of Salt Lake City, Utah

Nectarine Pasta Salad

1½ cups uncooked rotelle
  noodles or elbow macaroni
½ cup vegetable oil
½ cup white wine vinegar
3 tablespoons freeze-dried
  chopped chives
1½ teaspoons salt
1½ teaspoons dry mustard

1 teaspoon ground savory
½ teaspoon pepper
3 cups julienne strips cooked
  pork
1 pound (4 medium) fresh
  nectarines, sliced
1 small cucumber, sliced
Lettuce leaves

Cook rotelle noodles according to package directions; drain. Rinse with cold water; drain.

Combine oil, vinegar, chives, salt, mustard, savory, and pepper in a large bowl; mix well. Add pork, nectarines, cucumber, and pasta; toss gently. Cover and chill 1 hour. Serve on lettuce-lined salad plates. Yield: 8 servings.

A Taste of California
The San Francisco Home Economists in Business
San Francisco, California

Southwestern Pasta Salad with Cilantro Pesto

2 cups all-purpose flour
2 tablespoons chili powder
3 eggs
1 tablespoon olive oil
2 medium-size green peppers,
  thinly sliced
2 sweet red peppers, thinly
  sliced

2 sweet yellow peppers,
  thinly sliced
½ cup sliced green onions
3 tablespoons olive oil
1 (2-pound) boneless smoked
  turkey breast, thinly sliced
Cilantro Pesto

Position knife blade in food processor bowl. Add flour, chili powder, eggs, and 1 tablespoon olive oil. Top with cover, and process until dough forms a ball, leaving sides of bowl.

Turn dough out onto a lightly floured surface, and knead 4 to 6 times. Divide dough into thirds.

Working with one third at a time, pass dough through smooth rollers of pasta machine on widest setting. Generously dust dough with flour, and fold in half. Repeat rolling, dusting, and folding procedure 10 times or until dough becomes smooth and pliable. Pass each piece of dough, one at a time, through rollers of pasta machine, starting at widest setting. Continue moving width gauge to narrower settings, passing dough through rollers once at each setting and dusting with flour, if needed. Roll dough to about 1/16-inch thickness or to desired thickness. Pass each dough sheet through the cutting rollers of machine. Hang noodles on a wooden drying rack; dry no longer than 30 minutes. Repeat procedure with remaining portions of dough.

Fill a large Dutch oven two-thirds full with water. Add noodles; cook 2 to 3 minutes or until tender. Drain; place noodles in a large salad bowl, and set aside.

Sauté green peppers, red peppers, yellow peppers, and green onions in 3 tablespoons olive oil over medium heat until vegetables are crisp-tender. Add turkey; cook 1 minute or until thoroughly heated. Remove from heat; add to pasta. Pour Cilantro Pesto over pasta; toss gently to coat well. Yield: 10 to 12 servings.

Cilantro Pesto

**2 cups fresh cilantro,
  coarsely chopped**
2 large cloves garlic, halved
**½ cup coarsely chopped
  walnuts**

2 teaspoons salt
**½ cup grated Parmesan
  cheese**
1 cup olive oil

Position knife blade in food processor bowl; add first 5 ingredients. Top with cover, and process until smooth. With processor running, pour oil through food chute in a slow steady stream until combined. Use immediately or place in an airtight container, and refrigerate up to 1 week or freeze up to 6 months. Yield: 1¾ cups.

Purple Sage and Other Pleasures
The Junior League of Tucson, Arizona

Layered Pasta Salad

1½ cups uncooked medium
shell macaroni
1 tablespoon vegetable oil
2 cups shredded lettuce
1 cup (4 ounces) shredded
ham
3 hard-cooked eggs, sliced
1 (10-ounce) package frozen
green peas, thawed and
drained

1 cup (4 ounces) shredded
Monterey Jack cheese
1 cup mayonnaise
½ cup commercial sour
cream
2 teaspoons Dijon mustard
¼ cup sliced green onions
½ teaspoon salt
⅛ teaspoon pepper

Cook macaroni according to package directions; drain. Rinse
macaroni with cold water; drain. Combine macaroni and oil; toss
lightly to coat.

Layer lettuce, macaroni, ham, egg slices, peas, and cheese in a
large salad bowl. Combine mayonnaise and remaining ingredients,
and mix well. Spread mixture evenly over salad, sealing to edge of
bowl. Cover bowl tightly, and chill at least 12 hours. Toss gently
before serving. Yield: 8 to 10 servings.   Rosemary Bergling

Remembering Our Heritage
Herndon Covenant Church Women
Herndon, Kansas

Dance Festival Favorite

2 cups uncooked rotini
½ cup vegetable oil, divided
2 tablespoons sesame seeds
⅓ cup white wine vinegar
⅓ cup soy sauce
2 tablespoons sugar
½ teaspoon salt

¼ teaspoon pepper
3 cups chopped cooked
chicken
8 cups torn spinach
½ cup chopped fresh parsley
½ cup thinly sliced green
onions

Cook pasta according to package directions. Drain; rinse, and
drain again. Transfer to a large bowl.

Combine ¼ cup oil and sesame seeds in a small skillet. Cook over
medium-low heat 4 minutes or until golden. Remove from heat. Let
cool. Combine sesame seeds, remaining ¼ cup oil, vinegar, soy
sauce, sugar, salt, and pepper. Pour over cooked pasta. Add
chicken; toss gently. Cover and chill at least 6 hours.

Add spinach, parsley, and green onions to chilled mixture, and toss gently. Yield: 8 servings.

Even More Special
The Junior League of Durham and Orange Counties,
North Carolina

Cold Shrimp (or Chicken) and Pasta Medley

6 cups water
2 pounds unpeeled fresh
shrimp or 4 cups diced
cooked chicken
2 cups peeled, chopped
tomatoes
1 (14-ounce) can artichoke
hearts, drained and
quartered
¾ pound fresh mushrooms,
sliced

1½ cups frozen snow pea
pods, thawed
1½ cups commercial Italian
salad dressing, divided
1 (12-ounce) package
vermicelli, broken in half
¾ cup pine nuts
⅓ cup fresh basil or 3
teaspoons dried whole basil
¼ cup minced fresh parsley

Bring water to a boil; add shrimp, and cook 3 to 5 minutes. Drain well; rinse with cold water. Chill. Peel and devein shrimp.

Combine tomatoes, artichoke hearts, mushrooms, snow peas, and 1 cup salad dressing. Chill.

Cook vermicelli according to package directions; drain. Combine vermicelli and ½ cup salad dressing; toss well. Chill.

Combine vegetable mixture, vermicelli, and remaining ingredients in a large bowl, tossing well. Serve salad immediately. Yield: 10 to 12 servings.   Marty Johnson Margo

Superlatives
The Junior League of Oklahoma City, Oklahoma

Cold Pasta and Chicken Primavera

1 (8-ounce) package
  vermicelli
½ cup olive oil
½ cup wine vinegar
1 teaspoon Dijon mustard
1 clove garlic, crushed
1½ cups fresh snow pea
  pods, blanched
1 cup broccoli flowerets,
  blanched

12 cherry tomatoes, halved
  or 1 sweet red pepper,
  chopped
10 fresh mushrooms, sliced
2 cups cubed cooked chicken
⅓ cup chopped fresh basil
⅓ cup pine nuts
¼ teaspoon salt
¼ teaspoon freshly ground
  pepper

Cook vermicelli according to package directions. Drain; rinse with cold water, and drain.

Combine olive oil, vinegar, mustard, and garlic in a jar. Cover tightly, and shake vigorously. Pour ½ cup of oil mixture over vermicelli. Toss gently; chill at least 3 hours.

Combine snow peas, broccoli, tomatoes, and mushrooms in a large bowl. Add remaining ½ cup oil mixture; toss gently. Cover and chill 3 hours. Add chilled vegetable mixture, chicken, basil, pine nuts, salt, and pepper to pasta. Toss gently. Yield: 4 servings.

Susanne Bryson

Chord en Bleu
The Orchestra of Illinois Guild
Glenview, Illinois

Seafood Primavera with Pasta Shells

1 (12-ounce) package medium
  shell macaroni
3 tablespoons safflower oil
8 green onions, chopped
1 large clove garlic, minced
2 tablespoons vegetable oil
2 cups clam juice
¾ pound bay scallops
1½ pounds large fresh
  shrimp, peeled and
  deveined

2 large carrots, scraped and
  cut into julienne strips
2 large zucchini, cut into
  julienne strips
1 cup minced fresh parsley
1½ tablespoons dried whole
  dillweed
1½ teaspoons salt
½ teaspoon pepper
Herb Dressing

Cook macaroni according to package directions; drain. Rinse with cold water; drain again. Place macaroni in a large bowl; add safflower oil, and toss gently. Set aside.

Sauté onions and garlic in vegetable oil until tender. Add clam juice, and cook over medium heat until mixture is thoroughly heated. Add scallops, and cook until done. Remove scallops to a large bowl, using a slotted spoon. Add shrimp to liquid; cook, stirring frequently, 3 to 5 minutes or until shrimp are pink. Remove shrimp to large bowl with scallops. Add carrots to liquid; cook, stirring frequently, 5 minutes or until carrots are crisp-tender. Remove carrots to bowl with seafood, using a slotted spoon. Add zucchini to liquid; cook 20 seconds, stirring frequently. Remove zucchini to bowl with seafood mixture, using a slotted spoon. Discard liquid. Combine macaroni, seafood mixture, parsley, dillweed, salt, pepper, and Herb Dressing; toss gently until well coated. Cover and chill at least 8 hours, stirring occasionally. Yield: 10 servings.

Herb Dressing

1 large clove garlic, minced
½ cup chopped fresh parsley
1½ tablespoons dried whole dillweed
2 ounces grated Parmesan cheese
½ cup clam juice
⅓ cup safflower oil
2 teaspoons lemon juice
1 teaspoon salt
1 teaspoon pepper

Combine all ingredients in container of an electric blender; top with cover, and blend well. Cover and chill. Yield: 1¼ cups.

Carnegie Treasures Cookbook
Women's Committee, The Carnegie Museum of Art
Pittsburgh, Pennsylvania

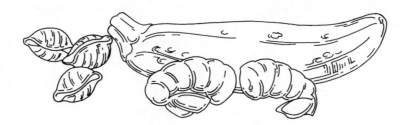

Pasta with Creamy Herb Sauce

1½ cups whipping cream
¼ cup unsalted butter or
   margarine
½ teaspoon salt
⅛ teaspoon ground nutmeg
Pinch of red pepper
¼ cup freshly grated
   Parmesan cheese
3 tablespoons chopped fresh
   basil

3 tablespoons chopped fresh
   mint leaves
3 tablespoons chopped fresh
   chives
3 tablespoons chopped fresh
   parsley
3 tablespoons chopped fresh
   watercress
1 (16-ounce) package angel
   hair pasta

Combine whipping cream and butter in a heavy saucepan over low heat. Add salt, nutmeg, and red pepper; simmer 15 minutes or until slightly thickened. Stir in cheese, basil, mint, chives, parsley, and watercress. Simmer 5 minutes.

Cook pasta according to package directions; drain. Place pasta on a warm platter, and top with sauce. Yield: 8 servings.

Tidewater on the Half Shell
The Junior League of Norfolk-Virginia Beach, Virginia

Fusilli and Broccoli
with Gorgonzola Sauce

1 (16-ounce) package fusilli
½ cup unsalted butter or
   margarine, divided
¼ cup freshly grated
   Parmesan cheese

⅓ cup minced fresh parsley
2 pounds fresh broccoli
1 cup whipping cream
½ pound Gorgonzola cheese,
   crumbled

Cook fusilli according to package directions, omitting salt; drain well. Combine fusilli, ¼ cup butter, Parmesan cheese, and parsley in a large bowl; toss gently.

Trim off large leaves of broccoli. Remove tough ends of lower stalks, and wash broccoli. Cut into flowerets, reserving stalks for use in another recipe. Place flowerets in a steaming rack over boiling water; cover and steam 2 minutes or until crisp-tender. Rinse with cold water; drain and combine with fusilli mixture.

Melt remaining ¼ cup butter in a medium saucepan over low heat; add cream, and bring to a boil. Cook 5 minutes, stirring constantly. Stir in Gorgonzola cheese; reduce heat to low, and cook, stirring constantly, until cheese melts. Pour cheese sauce over fusilli mixture, tossing gently to coat well. Serve immediately. Yield: 6 to 8 servings.   Barbara Hayford

Concertos for Cooks
The North Group, Symphony Women's Committee
Indiana State Symphony Society, Inc.
Indianapolis, Indiana

Pasta Primavera

½ cup unsalted butter or margarine
1 medium onion, minced
1 clove garlic, minced
1 pound fresh asparagus spears, diagonally sliced into 1-inch pieces
½ pound fresh mushrooms, sliced
1 small cauliflower, broken into flowerets
1 medium zucchini, cut into ¼-inch slices
1 small carrot, scraped and diagonally sliced
1 cup whipping cream

½ cup diluted canned chicken broth
2 tablespoons chopped fresh basil or 2 teaspoons dried whole basil
1 cup frozen green peas, thawed and drained
5 green onions, chopped
2 ounces prosciutto, chopped
½ teaspoon salt
¼ teaspoon pepper
1 (16-ounce) package fettuccine
1 cup freshly grated Parmesan cheese

Heat a wok or large skillet over medium high heat. Add butter. Sauté minced onion and garlic in butter 2 minutes. Add asparagus, mushrooms, cauliflower, zucchini, and carrot. Stir-fry 2 minutes. Increase heat to high. Add whipping cream, chicken broth, and basil. Bring to a boil. Cook, stirring constantly, 5 minutes or until slightly thickened. Stir in peas, green onions, and prosciutto. Cook 1 minute. Add salt and pepper.

Cook fettuccine according to package directions; drain. Place on a serving platter. Add vegetable mixture, and sprinkle with cheese. Toss gently. Yield: 10 servings.   Joan Gingrich

Feast and Fellowship
The St. Frances Guild
Atlanta, Georgia

Pasta with Red and Green Vegetables

1 pound fresh asparagus
  spears, diagonally sliced
  into 1-inch pieces
1 cup sliced zucchini
2 cups broccoli flowerets
2 cups fresh snow pea pods
1 cup sliced yellow squash
2 cloves garlic, minced
3 tablespoons vegetable oil,
  divided
4 large tomatoes, peeled,
  seeded, and chopped
¼ cup chopped fresh parsley
1 tablespoon dried whole
  basil

1¾ teaspoons salt, divided
¼ teaspoon pepper
1½ cups finely chopped
  smoked fully cooked ham
¾ cup plus 2 tablespoons
  butter or margarine,
  divided
½ pound fresh mushrooms,
  halved
3 quarts water
1 pound fresh linguine
1½ cups whipping cream
⅔ cup grated Parmesan
  cheese
⅓ cup pine nuts, toasted

Blanch first 5 ingredients separately in boiling water until crisp-tender; remove with a slotted spoon, and set aside.

Sauté garlic in 2 tablespoons oil in a large skillet over medium heat for 1 minute. Add tomatoes, parsley, basil, ¼ teaspoon salt, and pepper; cook over medium heat, stirring frequently, until tomatoes are tender. Set aside.

Sauté ham in 2 tablespoons butter in a medium skillet until thoroughly heated. Set aside.

Sauté mushrooms in ¼ cup butter in a large skillet. Stir in blanched vegetables; simmer just until vegetables are thoroughly heated. Set aside.

Combine 3 quarts water, 1½ teaspoons salt, and 1 tablespoon vegetable oil in a large Dutch oven; bring to a boil. Add linguine, and cook 3 to 4 minutes or until tender. Drain. Add ½ cup butter, cream, Parmesan cheese, and ham; toss gently.

Place linguine mixture in the center of a large serving platter. Spoon vegetable mixture around linguine. Pour tomato sauce over vegetable mixture, and sprinkle with toasted pine nuts. Yield: 8 to 10 servings.

Beyond Parsley
The Junior League of Kansas City, Missouri

Christmas Straw and Hay

½ (8-ounce) package linguine
½ (8-ounce) package spinach
   linguine
½ cup butter or margarine
½ cup julienne strips cooked
   ham
¾ cup cooked green peas
⅓ cup sliced pitted ripe
   olives
1 (2½-ounce) jar sliced
   mushrooms, drained
1 (2-ounce) jar sliced
   pimiento, drained and
   divided
2 egg yolks, beaten
1 cup whipping cream
1 cup grated Parmesan
   cheese, divided
Fresh parsley (optional)

Cook linguine in a large Dutch oven according to package directions. Drain well, and return cooked linguine to Dutch oven. Add butter, ham, peas, olives, mushrooms, and half of sliced pimiento; toss gently until butter melts.

Combine egg yolks and whipping cream in a small bowl. Add egg mixture to linguine mixture, tossing gently. Add ½ cup Parmesan cheese, and cook over medium heat until thickened, stirring gently. Place on a serving platter; garnish with remaining pimiento, cheese, and, if desired, parsley. Yield: 6 servings.

Christmas Memories Cookbook
Mystic Seaport Museum Stores
Mystic, Connecticut

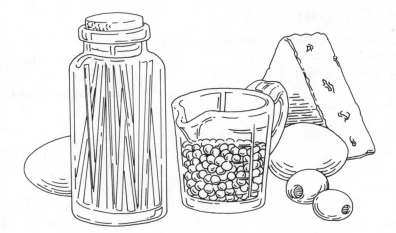

Pasta alla Melanzane

1 large eggplant
2 medium onions, chopped
2 green peppers, chopped
1 jalapeño pepper, minced
2 tablespoons olive oil
2 tablespoons butter or
margarine
4 (16-ounce) cans tomatoes,
drained and chopped

1 clove garlic, minced
1 teaspoon sugar
½ teaspoon seasoned salt
½ teaspoon lemon-pepper
seasoning
1 tablespoon vinegar
1 (12-ounce) package
vermicelli or thin spaghetti
Grated Parmesan cheese

Peel and cube eggplant; place in a bowl of cold salted water to cover. Set aside.

Sauté onion and peppers in olive oil and butter until vegetables are tender. Drain eggplant; add eggplant, tomatoes, garlic, sugar, salt, lemon-pepper seasoning, and vinegar to onion mixture. Cover and bring mixture to a boil; uncover and simmer 5 to 10 minutes or until thickened.

Cook vermicelli according to package directions. Drain well, and set aside.

Serve sauce over vermicelli; sprinkle with Parmesan cheese. Yield: 6 servings.   Mrs. Harlan Starr

Temptations
The Junior Service League of Rome, Georgia

Ricotta Gnocchi

2 tablespoons grated Romano
cheese
1 (16-ounce) carton ricotta
cheese
1 egg

1 egg yolk
Salt and pepper to taste
2 cups all-purpose flour
Commercial spaghetti sauce

Combine Romano cheese, ricotta cheese, egg, egg yolk, salt, and pepper in a large bowl; mix well. Gradually add flour, and mix until dough forms. Turn dough out onto a lightly floured surface, and knead 4 or 5 times or until dough is smooth and elastic.

Divide dough into fourths; shape each portion into a ball. Roll each ball on a floured surface to form a rope ¾-inch thick. Using kitchen shears dipped in flour, cut rope into ½-inch pieces, and dip in flour. Press thumbprint in each piece of dough. Cook gnocchi in boiling salted water to cover in a Dutch oven 10 minutes; drain. Serve with spaghetti sauce. Yield: 6 servings.   Marsha DeCaria

There Once Was a Cook . . .
The Wesley Institute, Inc.
Pittsburgh, Pennsylvania

Rigatoni alla Frank

1 (16-ounce) package rigatoni
½ pound hot bulk pork sausage
¼ pound ground veal
¼ pound ground beef
1 large onion, chopped
3 cloves garlic, minced
4 (8-ounce) cans tomato sauce
1 egg
¼ cup minced fresh parsley
3 tablespoons chopped fresh basil
½ teaspoon salt
¼ teaspoon pepper
2 cups (8 ounces) shredded Swiss cheese
1 cup (4 ounces) shredded mozzarella cheese
1 cup (4 ounces) shredded sharp Cheddar cheese
1 cup (4 ounces) grated Parmesan cheese
1 (16-ounce) carton ricotta cheese
1 egg
3 tablespoons chopped fresh basil
2 tablespoons minced fresh parsley
1 (4-ounce) can sliced mushrooms, drained
Grated Parmesan cheese

Cook rigatoni according to package directions; drain.

Combine meat, onion, and garlic in a large skillet. Cook over medium heat until meat is browned, stirring to crumble. Combine tomato sauce, 1 egg, ¼ cup parsley, 3 tablespoons basil, salt, and pepper; add to meat mixture. Cover and cook for 1 hour.

Combine Swiss cheese and next 3 ingredients; set aside. Combine ricotta cheese, 1 egg, 3 tablespoons basil, 2 tablespoons parsley, and mushrooms; set aside.

Spread one-third each of meat sauce, rigatoni, ricotta mixture, and cheese mixture in a 5-quart casserole. Repeat layers; sprinkle with additional Parmesan cheese. Bake at 325° for 50 minutes. Yield: 8 to 10 servings.

Cooking with the Santa Fe Opera
The Santa Fe Opera Guild
Santa Fe, New Mexico

Pastitsio II

1 large onion, chopped
½ cup butter or margarine
2 pounds ground beef
1 (8-ounce) can tomato sauce
1 tablespoon dried parsley
flakes
2 teaspoons salt
¼ teaspoon pepper
1 (3-inch) stick cinnamon

1 (1-pound) package elbow
macaroni
½ cup butter or margarine,
melted
2 cups (8 ounces) grated
Parmesan cheese, divided
½ teaspoon ground
cinnamon, divided
Cream Sauce

Sauté onion in ½ cup butter in a large skillet until tender. Add ground beef. Cook over medium heat until beef browns, stirring to crumble; drain. Add tomato sauce, parsley flakes, salt, pepper, and cinnamon stick. Cover, reduce heat, and simmer 30 minutes, stirring often. Remove cinnamon stick. Cook macaroni according to package directions; drain. Toss macaroni with ½ cup melted butter.

Sprinkle 2 tablespoons Parmesan cheese into a greased 3½-quart shallow baking dish. Spread half of macaroni into dish. Sprinkle with ⅔ cup Parmesan cheese. Sprinkle with ¼ teaspoon cinnamon. Top with beef mixture. Spread remaining macaroni over beef mixture. Top with ⅔ cup cheese and remaining cinnamon. Pour Cream Sauce over macaroni. Sprinkle with remaining cheese. Bake at 350° for 50 minutes or until golden. Yield: 12 servings.

Cream Sauce

½ cup butter or margarine
½ cup all-purpose flour
1 quart milk
5 egg yolks, slightly beaten

1 teaspoon salt
¼ teaspoon ground nutmeg
¼ teaspoon pepper

Melt butter in top of a double boiler over simmering water. Add flour, stirring until smooth. Cook 1 minute, stirring constantly. Gradually add milk. Cook, stirring constantly, until thickened. Gradually stir about one-fourth of hot mixture into yolks; add to remaining hot mixture, stirring constantly. Stir in salt, nutmeg, and pepper. Cook until thickened. Yield: 4 cups.

The Grecian Plate
Hellenic Ladies Society, St. Barbara Greek Orthodox Church
Durham, North Carolina

Lasagna Spinach Roll-Ups

1 (28-ounce) can whole
Italian-style tomatoes
1 pound Italian sausage
1 cup chopped onion
2 cloves garlic, minced
2 (6-ounce) cans tomato paste
1½ cups water
2 (4-ounce) cans mushroom
stems and pieces, drained
¼ cup chopped fresh parsley,
divided
1 teaspoon dried whole basil
1 teaspoon dried whole
oregano
¼ teaspoon pepper
⅛ teaspoon hot sauce

1 bay leaf
2 (10-ounce) packages frozen
chopped spinach, thawed
1 (16-ounce) carton ricotta
cheese
2 cups (8 ounces) shredded
mozzarella cheese
2 eggs, beaten
¼ cup plus 2 tablespoons
grated Romano cheese,
divided
½ teaspoon salt
⅛ teaspoon pepper
⅛ teaspoon ground nutmeg
12 lasagna noodles, cooked
and drained

Place tomatoes in container of an electric blender; top with cover, and process until smooth. Set aside. Remove sausage from casing. Cook sausage, onion, and garlic in a Dutch oven until meat is browned. Stir in pureed tomatoes, tomato paste, water, mushrooms, 2 tablespoons parsley, basil, oregano, ¼ teaspoon pepper, hot sauce, and bay leaf. Cover and simmer 45 minutes. Remove and discard bay leaf.

Drain spinach well, pressing between paper towels until barely moist. Combine spinach, 2 tablespoons parsley, ricotta cheese, mozzarella cheese, eggs, ¼ cup Romano cheese, salt, ⅛ teaspoon pepper, and nutmeg, stirring well.

Spread 1½ cups tomato mixture in a lightly greased 13- x 9- x 2-inch baking dish. Spread ⅓ cup spinach mixture on each lasagna noodle; roll up jellyroll fashion, starting at narrow end. Arrange lasagna rolls, seam side down, in pan. Pour remaining tomato sauce over rolls; top with remaining 2 tablespoons Romano cheese. Bake at 350° for 30 minutes or until bubbly. Let stand 10 minutes before serving. Yield: 12 servings.

Palette to Palate
The Junior League of St. Joseph and Albrecht Art Museum
St. Joseph, Missouri

Spinach Fettuccine "Muffins"

1 (8-ounce) package spinach fettuccine	1 cup ricotta cheese
	1 cup half-and-half
1¼ cups grated Parmesan cheese, divided	4 eggs
	2 teaspoons salt
1 cup crème fraîche	½ teaspoon white pepper

Cook fettuccine according to package directions, omitting salt; drain and set aside.

Generously butter muffin pans. Sprinkle 1 teaspoon Parmesan cheese into each cup.

Combine ½ cup Parmesan cheese, crème fraîche, ricotta cheese, half-and-half, eggs, salt, and pepper in container of an electric blender or food processor. Cover and process until smooth. Place 2 tablespoons cheese mixture into each muffin cup. Fill each muffin cup with equal amounts of fettuccine. Pour remaining cheese mixture over fettuccine to fill each cup. Sprinkle 1 teaspoon Parmesan cheese over each cup, and freeze 2 hours or until firm.

Place frozen muffin pans on oven rack at lowest position. Bake at 375° for 35 minutes (tops of muffins will be moist). Remove from pan, and serve immediately. Yield: 1½ dozen.

Taste of Today
BUNWC, North Shore Illinois Chapter
Northfield, Illinois

Bulgur and Cheese Casserole

2 tablespoons safflower oil	1 cup small-curd cottage cheese
1 medium onion, chopped	
1 clove garlic, minced	2 tablespoons chopped fresh parsley
1 cup uncooked bulgur wheat	
2 cups water	1 large tomato, sliced
1 egg	1 cup (4 ounces) shredded Cheddar cheese
¼ cup water	

Heat oil in a large skillet; sauté onion and garlic in oil. Add bulgur and 2 cups water; cook 20 minutes or until liquid is absorbed.

Combine egg and ¼ cup water; stir in cottage cheese and parsley. Place three-fourths of bulgur mixture on bottom of a 2-quart casserole. Layer tomato slices, cottage cheese mixture, and remaining bulgur in casserole. Sprinkle with Cheddar cheese. Bake at 350° for 30 minutes. Yield: 6 to 8 servings.

The Pride of Peoria: Recipes and Reminiscences
The Junior League of Peoria, Illinois

Jalapeño Grits Soufflé

1 tablespoon grated Parmesan
  cheese
1 cup milk
1 cup water
1½ teaspoons salt
1 cup uncooked quick-cooking
  grits
¼ cup plus 1 tablespoon
  unsalted butter or margarine
¼ teaspoon pepper

4 egg yolks
¾ cup (3 ounces) shredded
  sharp Cheddar cheese
¾ cup (3 ounces) shredded
  Monterey Jack cheese with
  jalapeño peppers
8 egg whites
¼ teaspoon cream of tartar
Sweet red and green pepper
  rings (optional)

Lightly butter a 2-quart soufflé dish. Cut a piece of aluminum foil long enough to circle the dish, allowing a 1-inch overlap. Fold foil lengthwise into thirds, and lightly butter one side. Wrap foil, buttered side against the dish, so that it extends 3 inches above the rim. Secure foil with string. Sprinkle 1 tablespoon Parmesan cheese in dish, and set aside.

Combine milk, water, and salt in a large saucepan. Bring to a boil; stir in grits. Reduce heat, and simmer, uncovered, 3 to 5 minutes or until thickened. Remove from heat. Add butter and pepper, stirring until butter melts. Add egg yolks and cheeses, stirring well.

Combine egg whites (at room temperature) and cream of tartar; beat at high speed of an electric mixer until stiff peaks form. Fold one-third of egg whites into cheese mixture; carefully fold in remaining egg whites.

Pour cheese mixture into prepared dish, spreading evenly. Bake on center rack of oven at 450° for 30 to 35 minutes or until puffed and golden brown. Remove collar. Garnish with pepper rings, if desired. Serve immediately. Yield: 10 to 12 servings.

Sounds Delicious!
The Tulsa Philharmonic Society
Tulsa, Oklahoma

Barley Casserole

½ cup butter or margarine
1½ cups uncooked pearl
  barley
1 cup sliced fresh
  mushrooms
1 cup chopped onion

3 cups diluted canned beef
  broth
1 (2-ounce) jar sliced
  pimiento, drained
¼ teaspoon salt
⅛ teaspoon pepper

Melt butter in a large skillet over medium heat. Add barley, mushrooms, and onion. Cook over medium heat, stirring constantly, until onion is tender and barley is browned.

Transfer mixture to a 2-quart casserole. Add beef broth, pimiento, salt, and pepper; stir gently. Cover and bake at 350° for 1 hour or until liquid is absorbed and barley is tender. Yield: 6 to 8 servings.

Gwen Cowley

Best of Friends
Friends of The Maitland Public Library
Maitland, Florida

Green Rice

2 cups hot cooked long-grain
  rice
1½ cups evaporated milk
1 cup (4 ounces) shredded
  sharp Cheddar cheese
1 cup chopped fresh parsley

⅓ cup butter or margarine,
  melted
3 eggs, separated
¼ cup chopped green pepper
2 tablespoons finely chopped
  onion

Combine cooked rice, evaporated milk, Cheddar cheese, chopped parsley, and melted butter in a large mixing bowl, stirring well. Add egg yolks, green pepper, and onion.

Beat egg whites (at room temperature) at high speed of an electric mixer until stiff peaks form. Gently fold into rice mixture. Pour into a greased 12- x 8- x 2-inch baking dish. Bake at 350° for 25 minutes or until lightly browned. Yield: 8 servings.

Gretchen Kite

A Dash of Down East
The Junior Guild of Rocky Mount, North Carolina

Fresh Lemon Rice

¼ cup butter or margarine
2½ cups uncooked long-grain rice
4½ cups diluted canned chicken broth
½ cup dry vermouth

1½ teaspoons salt
Pinch of white pepper
¼ cup minced fresh parsley
1 tablespoon plus 1 teaspoon grated lemon rind

Melt butter in a large Dutch oven. Add rice; cook over medium heat 2 minutes, stirring constantly. Add chicken broth, vermouth, salt, and pepper. Bring to a boil; cover, reduce heat, and simmer 20 minutes or until liquid is absorbed. Add parsley and lemon rind; toss gently. Yield: 8 to 10 servings.   Gay White

Celebration: A Taste of Arkansas
Sevier County Cookbook Committee
Lockesburg, Arkansas

Parsley Rice with Almonds and Jack Cheese

4 cups diluted canned chicken broth
2 cups uncooked long-grain rice
1 teaspoon salt
½ cup thinly sliced green onions

½ cup sliced almonds
¼ cup butter or margarine
½ cup chopped fresh parsley
1 (16-ounce) carton commercial sour cream
4 cups (16 ounces) shredded Monterey Jack cheese

Place chicken broth in a 2-quart saucepan. Bring to a boil. Stir in rice and salt; cover, reduce heat, and simmer 20 minutes or until liquid is absorbed.

Sauté onions and almonds in butter in a skillet over medium heat for 5 minutes. Add to rice. Stir in parsley and sour cream. Spread half the rice mixture in an ungreased 13- x 9- x 2-inch baking dish. Top with 2 cups cheese. Repeat layers with remaining rice mixture and cheese. Bake, uncovered, at 350° for 30 minutes or until golden. Serve immediately. Yield: 10 to 12 servings.

California Fresh
The Junior League of Oakland-East Bay, California

Rice and Vegetable Salad

8 cups hot cooked long-grain
  rice
Vinaigrette (recipe follows)
1 (10-ounce) package frozen
  green peas, blanched
1 sweet red pepper, cut into
  thin strips
1 green pepper, cut into thin
  strips
6 green onions, thinly sliced
2 shallots, finely chopped
1 cup currants
½ cup chopped black olives
½ cup chopped fresh
  dillweed
¼ cup chopped fresh parsley

Toss rice and vinaigrette in a bowl; add peas and remaining
ingredients; mix well. Serve immediately. Yield: 8 to 10 servings.

Vinaigrette

½ cup red wine vinegar
2 tablespoons Dijon mustard
2 tablespoons minced fresh
  parsley or chopped chives
2 teaspoons sugar
1 cup olive oil

Combine vinegar, mustard, parsley, and sugar. Gradually add oil;
stir, using a wire whisk, until mixture thickens. Yield: 2 cups.

Susan Dowdy

McComb's International Cuisine Affair
McComb Interdenominational Care Association
McComb, Mississippi

Wehani Rice

5 cups diluted canned
  chicken broth
2 cups uncooked brown rice
½ cup thinly sliced green
  onions

¼ cup plus 2 tablespoons
  unsalted butter or
  margarine
1 cup chopped pecans,
  toasted

Bring chicken broth to a boil in a large saucepan; add rice. Return to a boil; cover, reduce heat, and simmer 50 to 55 minutes or until rice is tender and liquid is absorbed. Set aside.

Sauté onions in butter in a large skillet until tender. Add rice and pecans; cook until thoroughly heated. Yield: 10 servings.

California Cooking
The Art Council, Los Angeles County Museum of Art
Los Angeles, California

Wild Rice with Mushrooms and Almonds

1 cup uncooked wild rice
½ cup slivered almonds
2 tablespoons chopped green
  onions
¼ cup butter or margarine

1 (10½-ounce) can chicken
  broth, diluted
1 (8-ounce) can mushrooms,
  drained

Rinse and drain rice; set aside. Sauté almonds and onions in butter until golden. Set aside. Pour rice into a lightly greased 1½-quart baking dish. Set aside.

Bring chicken broth to a boil in a small saucepan; stir into rice in baking dish. Stir in almond mixture and mushrooms. Cover and bake at 325° for 1½ hours or until rice is tender and liquid is absorbed. Yield: 6 to 8 servings.

Wild Rice, Star of the North
The 1006 Summit Avenue Society
St. Paul, Minnesota

Northwoods Wild Rice and Brussels Sprouts

¼ pound fresh brussels sprouts	3 tablespoons butter or margarine
2 tablespoons chopped green onions	¼ teaspoon salt
1 clove garlic, minced	¼ teaspoon pepper
	3 cups hot cooked wild rice

Wash brussels sprouts thoroughly, and remove discolored leaves. Cut off stem ends, and slash bottom of each sprout with a shallow X. Place sprouts in a medium saucepan; add water to cover, and bring to a boil. Cover, reduce heat, and simmer 5 minutes or until brussels sprouts are tender; drain and coarsley chop. Set aside.

Sauté onions and garlic in butter in a medium skillet until onions are tender.

Combine onion mixture, brussels sprouts, salt, pepper, and rice, stirring well. Serve immediately. Yield: 6 servings.

Look What's Cooking Now! Minnesota Heritage Cookbook Volume II
The American Cancer Society, Minnesota Division
Minneapolis, Minnesota

Pies & Pastries

Historical Pioneer Square, south of downtown Seattle, Washington, was built on top of the ruins of the former city center after it was destroyed by fire in 1889. The 20-block district is now comprised of Victorian brick and stone buildings which house stylish boutiques, excellent restaurants, and lively jazz clubs.

☆☆☆

Sugarless Apple Pie

Pastry for double-crust 9-inch
pie
1 (6-ounce) can frozen apple
juice concentrate, thawed
and undiluted
2 tablespoons cornstarch

1 tablespoon butter or
margarine
1 teaspoon ground cinnamon
¼ teaspoon ground nutmeg
6 cups peeled, sliced Golden
Delicious apples

Roll half of pastry to ⅛-inch thickness on a lightly floured surface.
Place in a 9-inch pieplate; set aside.

Combine apple juice and cornstarch in a saucepan; bring to a boil,
stirring frequently. Add butter, cinnamon, and nutmeg, mixing
well. Stir in apples. Spoon mixture into pastry shell.

Roll remaining pastry to ⅛-inch thickness; transfer to top of pie.
Trim off excess pastry along edges. Fold edges under and flute. Cut
slits in top of crust to allow steam to escape. Bake at 425° for 30
minutes. Reduce heat to 375° and bake an additional 30 minutes.
Yield: one 9-inch pie.   Mrs. Joe Hyche

Kitchen Sampler
The Junior Service League of Bessemer, Alabama

Pear and Apple Pie

3 cups peeled, sliced pears
3 cups peeled, sliced cooking
apples
¾ cup sugar
3 tablespoons all-purpose
flour
½ teaspoon ground cinnamon

¼ teaspoon salt
1 unbaked 9-inch pastry shell
½ cup firmly packed brown
sugar
½ cup finely chopped pecans
¼ cup all-purpose flour
¼ cup butter or margarine

Combine pears and apples; toss gently. Combine ¾ cup sugar, 3
tablespoons flour, cinnamon, and salt; add sugar mixture to pears
and apples. Spoon mixture into pastry shell.

Combine brown sugar, pecans, and flour; mix well. Cut in butter
with a pastry blender until mixture resembles coarse meal. Sprinkle
over pie. Cover pie with aluminum foil to prevent over browning.
Bake at 400° for 40 minutes. Remove foil; bake an additional 20
minutes. Yield: one 9-inch pie.   Diane Piasecki Nelson

The Pride of Peoria: Recipes and Reminiscences
The Junior League of Peoria, Illinois

Johnny Appleseed Sour Cream Pie

2 eggs, beaten
1 (8-ounce) carton
   commercial sour cream
½ cup sugar
2 tablespoons all-purpose
   flour
1 tablespoon lemon juice
1 teaspoon grated lemon rind
¼ teaspoon salt

2½ cups peeled, sliced
   cooking apples
⅓ cup raisins
1 unbaked 9-inch pastry shell
½ cup all-purpose flour
⅓ cup sugar
¼ teaspoon ground nutmeg
3 tablespoons butter or
   margarine

Combine first 7 ingredients; beat until blended. Add apples and raisins, stirring well. Pour filling into pastry shell. Bake at 400° for 10 minutes.

Combine ½ cup flour, ⅓ cup sugar, and nutmeg; cut in butter with a pastry blender until mixture resembles coarse meal. Sprinkle crumb mixture over pie. Bake an additional 30 to 35 minutes or until center is set and topping is browned. Chill thoroughly. Yield: one 9-inch pie.   Edward T. Meehan

The Mayors' Cookbook
Th United States Conference of Mayors
Washington, D.C.

Slice of the South Blackberry Pie

2¼ cups all-purpose flour
½ teaspoon salt
¾ cup cold unsalted butter or
   margarine
6 to 7 tablespoons cold water
Powdered sugar
¼ cup butter or margarine,
   melted

5 cups fresh blackberries
½ cup firmly packed brown
   sugar
¼ cup sugar
3 tablespoons cornstarch
2 tablespoons blackberry-
   flavored brandy
Sugar

Combine flour and salt; cut in ¾ cup butter with pastry blender until mixture resembles coarse meal. Sprinkle water (1 tablespoon at a time) evenly over surface; stir with a fork until dry ingredients are moistened. Shape into a ball.

Divide dough in half. Roll half of pastry to ⅛-inch thickness on a surface sprinkled with powdered sugar. Place in a 9-inch pieplate.

Combine melted butter and blackberries in a saucepan. Combine sugars and cornstarch; add to blackberry mixture, stirring well. Cook over medium heat until thoroughly heated. Stir in brandy. Spoon filling evenly into pastry shell.

Roll remaining pastry to ⅛-inch thickness; cut into ½-inch strips. Arrange strips, lattice fashion, across top of pie. Trim strips even with edges; fold edges under and flute. Sprinkle with sugar. Bake at 350° for 50 minutes to 1 hour. Yield: one 9-inch pie.

Upper Crust: A Slice of the South
The Junior League of Johnson City, Tennessee

Michigan Blueberry Pie

4 cups fresh blueberries
1 teaspoon lemon juice
Pastry for double-crust
  9-inch pie
1 cup sugar
3 to 4 tablespoons all-purpose
  flour
½ teaspoon grated lemon
  rind

Dash of salt
½ teaspoon ground cinnamon
½ teaspoon ground nutmeg
1 tablespoon butter or
  margarine
2 teaspoons milk
1 tablespoon sugar

Sprinkle blueberries with lemon juice; set aside.

Roll half of pastry to ⅛-inch thickness on a lightly floured surface, and place in a 9-inch pieplate.

Combine 1 cup sugar, flour, lemon rind, salt, cinnamon, and nutmeg. Add flour mixture to berries, stirring well. Pour into pastry shell, and dot with butter.

Roll out remaining pastry to ⅛-inch thickness. Place over filling; seal and flute edges. Cut slits in top of crust to allow steam to escape. Brush top of pastry lightly with milk. Sprinkle with 1 tablespoon sugar. Bake at 400° for 35 to 40 minutes or until golden brown. Cover edges with aluminum foil to prevent over browning, if necessary. Serve warm. Yield: one 9-inch pie.   Marilyn Witham

Some Enchanted Eating
Friends of the West Shore Symphony
Muskegon, Michigan

Molly's Butterscotch Pie

1 unbaked 9-inch pastry shell
1 cup firmly packed brown sugar
3 tablespoons all-purpose flour
¼ teaspoon salt
1½ cups milk
⅓ cup plus 1 tablespoon butter or margarine
3 eggs, separated
1 teaspoon vanilla extract
½ cup water
1 tablespoon cornstarch
½ cup sugar

Bake pastry shell at 400° for 5 minutes. Let cool.

Combine brown sugar, flour, and salt in top of a double boiler. Bring water to a boil; reduce heat. Gradually stir milk into brown sugar mixture; add butter. Cook over simmering water until butter melts. Beat egg yolks. Gradually stir about one-fourth of hot mixture into yolks; add to remaining hot mixture, stirring constantly. Cook over simmering water, stirring constantly, until thickened. Remove from heat; stir in vanilla. Spoon into pastry shell.

Combine water and cornstarch in a small saucepan. Bring to a boil, stirring constantly. Cook until thickened. Remove from heat; set aside to cool.

Beat egg whites (at room temperature) at high speed of an electric mixer 1 minute. Gradually add ½ cup sugar, 1 tablespoon at a time, beating until stiff peaks form and sugar dissolves. Add cooled cornstarch mixture, beating well. Spread meringue over hot filling, sealing to edge of pastry. Bake at 325° for 30 minutes or until browned. Serve warm or chilled. Yield: one 9-inch pie.

Jean Davis Brown

Perennials
The Junior Service League of Gainesville, Georgia

Chocolate Mousse Pie

3 cups chocolate wafer
  crumbs
½ cup butter or margarine,
  melted
1 pound dark semisweet
  chocolate
2 eggs

4 eggs, separated
4 cups whipping cream,
  divided
⅓ cup plus 2 tablespoons
  sifted powdered sugar,
  divided
Chocolate Leaves

Combine crumbs and melted butter; press firmly on bottom and up sides of a greased 10-inch springform pan. Chill thoroughly.

Place chocolate in top of a double boiler; bring water to a boil. Reduce heat to low; cook until chocolate melts. Remove from heat, and let cool. Add 2 eggs, and beat well. Add 4 egg yolks, and beat until mixture is smooth.

Beat egg whites (at room temperature) until stiff peaks form. Fold ½ cup beaten egg whites into chocolate mixture. Fold remaining egg whites into chocolate mixture.

Beat 2 cups whipping cream until foamy; gradually add ⅓ cup powdered sugar, beating until soft peaks form. Fold into chocolate mixture. Pour into chilled crust. Chill pie 6 hours or until firm.

Beat remaining 2 cups whipping cream until foamy; gradually add 2 tablespoons powdered sugar, beating until stiff peaks form. Carefully remove sides of pan; spread top with whipped cream, and top with Chocolate Leaves. Yield: one 10-inch pie.

Chocolate Leaves

3 to 4 (1-ounce) squares
  semisweet chocolate
1 teaspoon shortening

10 to 12 camelia or other
  waxy leaves

Combine chocolate and shortening in top of a double boiler; bring water to a boil. Reduce heat to low; cook until chocolate melts. Using a small paintbrush, paint a heavy coat of chocolate onto the back or ribbed side of each leaf. Chill until firm. Paint another coat of chocolate over the first one, and chill again. Once the chocolate is firm, gently and quickly pull the leaves away from the chocolate. Yield: 10 to 12 leaves.

Janet Joyce

Suncoast Seasons
The Dunedin Youth Guild, Inc.
Dunedin, Florida

Bourbon Chocolate Pie

1 cup sugar
2 eggs, slightly beaten
¼ cup cornstarch
½ cup butter or margarine,
  melted and cooled
3 tablespoons bourbon
1 cup chopped pecans
1 (6-ounce) package
  semisweet chocolate
  morsels

1 unbaked 9-inch pastry shell
1 cup whipping cream
½ teaspoon bourbon
2 tablespoons sifted
  powdered sugar

Combine first 5 ingredients in a medium mixing bowl; beat at medium speed of an electric mixer just until blended. Stir in pecans and chocolate morsels. Pour filling into pastry shell, and bake at 350° for 30 to 35 minutes. Let cool.

Beat whipping cream and bourbon until foamy; gradually add powdered sugar, beating until soft peaks form. Serve pie with whipped cream. Yield: one 9-inch pie.

Rare Collection
The Junior League of Galveston County, Texas

Old-Fashioned Chess Pie

1 cup butter or margarine,
  melted
3 cups sugar
6 eggs, slightly beaten
2 tablespoons cornmeal

3 tablespoons vinegar
1 tablespoon vanilla extract
1 unbaked 10-inch pastry
  shell

Combine butter and sugar, and mix well. Add eggs, cornmeal, vinegar, and vanilla; mix well. Pour filling into unbaked pastry shell. Bake at 300° for 15 minutes; increase heat to 350°, and bake 30 minutes or until pie is set. Cover edges with aluminum foil to prevent over browning, if necessary. Let cool completely on a wire rack. Yield: one 10-inch pie.   Helene Hamilton

McComb's International Cuisine Affair
McComb Interdenominational Care Association
McComb, Mississippi

Lemon Chess Pie

1½ cups sugar
½ cup butter or margarine, softened
4 eggs
2 teaspoons grated lemon rind
3 to 4 tablespoons lemon juice

2 tablespoons yellow cornmeal
2 tablespoons half-and-half or milk
2 teaspoons vanilla extract
Dash of salt
1 unbaked 9-inch pastry shell

Combine sugar, butter, and eggs; beat until blended. Add lemon rind, lemon juice, cornmeal, half-and-half, vanilla, and salt; beat until smooth. Pour into pastry shell. Bake at 325° for 1 hour or until pie is set. Cool completely on a wire rack. Yield: one 9-inch pie.

Putting on the Grits
The Junior League of Columbia, South Carolina

Key Lime Pie

1 cup sugar
¼ cup all-purpose flour
3 tablespoons cornstarch
¼ teaspoon salt
2 cups water
3 eggs, separated
1 tablespoon butter or margarine

Grated rind of 1 Key lime
¼ cup Key lime juice
1 baked 9-inch pastry shell
¼ teaspoon cream of tartar
¼ cup plus 2 tablespoons sugar

Combine 1 cup sugar, flour, cornstarch, and salt in a saucepan; stir in water. Cook over low heat, stirring constantly, until thickened. Beat egg yolks until foamy. Stir one-fourth of hot mixture into egg yolks; add to remaining hot mixture. Cook over medium heat 2 minutes, stirring constantly. Remove from heat; add butter, rind, and juice, stirring until butter melts. Spoon into pastry shell.

Beat egg whites (at room temperature) and cream of tartar at high speed of an electric mixer 1 minute. Gradually add remaining sugar, 1 tablespoon at a time, beating until stiff peaks form. Spread meringue over filling, sealing to edge of pastry. Bake at 425° for 5 to 6 minutes or until lightly browned. Chill. Yield: one 9-inch pie.

Peachtree Bouquet
The Junior League of DeKalb County, Georgia

Maple Chiffon Pie

1¼ cups vanilla wafer
  crumbs
¼ cup chopped walnuts
¼ cup butter or margarine,
  melted
2 tablespoons sugar
1 envelope unflavored gelatin
¼ cup cold water

2 eggs, separated
¾ cup maple-flavored syrup,
  divided
⅛ teaspoon salt
1 cup milk
½ cup whipping cream,
  whipped
1 teaspoon vanilla extract

Combine vanilla wafer crumbs, walnuts, butter, and sugar; mix well. Press mixture into bottom and up sides of a lightly greased 10-inch pieplate. Bake at 375° for 5 to 8 minutes. Cool.

Soften gelatin in cold water; set aside.

Combine egg yolks, ½ cup syrup, and salt in top of a double boiler; beat well. Gradually add milk to yolk mixture, stirring constantly. Bring water in bottom of double boiler to a boil. Reduce heat to medium-low; cook, stirring constantly, until mixture coats a metal spoon. Remove from heat. Stir in softened gelatin. Chill until slightly thickened.

Beat egg whites (at room temperature) until foamy; gradually add remaining ¼ cup syrup. Beat until stiff peaks form. Fold into chilled gelatin mixture. Fold in whipped cream and vanilla. Spoon filling into cooled piecrust. Chill pie for 3 hours or until firm. Yield: one 10-inch pie.   Katherine Edmunds

The Vermont Symphony Cookbook
The Vermont Symphony Orchestra
Burlington, Vermont

Frost-on-the-Pumpkin Pie

1 tablespoon unflavored
  gelatin
¼ cup cold water
3 eggs, separated
⅓ cup sugar
1¼ cups cooked, mashed
  pumpkin
½ cup milk
½ teaspoon ground allspice

1 teaspoon ground cinnamon,
  divided
¼ teaspoon ground ginger
¼ teaspoon ground nutmeg
1½ cups sifted powdered
  sugar, divided
1 cup whipping cream
½ teaspoon vanilla extract
1 baked 9-inch pastry shell

Soften gelatin in cold water; set aside.

Beat egg yolks at high speed of an electric mixer until thick and lemon colored. Gradually add ⅓ cup sugar, beating until mixture is thickened. Add pumpkin, milk, allspice, ½ teaspoon cinnamon, ginger, and nutmeg, mixing well.

Pour pumpkin mixture into a medium saucepan. Cook over medium heat, stirring constantly, 5 minutes or until thickened. Remove from heat; add gelatin mixture, and stir until gelatin dissolves. Let cool completely; chill.

Combine 1¼ cups powdered sugar and remaining ½ teaspoon cinnamon; stir and set aside. Beat whipping cream and vanilla until foamy. Gradually add powdered sugar mixture, beating until light and fluffy. Chill; set aside.

Beat egg whites (at room temperature) at high speed of electric mixer until foamy. Gradually add remaining ¼ cup powdered sugar, 1 tablespoon at a time, beating until stiff peaks form. Fold egg whites into chilled pumpkin mixture.

Carefully spread half of the pumpkin mixture evenly in pastry shell. Spoon half of the whipped cream mixture over pumpkin layer. Repeat layers, ending with whipped cream mixture, and sealing to edge of pastry. Chill for several hours or until set. Yield: one 9-inch pie.

First There Must Be Food
Northwestern Memorial Hospital
Chicago, Illinois

Orange Cloud Pie

1 envelope unflavored gelatin
½ cup sugar
⅛ teaspoon salt
1 cup water
3 egg yolks
1 (6-ounce) can frozen orange
    juice concentrate, thawed
    and undiluted

3 egg whites
¼ cup superfine sugar
1 baked 10-inch pastry shell
Sliced almonds, toasted
    (optional)
Whipped cream (optional)

Combine gelatin, ½ cup sugar, salt, and water in top of a double boiler. Bring water to boil; reduce heat to medium, and cook, stirring constantly, until gelatin dissolves.

Beat egg yolks until thick and lemon colored. Gradually stir about one-fourth of hot mixture into yolks; add to remaining hot mixture, stirring constantly. Cook over medium heat, stirring constantly, until mixture coats a metal spoon. Remove from heat; add orange juice, and blend. Chill until mixture begins to thicken.

Beat egg whites (at room temperature) at high speed of an electric mixer 1 minute. Gradually add superfine sugar, 1 tablespoon at a time, beating until stiff peaks form and sugar dissolves (2 to 4 minutes). Fold egg whites into orange juice mixture; pour into pastry shell. Chill until set. Garnish with almonds and whipped cream, if desired. Yield: one 10-inch pie.   Jane Paynter

Angel Food
St. Anne's Church
Annapolis, Maryland

Raspberry Bavarian Pie

1 (10-ounce) package frozen
    raspberries, partially
    thawed and drained
2 egg whites
1 cup sugar
1 tablespoon lemon juice

¼ teaspoon vanilla extract
¼ teaspoon almond extract
⅛ teaspoon salt
1 cup whipping cream,
    whipped
Pastry (recipe follows)

Combine raspberries, egg whites (at room temperature), sugar, lemon juice, flavorings, and salt; beat until soft peaks form. Fold in whipped cream; pour filling into pastry shell. Freeze 8 hours or until firm. Yield: one 10-inch pie.

Pastry

⅓ **cup butter or margarine,
  softened**
2½ **tablespoons sugar**
¼ **teaspoon salt**

1 **egg yolk**
1 **cup all-purpose flour**
⅓ **cup finely chopped
  almonds**

Cream butter; gradually add sugar and salt, beating until light and fluffy. Add egg yolk, and beat well. Combine flour and almonds; gradually add to creamed mixture, mixing well.

Press firmly into bottom and up sides of a lightly greased 10-inch pieplate. Bake at 400° for 12 minutes or until lightly browned. Cool completely. Yield: one 10-inch pastry shell.

Concertos for Cooks
The North Group, Symphony Women's Committee
Indiana State Symphony Society, Inc.
Indianapolis, Indiana

Mocha Alaskan Pie

1 **cup chocolate wafer crumbs**
¼ **cup butter or margarine,
  melted**
1 **tablespoon sugar**
1 **quart coffee ice cream,
  softened**
1 **(5½-ounce) can chocolate
  syrup**

½ **cup chopped pecans**
3 **egg whites**
½ **teaspoon vanilla extract**
¼ **teaspoon cream of tartar**
¼ **cup plus 2 tablespoons
  sugar**

Combine crumbs, melted butter, and 1 tablespoon sugar; press firmly into a 9-inch pieplate. Bake at 350° for 10 minutes. Let cool.

Spoon ice cream into crust; freeze until firm. Drizzle syrup over frozen ice cream. Sprinkle with pecans. Freeze until firm.

Combine egg whites (at room temperature), vanilla, and cream of tartar. Beat until foamy. Gradually add remaining sugar, 1 tablespoon at a time, beating until stiff peaks form and sugar dissolves (2 to 4 minutes). Spread meringue over frozen pie, sealing to edge. Freeze until firm.

Bake frozen pie at 450° for 2 to 3 minutes or until meringue is browned. Serve immediately. Yield: one 9-inch pie.

Purple Sage and Other Pleasures
The Junior League of Tucson, Arizona

Triple Chocolate Sin

1¼ cups graham cracker
crumbs
3 tablespoons sugar
3 tablespoons cocoa
⅓ cup butter or margarine,
melted
4 (3-ounce) packages cream
cheese, softened
¾ cup sugar
2 eggs
1 tablespoon vanilla extract
1 tablespoon crème de cacao
1 (8-ounce) carton
commercial sour cream

1 (1-ounce) square unsweetened
chocolate, grated
1½ teaspoons instant coffee
granules
2 tablespoons boiling water
4 (1-ounce) squares semisweet
chocolate
4 eggs, separated
⅓ cup sugar
½ teaspoon vanilla extract
2 tablespoons dark rum,
divided
1 cup whipping cream
Grated chocolate

Combine graham cracker crumbs, 3 tablespoons sugar, and cocoa, mixing well. Add melted butter, stirring well. Press crumb mixture evenly into bottom and up sides of a 9-inch pieplate. Bake at 350° for 8 minutes; let cool.

Beat cream cheese at high speed of an electric mixer until light and fluffy; gradually add ¾ cup sugar, mixing well. Add eggs, one at a time, beating well after each addition. Stir in 1 tablespoon vanilla and crème de cacao; beat until blended. Pour into prepared pan. Bake at 350° for 30 minutes or until set. Let cool 10 minutes on a wire rack. Spread sour cream over cooled layer. Sprinkle with 1 ounce grated chocolate. Chill until firm.

Sprinkle coffee granules over boiling water in top of a double boiler; bring water in bottom of double boiler to a boil. Reduce heat to low; add semisweet chocolate, and cook, stirring occasionally, until chocolate melts. Set aside.

Beat egg yolks at high speed of an electric mixer until thick and lemon colored. Gradually add ⅓ cup sugar, beating constantly. Gradually stir in melted chocolate mixture, ½ teaspoon vanilla, and 1 tablespoon rum until well blended.

Beat egg whites (at room temperature) until stiff peaks form. Stir one-fourth of egg whites into chocolate mixture. Fold chocolate mixture into remaining egg whites. Spread chocolate mixture over chilled layer. Chill thoroughly.

Beat whipping cream until stiff peaks form; add remaining rum. Spread whipped cream mixture over chocolate layer. Sprinkle with grated chocolate. Yield: one 9-inch pie.

Brunch Basket
The Junior League of Rockford, Illinois

Coffee Toffee Pie

1½ cups all-purpose flour
¾ cup finely chopped pecans
¼ cup plus 2 tablespoons butter or margarine, melted
¼ cup firmly packed brown sugar
1 (1-ounce) square unsweetened chocolate, grated
1 tablespoon water
1 teaspoon vanilla extract
¾ cup butter or margarine, softened
1 cup sugar

1½ (1-ounce) squares unsweetened chocolate, melted
1 tablespoon instant coffee powder
3 eggs
2 cups whipping cream
2 tablespoons instant coffee powder
2 tablespoons Kahlúa or other coffee-flavored liqueur
½ cup sifted powdered sugar
Chocolate curls (optional)

Combine first 7 ingredients; mix well. Press firmly into 2 greased 9-inch pieplates. Bake at 350° for 15 minutes. Let cool completely.

Cream ¾ cup butter; gradually add 1 cup sugar, beating at medium speed of an electric mixer until light and fluffy. Add melted chocolate and 1 tablespoon coffee powder; beat well. Add eggs, one at a time, beating well after each addition. Pour filling into baked piecrusts. Cover and chill 8 hours.

Before serving, beat whipping cream, 2 tablespoons coffee powder, and Kahlúa until soft peaks form. Gradually add powdered sugar, beating well. Spread over chilled pies. Garnish with chocolate curls, if desired. Yield: two 9-inch pies.

Uptown Down South
The Junior League of Greenville, South Carolina

Florida Pecan Pie

3 eggs, beaten
1 cup dark corn syrup
½ cup sugar
⅓ cup orange juice
1 tablespoon grated orange
  rind

1 tablespoon all-purpose flour
¼ teaspoon salt
1¼ cups chopped pecans
1 unbaked 9-inch pastry shell
¾ cup pecan halves
Whipped cream

Combine eggs, corn syrup, sugar, orange juice, orange rind, flour, and salt in a large mixing bowl; beat at medium speed of an electric mixer until blended. Stir in chopped pecans.

Pour filling into unbaked pastry shell, and top with pecan halves. Bake at 350° for 55 minutes to 1 hour. Serve with whipped cream. Yield: one 9-inch pie.

Gulfshore Delights
The Junior League of Fort Myers, Florida

Easy Peach Cobbler

4 cups peeled, sliced fresh
  peaches
½ cup butter or margarine,
  softened
¾ cup sugar
1 cup all-purpose flour
1 teaspoon baking powder

½ teaspoon salt
½ cup milk
½ teaspoon vanilla extract
¾ cup sugar
1 teaspoon cornstarch
1 cup boiling water

Place peaches in a lightly greased 12- x 8- x 2-inch baking dish. Set aside. Cream butter; gradually add ¾ cup sugar, beating well at medium speed of an electric mixer.

Combine flour, baking powder and salt; add to creamed mixture, mixing well. Stir in milk and vanilla. Pour batter over peaches.

Combine remaining ¾ cup sugar and cornstarch; stir in water. Pour mixture over batter, and bake at 375° for 45 to 50 minutes. Yield: 8 servings.　　　　　　　　　　　　　　　Velma Goff

The Best of Mississippi's Old and New Recipes
Mississippi Order of the Eastern Star
Woodville, Mississippi

Hot Apple Cobbler with Cinnamon Ice Cream

½ cup butter or margarine, melted
1½ cups sugar
1 cup all-purpose flour
1 tablespoon baking powder
½ teaspoon salt
1 cup milk
4 cups thinly sliced, peeled, and cored cooking apples

1½ cups firmly packed brown sugar
1½ teaspoons ground cinnamon
¼ teaspoon ground allspice
Cinnamon Ice Cream

Pour melted butter into a 13- x 9- x 2-inch baking dish. Combine 1½ cups sugar, flour, baking powder, and salt; stir in milk, mixing until smooth. Pour into prepared dish. Arrange apples evenly over batter. Combine brown sugar, cinnamon, and allspice; sprinkle over apples. Bake at 350° for 1 hour or until top is golden brown. Spoon into individual serving bowls, and top each with Cinnamon Ice Cream. Yield: 8 to 10 servings.

Cinnamon Ice Cream

1 quart vanilla ice cream, softened
½ cup sugar

1 tablespoon ground cinnamon

Combine all ingredients in a large mixing bowl, mixing well. Freeze until firm. Yield: 1 quart.   Rose Betty Williams

Sampler
The Women's Art Guild, Laguna Gloria Art Museum
Austin, Texas

Fresh Strawberry Almond Tart

¾ cup all-purpose flour
⅓ cup ground almonds
2 tablespoons sifted
  powdered sugar
½ cup cold butter or
  margarine, cut into pieces
½ cup almond paste
¼ cup sifted powdered sugar
2 tablespoons butter or
  margarine, softened

1 egg yolk
½ cup apricot preserves
1 tablespoon Cognac
2 pints large fresh
  strawberries, hulled and
  halved
1 cup whipping cream
1 tablespoon sugar
1 teaspoon vanilla extract

Combine flour, ground almonds, and 2 tablespoons powdered sugar. Cut in cold butter with a pastry blender until mixture resembles coarse meal. Press flour mixture into bottom of an ungreased 11-inch tart pan. Place on a baking sheet, and bake at 425° for 8 to 10 minutes or until golden brown. Let crust cool completely on a wire rack.

Combine almond paste, ¼ cup powdered sugar, 2 tablespoons butter, and egg yolk. Beat at medium speed of an electric mixer until well blended. With buttered fingers, spread almond paste mixture over cooled crust.

Place preserves in a saucepan over medium heat. Cook until preserves are melted, stirring frequently. Strain preserves through a sieve. Stir in Cognac.

Arrange strawberries, cut side down, over tart filling. Spoon preserves over strawberries. Chill tart thoroughly.

Beat whipping cream at high speed of an electric mixer until soft peaks form. Gradually blend in 1 tablespoon sugar and vanilla. Pipe whipped cream mixture in a decorative design between strawberries on tart. Chill tart thoroughly. Cut into wedges to serve. Yield: 10 servings.

Beyond Parsley
The Junior League of Kansas City, Missouri

Poultry

*In the center of the North Pacific Ocean lies Waikiki Beach,
a resort on Oahu in the southeastern section of Honolulu.
Diamond Head, the 761-foot-high landmark, rises above the
palm tree-lined beaches. Honolulu became the capital of
Hawaii in 1820.*

☆☆☆

Chicken Macadamia

1 cup macadamia nuts,
  chopped
2 tablespoons butter or
  margarine
1 onion, minced
2 eggs
½ cup all-purpose flour
¼ cup cornstarch
¼ cup cold water
2 tablespoons vegetable oil

2 tablespoons soy sauce
2 tablespoons brandy
1 teaspoon ground ginger
¼ teaspoon pepper
6 chicken breast halves,
  skinned and boned
Vegetable oil
Sweet-and-Sour Sauce
1 green onion, diced

Combine nuts and butter in a 12- x 8- x 2-inch baking dish. Bake at 350° for 10 minutes, stirring occasionally. Remove nuts; set aside.

Combine minced onion and next 9 ingredients in container of an electric blender. Cover and blend at high speed until smooth. Pour mixture into 12- x 8- x 2-inch baking dish; add chicken. Cover and marinate in refrigerator 30 minutes.

Heat ¼ inch of vegetable oil in a skillet; add chicken, and fry 10 to 15 minutes or until golden brown, turning to brown both sides. Drain on paper towels. Serve with Sweet-and-Sour Sauce, and sprinkle with toasted nuts and green onion. Yield: 6 servings.

Sweet-and-Sour Sauce

1 cup water
1 small sweet red pepper,
  diced
3 tablespoons dark brown
  sugar
1 teaspoon soy sauce

1 chicken-flavored bouillon
  cube
1 tablespoon plus 1 teaspoon
  cornstarch
2 tablespoons cider vinegar

Combine water and red pepper in a saucepan; bring to a boil. Reduce heat, and simmer, uncovered, 1 minute. Add sugar, soy sauce, and bouillon cube; stir well. Combine cornstarch and vinegar, stirring until blended. Add to hot mixture, stirring constantly. Cook over medium heat, stirring constantly, until thickened and smooth. Yield: about 1½ cups.   Nancy Hannah

Culinary Arts & Crafts
The Park Maitland School
Maitland, Florida

Michael's Marvelous Chicken

2 cups water
¼ pound unpeeled fresh
　shrimp
1 (8-ounce) carton unsalted
　whipped butter
6 fresh mushrooms, finely
　chopped
3 large green onions, finely
　chopped
½ pound fresh lump
　crabmeat, drained and
　flaked
½ teaspoon salt
½ teaspoon dried whole basil

¼ teaspoon poultry seasoning
1 clove garlic, minced
1 tablespoon lemon juice
8 chicken breast halves,
　skinned and boned
½ cup Chablis or other dry
　white wine
Butter
Paprika
4 fresh mushrooms, sliced
1 green onion, finely chopped
3 tablespoons butter or
　margarine

Bring 2 cups water to a boil; add shrimp, and cook 3 to 5 minutes. Drain well; rinse with cold water. Peel and devein shrimp. Combine whipped butter and next 3 ingredients; add shrimp. Add salt, basil, poultry seasoning, garlic, and lemon juice; mix well.

Place each chicken breast half between 2 sheets of wax paper; flatten to ¼-inch thickness, using a meat mallet or rolling pin. Place 2 tablespoons of shrimp mixture in center of each chicken breast; fold chicken over filling. Place chicken, folded side down, in a 13- x 9- x 2-inch baking dish. Pour wine over chicken, dot each breast with butter, and sprinkle with paprika. Cover and bake at 350° for 15 minutes; uncover, and bake an additional 10 minutes or until chicken is tender.

Pour liquid from casserole into saucepan, bring to a boil. Add sliced mushrooms and chopped green onion. Reduce heat, and simmer until liquid is reduced by half. Stir 3 tablespoons butter butter into sauce, 1 tablespoon at a time. Pour sauce over chicken. Yield: 8 servings.

Michael Norton and friends

Charleston Receipts Repeats
The Junior League of Charleston, South Carolina

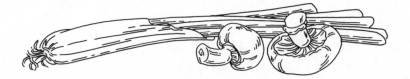

Chicken and Grapes

8 chicken breast halves,
  skinned and boned
2 tablespoons butter
½ cup Chablis or other dry
  white wine
1 tablespoon plus 1½
  teaspoons orange
  marmalade

1½ teaspoons dried whole
  tarragon
1 cup whipping cream
2 teaspoons cornstarch
2 teaspoons water
1½ cups seedless green
  grapes
Hot cooked rice

Brown chicken in butter in a skillet over medium heat. Add wine, marmalade, and tarragon. Cover and simmer 20 minutes or until chicken is tender. Remove chicken from skillet. Add cream to drippings in skillet. Bring to a rolling boil. Combine cornstarch and water; add to cream mixture. Simmer until thickened. Add chicken and grapes to mixture in skillet; cook until thoroughly heated. Serve over rice. Yield: 4 servings.   Libby Berry Payne

Superlatives
The Junior League of Oklahoma City, Oklahoma

Old Port Mustard Chicken

2 tablespoons Dijon mustard
8 chicken breast halves,
  skinned and boned
2 teaspoons dried whole
  tarragon

½ cup soft breadcrumbs
¼ cup butter or margarine,
  melted

Spread half of mustard on one side of each chicken breast half, and sprinkle with half each of tarragon and breadcrumbs; drizzle with half of butter. Turn chicken breasts over, and repeat procedure with remaining mustard, tarragon, breadcrumbs, and butter.

Place chicken on a broiler rack, and broil 2 to 4 minutes on each side, or until tender. Yield: 4 servings.   John O. Robertson

The Maine Ingredient
Southern Coastal Family Planning, Inc.
Portland, Maine

Chicken Breasts with Tomato-Tarragon Cream Sauce

¼ cup all-purpose flour
¼ teaspoon salt
¼ teaspoon pepper
¼ teaspoon red pepper
8 chicken breast halves, skinned and boned
¼ cup butter or margarine
1½ tablespoons chopped shallots
¾ cup Chablis or other dry white wine
1 cup coarsely chopped tomatoes
1½ teaspoons lemon juice
¾ cup whipping cream
2 teaspoons chopped fresh tarragon
½ teaspoon salt
¼ teaspoon pepper

Combine first 4 ingredients; dredge chicken in flour mixture. Melt butter in a large skillet; sauté chicken until golden brown. Add shallots, and cook 2 minutes, stirring constantly. Add wine, stirring to dissolve brown particles. Add tomatoes, lemon juice, and cream; bring to a boil, and cook until cream is reduced and coats chicken. Stir in seasonings. Yield: 4 servings.   Paul Roller

Philadelphia Homestyle Cookbook
The Norwood-Fontbonne Academy Home and School
Philadelphia, Pennsylvania

Chicken with Oyster Sauce

12 chicken breast halves, skinned and boned
Salt and pepper to taste
¼ cup minced shallots, divided
½ cup butter or margarine, divided
½ cup Chablis or other dry white wine
½ teaspoon dried whole thyme
1 (12-ounce) container fresh Standard oysters, undrained
1 clove garlic, minced
¼ cup plus 2 tablespoons all-purpose flour
1 cup half-and-half
Salt and pepper to taste
½ cup soft breadcrumbs
2 tablespoons grated Parmesan cheese

Sprinkle chicken with salt and pepper. Set aside. Sauté 2 tablespoons shallots in ¼ cup butter in a large skillet; add chicken, and brown on all sides. Add wine and thyme. Cover and bring to a boil over medium-high heat. Reduce heat, and simmer 15 to 20 minutes or until chicken is tender. Transfer chicken to a shallow 2-quart casserole, and keep warm. Reserve liquid.

Drain oysters, reserving liquid. Add enough reserved wine liquid to oyster liquid to equal 1½ cups. Set oysters and liquid aside.

Sauté remaining shallots and garlic in ¼ cup butter in a saucepan. Add flour; stir until smooth. Gradually add half-and-half and 1½ cups liquid. Bring to a boil over medium heat, stirring constantly. Cook 5 minutes or until thickened. Add salt and pepper to taste. Add oysters; cook 2 minutes. Pour oyster sauce over chicken.

Combine breadcrumbs and Parmesan cheese; sprinkle over casserole. Bake, uncovered, at 375° for 20 to 30 minutes or until golden brown. Yield: 8 servings.   Charlotte Breytspraak

Acornucopia
The Valley Hospital Auxiliary
Ridgewood, New Jersey

Picnic Stuffed Chicken Breasts

8 slices bacon
1 large onion, finely chopped
1 (10-ounce) package frozen chopped spinach, thawed and well drained
1 egg, slightly beaten
½ cup seasoned croutons, slightly crushed
½ teaspoon garlic salt
8 chicken breast halves, skinned and boned
½ teaspoon salt
⅛ teaspoon pepper
3 tablespoons vegetable oil

Fry bacon in a large skillet over medium heat until crisp; drain and crumble. Reserve 2 tablespoons drippings in skillet.

Sauté onion in bacon drippings until tender. Remove from heat; stir in spinach, egg, croutons, garlic salt, and crumbled bacon.

Cut a pocket in thick side of each breast half. Spoon spinach mixture evenly into pockets; secure with wooden picks. Sprinkle with salt and pepper; brown chicken in hot oil over medium heat. Reduce heat; cook 12 minutes or until tender. Drain on paper towels; remove wooden picks. Serve hot or cold. Yield: 8 servings.

Beyond Parsley
The Junior League of Kansas City, Missouri

Peanut Chicken with Mustard Sauce

6 chicken breast halves,
  skinned and boned
½ cup butter or margarine,
  divided
¼ cup plus 1 tablespoon
  Dijon mustard, divided
1½ cups finely chopped
  roasted peanuts

3 tablespoons peanut oil
1 (8-ounce) carton
  commercial sour cream
¼ cup chopped fresh parsley
¼ teaspoon salt
¼ teaspoon pepper
Fresh parsley sprigs
  (optional)

Place each piece of chicken between 2 sheets of wax paper; flatten to ¼-inch thickness, using a meat mallet or rolling pin.

Melt ¼ cup plus 2 tablespoons butter in a saucepan over medium heat. Add 3 tablespoons mustard; stir using a wire whisk until smooth. Spread mustard mixture on both sides of chicken; coat completely with peanuts.

Melt remaining 2 tablespoons butter in a large skillet over medium heat. Stir in oil. Sauté chicken breasts 3 to 4 minutes on each side or until golden brown. Remove chicken, and drain on paper towels. Arrange chicken on a serving platter; keep warm.

Combine sour cream, remaining 2 tablespoons mustard, chopped parsley, salt, and pepper in a small saucepan over medium heat. Cook, stirring constantly, until smooth and thoroughly heated. Spoon sauce over chicken; garnish with parsley sprigs, if desired. Yield: 6 servings.   Donna Steel Matteson

Celebration: A Taste of Arkansas
The Sevier County Cookbook Committee
Lockesburg, Arkansas

Cold Ginger Chicken

1 cup vegetable oil
½ cup grated fresh
  gingerroot
4 green onions, minced
4 cloves garlic, crushed

1 teaspoon coarse salt
6 chicken breast halves,
  skinned and boned
Fresh watercress

Combine vegetable oil, grated gingerroot, minced green onions, garlic, and salt in a small mixing bowl; mix well. Cover and refrigerate at least 2 hours.

Cook chicken in boiling water to cover for 10 minutes or until tender; drain well. Cover chicken, and chill thoroughly. Cut chicken into 2-inch pieces.

Arrange watercress on a serving platter; arrange chicken pieces on watercress, and serve with chilled gingerroot mixture. Yield: 4 to 6 servings.

Maui Cooks: A Collection of Island Recipes
Kokua Services
Pukalani, Maui, Hawaii

Country Captain Chicken

¼ cup all-purpose flour
½ teaspoon pepper
⅛ teaspoon salt
1 (2½- to 3-pound) broiler-fryer, cut up
3 tablespoons butter or margarine
3 tablespoons vegetable oil
1 large onion, chopped
½ cup chopped green pepper
3 cloves garlic, minced
2 (14½-ounce) cans stewed tomatoes, undrained
1 tablespoon curry powder
1 cup chopped dry roasted peanuts
½ cup golden raisins
Hot cooked rice

Combine flour, pepper, and salt. Skin chicken if desired. Dredge chicken in flour mixture. Heat butter and oil in a large skillet over medium heat; add chicken, and cook until golden brown. Remove chicken from skillet; set aside.

Reduce heat to low, and sauté onion, green pepper, and garlic in pan drippings until tender. Add tomatoes and curry powder; stir well. Return chicken to mixture in skillet. Cover and cook 25 to 30 minutes or until chicken is tender. Remove chicken to a large serving platter; set aside.

Cook sauce over medium-high heat, stirring constantly, until liquid is reduced and sauce is thickened. Stir in peanuts and raisins. Spoon rice around chicken on platter; pour sauce over chicken and rice. Yield: 4 servings.   Marion Cunningham

California Fresh
The Junior League of Oakland-East Bay, California

Cranberry Glazed Chicken

½ cup all-purpose flour
1 teaspoon salt
⅛ teaspoon pepper
1 (3- to 3½-pound)
broiler-fryer, cut up
3 tablespoons butter or
margarine
1½ cups fresh cranberries

1 cup firmly packed brown
sugar
¾ cup water
1 tablespoon all-purpose flour
½ teaspoon ground cinnamon
¼ teaspoon ground cloves
¼ teaspoon ground allspice
1 tablespoon wine vinegar

Combine ½ cup flour, salt, and pepper. Skin chicken, if desired. Dredge chicken in flour mixture.

Melt butter in a large skillet over medium heat. Add chicken, and cook 30 minutes or until golden brown. Remove chicken, and drain on paper towels; keep warm.

Add cranberries, brown sugar, and water to pan drippings in skillet; cook for 5 minutes or until cranberry skins pop. Blend together 1 tablespoon flour, cinnamon, cloves, allspice, and vinegar. Add vinegar mixture to cranberry mixture, and cook until thickened, stirring constantly.

Return chicken to mixture in skillet, and baste with cranberry mixture; cover and simmer 30 minutes, turning chicken occasionally. Yield: 4 to 6 servings.   Stephen R. Reed

The Mayors' Cookbook
The United States Conference of Mayors
Washington, D.C.

Chicken Fiesta

1 cup sliced fresh
mushrooms
¼ cup red wine vinegar
¼ cup olive oil
¼ cup pitted Spanish green
olives
¼ cup capers plus 1
tablespoon juice
2 tablespoons chopped fresh
oregano
1 teaspoon salt

½ teaspoon pepper
12 small cloves garlic, minced
3 bay leaves
2 (2½- to 3-pound) broiler-
fryers, cut up
½ cup Chablis or other dry
white wine
½ cup firmly packed brown
sugar
2 tablespoons minced fresh
parsley

Combine first 10 ingredients in a large bowl; mix well. Add chicken, turning to coat with marinade; cover and marinate in refrigerator at least 12 hours.

Arrange chicken in two 12- x 8- x 2-inch baking dishes. Remove and discard bay leaves from marinade. Pour marinade and wine over chicken; sprinkle sugar evenly over chicken. Bake at 350° for 50 minutes or until tender, basting often with marinade.

Using a slotted spoon, remove chicken, olives, mushrooms, and capers to a large serving platter. Spoon ½ cup pan juices over chicken; sprinkle with parsley. Yield: 6 to 8 servings.

Some Like It South!
The Junior League of Pensacola, Florida

Rosemary Chicken

2 tablespoons cracked pepper
⅔ cup fresh lemon juice
¼ cup plus 2 tablespoons olive oil
1 tablespoon salt

3 tablespoons dried whole rosemary
2 (2½- to 3-pound) broiler-fryers, cut up

Combine all ingredients, except chicken, in a large shallow container; mix well. Add chicken, turning to coat pieces; cover and marinate in refrigerator 12 hours.

Remove chicken from marinade, reserving marinade. Place chicken on grill over medium coals. Grill chicken 15 to 20 minutes on each side or until done, turning and basting frequently with reserved marinade. Yield: 8 servings.

Note: To bake chicken, remove chicken from marinade; arrange in two 12- x 8- x 2-inch baking dishes. Pour marinade over chicken. Bake, uncovered, at 425° for 40 to 45 minutes or until tender, basting occasionally.

California Cooking
The Art Council, Los Angeles County Museum of Art
Los Angeles, California

Korean Roast Chicken

8 chicken thighs
½ cup soy sauce
½ cup minced green onions
3 tablespoons dark sesame oil
3 tablespoons honey
2 teaspoons minced fresh garlic
  or ¼ teaspoon garlic powder

2 teaspoons minced fresh
  gingerroot or ¼ teaspoon
  ground ginger
½ teaspoon pepper

Place chicken, skin side down, in a large baking dish. Combine soy sauce and remaining ingredients, stirring well. Pour over chicken. Bake, uncovered, at 375° for 45 minutes. Remove from oven; turn each piece, and continue baking 10 to 15 minutes or until done. Yield: 4 servings.   Alice Whitmore

Angel Food
St. Anne's Church
Annapolis, Maryland

Guamanian Chicken

2½ cups soy sauce
1 cup fresh lime juice
1 cup catsup
1 cup sugar
1 medium onion, chopped

Grated rind of 5 limes (about
  ¼ cup)
10 pounds chicken thighs
Finadene Sauce

Combine first 6 ingredients, stirring well. Place chicken thighs in a large shallow container. Pour marinade over chicken. Cover and marinate in refrigerator at least 24 hours. Remove chicken from marinade, reserving marinade. Grill chicken over medium-hot coals 8 minutes on each side or until done, basting frequently with marinade. Serve with Finadene Sauce. Yield: 12 servings.

Finadene Sauce

½ cup chopped onion
½ cup fresh lime juice

⅓ cup soy sauce
4 to 5 drops hot sauce

Combine all ingredients; stir well. Yield: about 1¼ cups.

Maui Cooks: A Collection of Island Recipes
Kokua Services
Pukalani, Maui, Hawaii

Chicken Tetrazzini Glencrest

1 (5½- to 6-pound) hen
¼ cup butter or margarine
¼ cup all-purpose flour
1½ cups whipping cream
¼ cup dry sherry
1 teaspoon lemon juice
1 teaspoon salt
¼ teaspoon pepper
1 medium onion, chopped

½ green pepper, chopped
2 tablespoons butter or margarine
1 pound fresh mushrooms, sliced
1 (8-ounce) package thin spaghetti
1 cup grated Parmesan cheese

Place chicken in a large Dutch oven; add water to cover. Bring to a boil; cover and simmer 1½ hours or until chicken is tender. Remove chicken from Dutch oven, reserving broth. Bone chicken; chop meat, and set aside.

Melt ¼ cup butter in a heavy saucepan over low heat; add flour, stirring until smooth. Cook 1 minute, stirring constantly. Combine 2 cups chicken broth, cream, sherry, lemon juice, salt, and pepper. Gradually add broth mixture to roux; stir constantly, using a wire whisk, until thickened and smooth. Set aside.

Sauté onion and green pepper in 2 tablespoons butter; add mushrooms, and cook until tender. Add vegetables and chopped chicken to cream sauce; stir well.

Cook spaghetti according to package directions in remaining broth plus enough water to equal 2 quarts.

Drain spaghetti, and place in a 13- x 9- x 2-inch baking dish. Spoon chicken mixture over top; sprinkle with Parmesan cheese. Bake at 350° for 30 minutes. Yield: 10 servings.

Bluegrass Winners
The Garden Club of Lexington, Kentucky

Chicken Enchiladas

12 corn tortillas
Vegetable oil
2 cups (8 ounces) shredded
   Monterey Jack cheese,
   divided
¼ cup butter or margarine
¾ cup finely chopped onion
3 tablespoons all-purpose
   flour

2 cups diluted canned
   chicken broth
1 (8-ounce) carton
   commercial sour cream
2 cups finely chopped cooked
   chicken
1 (4-ounce) can chopped
   green chiles

Fry tortillas, one at a time, in 2 tablespoons oil in a medium skillet 5 seconds on each side or just until tortillas are softened; add additional oil, if necessary. Drain on paper towels.

Place 2 tablespoons cheese on each tortilla; roll up and place, seam side down, in a 12- x 8- x 2-inch baking dish. Set aside.

Melt butter in large skillet over medium heat; sauté onion until tender. Add flour, stirring until smooth. Cook 1 minute, stirring constantly. Add broth; cook over medium heat, stirring constantly, until thickened and bubbly. Stir in sour cream, chicken, and chiles. Pour over tortillas. Sprinkle remaining cheese on top; bake at 350° for 30 minutes. Yield: 6 servings.   Vicki Layton

Deep in the Heart
The Junior Forum of Dallas, Texas

Chicken and Pork Fajitas with Salsa

4 chicken breast halves,
   skinned and boned
1 (2-pound) boneless pork
   loin roast, trimmed
½ cup olive oil
¼ cup plus 2 tablespoons
   fresh lime juice
1 tablespoon ground cumin
2 cloves garlic, crushed

1 jalapeño pepper, seeded
   and chopped
¼ teaspoon salt
8 flour tortillas
Tomato Avocado Salad
Salsa
1½ cups (6 ounces) shredded
   Monterey Jack cheese

Cut chicken and pork into ¼-inch-thick slices. Combine oil, lime juice, cumin, garlic, pepper, and salt in a large bowl. Add chicken and pork, stirring well. Cover and marinate in refrigerator 1 hour.

Cover a hot grill with a layer of heavy-duty aluminum foil. Puncture several holes in foil for ventilation. Remove meat from marinade, reserving marinade. Place chicken and pork on foil-covered grill. Grill over hot coals 6 to 8 minutes or until tender, basting frequently with marinade.

Wrap tortillas in aluminum foil, and bake at 325° for 15 minutes. Place even amounts of meat, Tomato Avocado Salad, Salsa, and shredded cheese down the center of each tortilla. Roll up tortillas, and serve immediately. Yield: 8 servings.

Tomato Avocado Salad

6 slices bacon
3 tablespoons vegetable oil
1 tablespoon vinegar
½ teaspoon salt
⅛ teaspoon pepper
3 drops hot sauce

2 medium avocados, peeled and cubed
2 medium tomatoes, peeled, seeded, and cubed
1 small onion, chopped

Cook bacon in a large skillet until crisp; remove bacon, crumble, and set aside.

Combine oil, vinegar, salt, pepper, and hot sauce in a medium mixing bowl. Add avocados. Stir in crumbled bacon, tomatoes, and onion. Cover and chill 2 hours. Yield: 8 servings.

Salsa

1 (14½-ounce) can stewed tomatoes or 4 small tomatoes
1 medium onion, quartered
1 green pepper

2 to 3 jalapeño peppers, seeded
½ teaspoon garlic powder
¼ teaspoon salt
⅛ teaspoon pepper

Combine all ingredients in food processor bowl fitted with knife blade. Top with cover, and process until vegetables are coarsely chopped and mixture is well blended. Cover and chill. Yield: 4 cups.

Palette to Palate
The Junior League of St. Joseph and Albrecht Art Museum
St. Joseph, Missouri

Famous Hot Browns

⅓ cup plus 1 tablespoon
  butter or margarine, divided
1 medium onion, chopped
⅓ cup all-purpose flour
3 cups milk
1 teaspoon salt
½ teaspoon crushed red
  pepper
1 (6-ounce) package process
  American cheese, cubed

2 eggs, beaten
8 slices whole wheat bread,
  toasted
1 pound sliced cooked
  chicken or turkey breast
8 slices bacon, cooked
Grated Parmesan cheese
Paprika

Melt ⅓ cup butter in a saucepan. Add onion, and sauté 3 minutes or until tender. Add flour, stirring until blended. Gradually add milk, salt, and red pepper; cook over medium heat, stirring constantly, until thickened. Add American cheese, stirring until cheese melts. Stir about one-fourth of hot mixture into eggs; add to remaining hot mixture. Stir in remaining 1 tablespoon butter. Cook over medium heat 1 minute, stirring constantly. Remove from heat.

Slice 4 slices of toast in half diagonally. Place 2 slices, cut side in, with one whole slice in the center, on an ovenproof plate or baking sheet. Repeat with remaining toast. Top with chicken, cheese sauce, and bacon. Sprinkle with Parmesan cheese and paprika. Broil sandwiches 6 inches from heat until golden brown. Yield: 4 servings.

To Market, To Market
The Junior League of Owensboro, Kentucky

Chicken-on-a-Skewer

⅔ cup soy sauce
¼ cup vegetable oil
¼ cup Chablis or other dry
  white wine
½ cup minced onion
2 cloves garlic, crushed
10 chicken breast halves,
  skinned, boned, and cut
  into 1½-inch pieces

5 medium-size green or red
  peppers, cut into 1-inch
  pieces
2 (15¼-ounce) cans
  unsweetened pineapple
  chunks, drained
Hot cooked rice

Combine first 5 ingredients; stir well. Add chicken, turning to coat. Cover and marinate in refrigerator 30 minutes.

Cook green pepper in boiling water 2 minutes; drain and cool.
Remove chicken from marinade, reserving marinade. Alternate chicken, green pepper, and pineapple chunks on skewers. Grill over medium-hot coals 15 minutes or until done, turning and basting frequently with marinade. Serve kabobs over hot cooked rice. Yield: 10 servings.   Dannie Compton Weatherly

Vintage Vicksburg
The Junior Auxiliary of Vicksburg, Mississippi

Peking Turkey

1 (12- to 14-pound) turkey
8 cups water
⅓ cup honey
3 tablespoons hoisin sauce
2 tablespoons soy sauce
1 tablespoon plus 1½
   teaspoons black bean sauce

1 tablespoon five spice
   powder
1 bunch fresh cilantro
6 green onions, cut into
   1-inch pieces
4 stalks celery, cut into
   1-inch pieces

Remove giblets and neck from turkey; reserve for other uses. Rinse turkey thoroughly with cold water; pat dry. Place turkey on a roasting rack, breast side down. Combine water and honey in a saucepan; bring to a boil. Pour half of boiling liquid over turkey. Turn turkey breast side up, and pour remaining boiling liquid over turkey. Cover and refrigerate 8 hours.

Combine hoisin sauce and next 3 ingredients, stirring well. Rub sauce mixture inside cavity of turkey. Stuff cilantro, green onions, and celery into cavity of turkey; close cavity with skewers. Lift wing tips up and over back, and tuck under bird. Insert meat thermometer in meaty part of thigh, making sure it does not touch bone.

Bake at 350° for 3 to 4 hours or until meat thermometer registers 185°, basting frequently with pan juices. If turkey starts to brown too quickly, cover loosely with aluminum foil. Turkey is done when drumsticks move up and down easily. Let stand 15 minutes. Remove stuffing, and serve with turkey. Yield: 20 to 24 servings.

Look What's Cooking Now! Minnesota Heritage Cookbook Volume II
The American Cancer Society, Minnesota Division
Minneapolis, Minnesota

Quail in Red Wine

6 quail, cleaned
½ cup brandy
¼ cup plus 2 tablespoons all-purpose flour
½ cup plus 2 tablespoons butter or margarine, divided
2 cups sliced fresh mushrooms
1 (10½-ounce) can beef consommé, undiluted
1 cup Burgundy or other dry red wine
1 celery stalk, cut into 2-inch pieces
⅛ teaspoon salt
⅛ teaspoon pepper
½ cup fresh orange juice
Hot cooked wild rice

Rub quail with a cloth towel soaked in brandy. Dredge quail in flour, and sauté in ¼ cup plus 2 tablespoons butter in a large skillet 10 minutes.

Sauté sliced mushrooms in remaining ¼ cup butter in a skillet 4 minutes. Add sautéed mushrooms, consommé, wine, celery, salt, and pepper to quail. Cover and simmer 20 to 30 minutes or until quail is tender. Remove celery, using a slotted spoon. Stir in orange juice. Cook until thoroughly heated. Serve with hot cooked wild rice. Yield: 3 servings.   Beverly S. McElroy

Mountain Measures: A Second Serving
The Junior League of Charleston, West Virginia

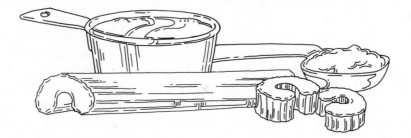

Cinnamon and Plum Duckling

1 (4- to 5-pound) dressed
  duckling
2 tablespoons unsalted butter
  or margarine
1 (3-inch) stick cinnamon
1 cup shallots or pearl onions
4 large plums, sliced
½ teaspoon salt

½ teaspoon freshly ground
  pepper
¼ cup damson plum jam
⅛ teaspoon ground cinnamon
⅛ teaspoon ground allspice
⅛ teaspoon ground ginger
Fresh watercress

Remove giblets and neck from duckling; reserve for other uses, if desired. Rinse duckling, and pat dry with paper towels. Melt butter in a large skillet; add cinnamon stick and shallots. Cook over medium heat until shallots are lightly browned. Add plums; toss until well coated. Set aside.

Combine salt and pepper; rub on duckling and in cavity of duckling. Spoon plum mixture into cavity; place cinnamon stick in center of mixture. Close cavity with skewers; truss duckling. Prick skin with a fork at 2-inch intervals. Place duckling on side on rack in a roasting pan. Pour 1 cup water into pan. Bake at 425° for 45 minutes, turning every 15 minutes, ending with breast side up.

Combine plum jam, ground cinnamon, allspice, and ginger. Reduce heat to 350°. Insert meat thermometer in thigh, making sure it does not touch bone. Baste duckling with jam mixture, and bake 1 hour or until meat thermometer registers 185°, basting frequently with jam mixture. Place duckling on a serving platter. Remove stuffing from duckling, and arrange around duckling on serving platter. Garnish with fresh watercress. Yield: 4 servings.

Taste of Today
BUNWC, North Shore Illinois Chapter
Northfield, Illinois

Baked Goose

1 (9- to 10-pound) dressed
  goose
½ teaspoon onion powder
½ teaspoon garlic powder
½ teaspoon pepper
2 cups peeled, chopped
  cooking apples
¾ cup chopped onion
Soy sauce
Butter or margarine, melted

Bacon slices, uncooked
1 cup Chablis or other dry
  white wine
⅓ cup water
2 slices onion
1 jalapeño pepper, chopped
1 tablespoon Worcestershire
  sauce
¼ teaspoon hot sauce

Remove giblets and neck from goose, reserving for use in other recipes, if desired. Rinse goose thoroughly with water; pat dry. Prick skin with a fork at 2-inch intervals. Combine onion powder, garlic powder, and pepper; rub 1 teaspoon of mixture in cavity of goose. Combine apples and chopped onion; spoon into cavity of goose. Close cavity with skewers; truss goose. Place goose, breast side up, in a roasting pan. Rub outside of goose with soy sauce. Rub the breast with butter. Sprinkle with remaining garlic powder mixture. Cover breast with bacon slices. Pour wine and water over goose; add onion slices, jalapeño pepper, Worcestershire sauce, and hot sauce.

Insert meat thermometer in thigh, making sure it does not touch bone. Bake, uncovered, at 400° for 30 minutes. Reduce heat to 325°; bake 1½ hours or until meat thermometer registers 185°, basting every 30 minutes with pan drippings. Yield: 5 to 7 servings.

Rockport Collection
The Rockport Art Association
Rockport, Texas

Salads &
Salad Dressings

Gathering fresh herbs is a pleasant task in the garden of a home in Williamsburg, Virginia. The colonial capital, situated between the James and York rivers, captures the eighteenth-century spirit of America with its formal gardens and craft shops.

☆☆☆

Molded Gazpacho Salad

3 envelopes unflavored gelatin
2 cups water
1 (14½-ounce) can stewed
  tomatoes, undrained
2 (8-ounce) cans tomato sauce
½ cup wine vinegar
1 tablespoon Worcestershire
  sauce
10 to 12 drops hot sauce
1½ teaspoons salt

½ teaspoon ground cumin
1 clove garlic, crushed
½ cup finely chopped onion
⅔ cup finely chopped celery
¾ cup seeded and finely
  chopped cucumber
1 cup finely chopped green
  pepper
Lettuce leaves (optional)
Lemon wedges (optional)

Sprinkle gelatin over water in a small saucepan; cook over low heat, stirring constantly, until gelatin dissolves. Remove from heat.

Drain tomatoes, reserving liquid; chop tomatoes. Combine gelatin mixture, tomatoes, reserved liquid, tomato sauce, vinegar, Worcestershire sauce, hot sauce, salt, and cumin in a medium bowl; stir well. Add garlic, onion, celery, cucumber, and green pepper. Chill until mixture is the consistency of unbeaten egg white. Pour into a lightly oiled 8-cup mold; chill 8 hours or until firm. Unmold onto a serving platter lined with lettuce leaves, and garnish with lemon wedges, if desired. Yield: 12 to 14 servings.   Mitzi Gaynor

Suncoast Seasons
The Dunedin Youth Guild, Inc.
Dunedin, Florida

Southern Caviar

2 (15-ounce) cans black-eyed
  peas, drained
½ cup chopped purple onion
½ cup chopped green pepper
½ clove garlic

¼ cup vinegar
¼ cup vegetable oil
¼ cup sugar
½ teaspoon salt
⅛ teaspoon pepper

Combine peas, onion, green pepper, and garlic in a large bowl. Combine vinegar and remaining ingredients in a jar; cover tightly, and shake vigorously. Pour over pea mixture, and toss gently. Cover and chill 12 hours. Remove garlic clove, and drain before serving. Yield: 6 to 8 servings.   Patricia Franklin Rauch

Perennials
The Junior Service League of Gainesville, Georgia

Quaker Coleslaw

2 eggs, beaten
¼ cup cider vinegar
¼ cup water
½ cup sugar
2 tablespoons butter or
　margarine
⅛ teaspoon salt
⅛ teaspoon pepper
1 (8-ounce) carton
　commercial sour cream
1 medium cabbage, shredded

Combine first 7 ingredients in top of a double boiler; bring water to a boil. Reduce heat to low; cook until mixture thickens. Stir in sour cream; cook just until heated. Pour hot dressing over cabbage, and toss. Let stand until cool. Cover with a cloth, and refrigerate overnight. Yield: 6 servings. 　　　　　　　　　Judy Genrich

Recipes from Woodruff Place
The Woodruff Place Civic League
Indianapolis, Indiana

Green Bean, Walnut, and Feta Salad

1½ pounds fresh green beans
¾ cup olive oil
½ cup loosely packed fresh
　mint leaves
¼ cup white wine vinegar
¾ teaspoon salt
1 clove garlic, minced
¼ teaspoon pepper
1 cup chopped walnuts,
　toasted
1 cup chopped red onion
1 cup crumbled feta cheese

Wash beans; trim ends, and remove strings, if necessary. Cut beans in half crosswise. Cook beans in a small amount of boiling water 5 minutes or until tender; drain and plunge into ice water. Drain again, and pat dry. Cover and chill.

Combine olive oil and next 5 ingredients in container of an electric blender or food processor. Top with cover, and process 20 seconds or until well blended.

Arrange beans in a serving bowl. Top with walnuts, onion, and feta cheese. Pour dressing over salad just before serving, and toss well. Yield: 6 servings. 　　　　　　　　　Susan Kokx

The Maine Ingredient
Southern Coastal Family Planning, Inc.
Portland, Maine

Green Beans Picante

1 pound fresh green beans	Freshly ground pepper to
¾ cup water	taste
1 (8-ounce) carton	¾ teaspoon curry powder
commercial sour	1 small white onion, thinly
cream	sliced
¼ cup mayonnaise	1 cucumber, peeled and
2 tablespoons white wine	sliced
vinegar	Lettuce leaves
2 tablespoons sugar	2 hard-cooked eggs, finely
1 teaspoon salt	chopped

Wash beans; trim ends, and remove strings. Combine beans and water in a large saucepan; bring to a boil. Cover, reduce heat, and cook 6 to 8 minutes or until crisp-tender; drain and set aside.

Combine sour cream, mayonnaise, vinegar, sugar, salt, pepper, and curry powder in a large bowl; mix well. Add beans, onion, and cucumber; toss gently. Cover and chill 2 to 3 hours.

To serve, arrange lettuce leaves on a serving platter. Spoon green bean mixture over lettuce, and sprinkle with chopped egg. Yield: 6 servings.   Mrs. Raymond Suelflow

Acornucopia
The Valley Hospital Auxiliary
Ridgewood, New Jersey

Pea Salad

2 (10-ounce) packages frozen	12 slices bacon, cooked and
tiny green peas, thawed	crumbled
2 cups chopped celery	1 cup commercial sour cream
1 cup cashews	¼ teaspoon salt
½ cup chopped green onions	¼ teaspoon pepper

Combine peas, celery, cashews, green onions, and bacon in a large bowl. Add sour cream, salt, and pepper; toss lightly to coat. Cover and chill thoroughly. Yield: 8 to 10 servings.

Sassafras!
The Junior League of Springfield, Missouri

Snow Pea, Yellow Bell Pepper, and Mushroom Salad

½ pound fresh snow pea
  pods
1 large sweet red or yellow
  pepper, cut into thin strips
½ pound fresh mushrooms,
  sliced
¼ cup vegetable oil
3 tablespoons white wine
  vinegar

2 tablespoons sugar
2 teaspoons sesame oil
1 teaspoon pepper
½ teaspoon salt
2 tablespoons sesame seeds,
  toasted

Trim ends from snow peas; place in a steaming basket. Plunge basket into boiling water, and remove immediately. Place snow peas in ice water to cool quickly. Remove from water, and refrigerate. Combine snow peas, pepper strips, and mushrooms in a large salad bowl. Set aside.

Combine vegetable oil, vinegar, sugar, sesame oil, pepper, and salt in a jar. Cover tightly, and shake vigorously. Pour over vegetables, and toss gently to coat. Sprinkle with toasted sesame seeds. Serve immediately. Yield: 6 servings.

California Cooking
The Art Council, Los Angeles County Museum of Art
Los Angeles, California

Spinach Salad with Strawberries

1 pound fresh spinach
1 pint fresh strawberries,
  hulled and halved
½ cup sugar
2 tablespoons sesame
  seeds
1 tablespoon poppy seeds

1½ teaspoons minced onion
¼ teaspoon Worcestershire
  sauce
¼ teaspoon paprika
½ cup vegetable oil
¼ cup cider vinegar

Remove stems from spinach; wash leaves thoroughly, and pat dry. Tear into bite-size pieces. Combine spinach and strawberries in a large salad bowl, tossing gently.

Combine sugar and remaining ingredients in container of an electric blender; top with cover, and process at low speed for 30 seconds. Drizzle dressing over spinach and strawberries; toss gently. Yield: 4 to 6 servings.

Clock Wise Cuisine
The Junior League of Detroit, Michigan

New Potato Salad with Roquefort

¼ cup finely chopped shallots
3 tablespoons tarragon vinegar
1 teaspoon Dijon mustard
¾ teaspoon salt
½ teaspoon freshly ground pepper
½ cup olive oil
2 tablespoons minced fresh parsley
1 (3-ounce) package Roquefort cheese, crumbled

½ cup whipping cream
10 strips bacon, cooked, crumbled, and divided
2 pounds new potatoes, unpeeled and sliced
Lettuce leaves
1 cup fresh watercress sprigs
2 tablespoons chopped fresh chives

Combine shallots, vinegar, mustard, salt, and pepper in a small bowl; add oil, 1 tablespoon at a time, stirring with a wire whisk until smooth. Add parsley, stir well. Set aside ¼ cup dressing. Add Roquefort cheese, cream, and half of crumbled bacon to remaining dressing; stir well, and set aside.

Cook potatoes, covered, in boiling water to cover 10 to 15 minutes or until almost tender; drain. Slice potatoes, leaving skins intact, and place in a large bowl. Pour reserved ¼ cup dressing over potatoes, tossing gently to coat well.

Arrange potato slices in rows on a lettuce-lined plate; garnish with watercress sprigs between rows of potatoes. Drizzle Roquefort mixture over potatoes. Sprinkle with remaining crumbled bacon and chopped chives. Yield: 6 servings.

Taste the Seasons
Woodside-Atherton Auxiliary to Children's Hospital at Stanford
Menlo Park, California

Layered Walnut Salad

1 cup coarsely chopped
walnuts
1 teaspoon vegetable oil
¼ teaspoon garlic salt
⅛ teaspoon dried whole
dillweed
4 cups shredded lettuce
6 to 8 cherry tomatoes,
halved
1 cup (4 ounces) shredded
Cheddar cheese

1 (10-ounce) package frozen
green peas, thawed and
drained
¾ cup mayonnaise
½ cup commercial sour
cream
1 tablespoon lemon juice
1 teaspoon prepared mustard
½ teaspoon salt

Place walnuts in a small saucepan; cover with water, and bring to a
boil; cover and cook 3 minutes. Remove from heat, drain walnuts.
Combine walnuts, oil, garlic salt, and dillweed; toss lightly to coat.
Toast walnuts at 350° for 10 minutes. Remove from oven; cool.

Layer toasted walnuts, lettuce, tomatoes, cheese, and peas in a
2-quart salad bowl. Set aside.

Combine mayonnaise and remaining ingredients; mix well.
Spread over top of salad, sealing to edge of bowl. Cover and
refrigerate at least 8 hours. Toss salad before serving. Yield:
6 servings.   Arvilla Dammann

Armour Centennial Cookbook
The Armour Centennial Committee
Armour, South Dakota

Festive Cornbread Salad

6 cups crumbled cornbread
2 cups mayonnaise
2 large tomatoes, diced
1 large green pepper,
chopped

¾ cup chopped green onions
¾ cup chopped pecans
2 stalks celery, chopped
1 (4-ounce) jar sliced
pimiento, drained

Combine all ingredients, stirring well. Cover and chill at least 2
hours. Yield: 8 to 10 servings.   Debbi Arnold

Deep in the Heart
The Junior Forum of Dallas, Texas

Missouri Spring Salad with Walnuts

1 head red leaf lettuce, torn	½ pound fresh arugula, torn
1 bunch fresh watercress, torn	1 cup walnut halves
	Dressing (recipe follows)

Combine all ingredients, except dressing, in a large salad bowl. Toss with dressing. Yield: 8 servings.

Dressing

½ cup walnut oil	2 teaspoons salt
½ cup olive oil	2 teaspoons sugar
⅓ cup red wine vinegar	¼ teaspoon pepper

Combine all ingredients in a jar; cover tightly, and shake vigorously. Chill. Shake well before serving. Yield: 1⅓ cups.

Beyond Parsley
The Junior League of Kansas City, Missouri

Salata Meh Kritharaki (Orzo Salad)

4 cups water	1 tomato, cut into wedges
½ teaspoon salt	⅓ cup olive oil
1 cup uncooked orzo	¼ cup lemon juice
¾ cup crumbled feta cheese	½ teaspoon salt
3 tablespoons minced fresh parsley	¼ teaspoon pepper
3 tablespoons minced fresh basil or dillweed	

Combine water and ½ teaspoon salt in a heavy saucepan; bring to a boil. Gradually add orzo, stirring constantly. Cover, reduce heat, and simmer, stirring frequently, 15 minutes or until orzo is tender and water is absorbed. Drain; rinse with cold water, and drain.

Combine orzo, feta cheese, parsley, basil, and tomato in a large bowl. Set aside. Combine oil and remaining ingredients in a jar; cover tightly, and shake vigorously. Toss salad with dressing. Cover and chill. Toss salad again just before serving. Yield: 6 servings.

The Grecian Plate
The Hellenic Ladies Society, St. Barbara Greek Orthodox Church
Durham, North Carolina

Curried Rice Salad

3⅓ quarts water
2 teaspoons salt
2 cups uncooked long-grain rice
8 large fresh mushrooms, sliced
2 tablespoons vegetable oil
4 small zucchini, quartered lengthwise and cut into ½-inch slices
⅓ cup minced green onions
⅔ cup minced sweet red pepper
4 tablespoons minced fresh parsley
2 tablespoons dry sherry
⅓ cup fresh lemon juice
2 teaspoons salt
2 teaspoons curry powder
¼ teaspoon red pepper
⅔ cup vegetable oil
Lettuce leaves (optional)

Combine water and 2 teaspoons salt in a large saucepan; bring to a boil. Gradually add rice, stirring constantly until water returns to a boil. Boil 10 minutes or until rice is tender. Drain rice in a large colander, and rinse with cold water. Place rice in colander over a pan of boiling water, cover with a towel and pan lid; steam 15 minutes or until rice is fluffy.

Sauté mushrooms in 2 tablespoons oil in a large skillet for 1 to 2 minutes. Add zucchini and onions; sauté 1 to 2 minutes or until vegetables are crisp-tender.

Combine rice, sweet red pepper, parsley, and vegetables in a large bowl; toss gently. Combine sherry, lemon juice, 2 teaspoons salt, curry powder, and pepper. Gradually add ⅔ cup oil; beat with a wire whisk until blended. Pour dressing over salad, and toss gently. Serve salad over lettuce leaves, if desired. Yield: 12 servings.

Silver Soirees
The Service Guild of Birmingham, Alabama

James Levine's Classic Chicken Salad

4 chicken breasts, skinned and boned (about 2½ pounds)
2 carrots, quartered
2 stalks celery, quartered
1 medium onion, quartered
1 (8-ounce) bottle Italian salad dressing
1 cup chopped celery
4 hard-cooked eggs, sliced
2 tablespoons capers
Salt and pepper to taste
1 cup mayonnaise
1 tablespoon whipping cream

Combine chicken, carrots, 2 stalks celery, onion, and water to cover in a large saucepan; bring to a boil; cover, reduce heat, and simmer 35 minutes or until chicken is tender. Drain chicken; cool and cut into bite-size pieces. Discard broth and vegetables. Combine chicken and Italian dressing in a medium bowl; mix well. Cover and refrigerate at least 12 hours, stirring occasionally. Drain and discard marinade.

Combine chicken, 1 cup celery, eggs, capers, salt, and pepper in a large bowl; set aside. Combine mayonnaise and cream; stir well. Pour mayonnaise mixture over chicken mixture, tossing until well coated. Cover and chill thoroughly. Yield: 8 servings.

Noteworthy
The Ravinia Festival
Highland Park, Illinois

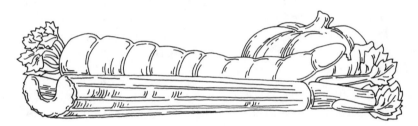

Bahamian Chicken Salad

1 (8-ounce) can pineapple tidbits, undrained
1 (11-ounce) can mandarin oranges, drained
1 (3-ounce) jar chutney
4 cups chopped cooked chicken
2 medium bananas, peeled and cut into ½-inch slices
½ cup mayonnaise
¼ cup sour cream
1 teaspoon curry powder
¼ teaspoon salt
¼ teaspoon pepper

Drain pineapple, reserving 2 tablespoons of juice. Reserve remaining juice for use in other recipes. Set aside.

Combine pineapple tidbits and next 4 ingredients in a large bowl; toss gently, and set aside.

Combine 2 tablespoons pineapple juice, mayonnaise, sour cream, curry powder, salt, and pepper; stir well, and add to chicken mixture. Toss gently to coat. Cover and chill. Yield: 6 servings.

The Stenciled Strawberry Cookbook
The Junior League of Albany, New York

Old Pueblo Club Salad

1 cup vegetable oil
⅓ cup red wine vinegar
1 teaspoon sugar
1 teaspoon salt
1 teaspoon freshly ground pepper
1 teaspoon dried whole oregano
½ teaspoon dried whole tarragon
1 tablespoon Worcestershire sauce
2 tablespoons anchovy paste
1 head iceberg lettuce, torn
1 head romaine, torn
½ head endive, torn
2 ounces ham, cut into julienne strips
2 ounces turkey, cut into julienne strips
2 ounces salami, cut into julienne strips
2 ounces Monterey Jack cheese, cut into julienne strips
2 ounces Cheddar cheese, cut into julienne strips
½ cup garbanzo beans
1 (6-ounce) package croutons
¼ cup grated Parmesan cheese
¼ cup shredded red cabbage
¼ cup shredded carrot
Fresh watercress sprigs (optional)

Combine oil, vinegar, sugar, salt, pepper, oregano, tarragon, Worcestershire sauce, and anchovy paste in container of an electric blender; top with cover, and process 30 seconds. Set aside.

Combine salad greens, ham, turkey, salami, Monterey Jack cheese, Cheddar cheese, and garbanzo beans in a large bowl. Pour dressing over salad, and toss gently. Add croutons, and toss well.

Garnish with Parmesan cheese, red cabbage, carrot, and, if desired, watercress. Serve immediately. Yield: 10 to 12 servings.

Purple Sage and Other Pleasures
The Junior League of Tucson, Arizona

Smoked Turkey, Apple, and Walnut Salad

2 pounds smoked turkey, cut into julienne strips
3 medium-size Granny Smith apples, cored and diced
6 stalks celery, thinly sliced
6 cups chopped fresh watercress
Salt and pepper to taste
1 tablespoon plus 2 teaspoons fresh lemon juice

1 tablespoon plus 1 teaspoon Dijon mustard
1 egg yolk
¼ teaspoon salt
¼ teaspoon pepper
½ cup olive oil
½ cup vegetable oil
Romaine lettuce leaves
1 cup chopped walnuts, toasted
Fresh watercress sprigs

Combine turkey, apple, celery, and chopped watercress in a large bowl. Season with salt and pepper to taste.

Combine lemon juice, mustard, egg yolk, ¼ teaspoon salt, and ¼ teaspoon pepper in container of an electric blender; gradually add oils in a slow steady stream, processing until thickened and smooth.

Pour dressing over turkey mixture, and toss gently to coat. Cover and refrigerate 1 to 4 hours.

Mound salad on a lettuce-lined platter. Sprinkle with walnuts, and garnish with watercress sprigs. Yield: 10 servings.

San Francisco Encore
The Junior League of San Francisco, California

Oregon Blue Cheese Dressing

1 cup mayonnaise
1 (8-ounce) carton commercial sour cream
1½ (4-ounce) packages blue cheese, crumbled
¼ cup olive oil

1 tablespoon milk
1 teaspoon cider vinegar
1 clove garlic, minced
⅛ teaspoon dry mustard
⅛ teaspoon freshly ground pepper

Combine all ingredients in a small bowl; stir until well blended. Cover and chill. Serve over fruit or salad greens. Yield: 3 cups.

Oregon Sampler: Resorts & Recipes
The Assistance League of Corvallis, Oregon

Green Mill House Dressing

2 cups vegetable oil
½ cup white wine vinegar
¼ cup finely chopped onion
¼ cup finely chopped green
  pepper
3 tablespoons finely chopped
  fresh parsley

1 tablespoon sugar
1 teaspoon salt
½ teaspoon crushed red
  pepper
2 tablespoons Dijon mustard

Combine all ingredients in a jar. Cover tightly, and shake vigorously. Chill thoroughly. Shake well before serving. Serve dressing over salad greens. Yield: 3½ cups.

Look What's Cooking Now! Minnesota Heritage Cookbook Volume II
The American Cancer Society, Minnesota Division
Minneapolis, Minnesota

Green Salad Vinaigrette Dressing

⅓ cup olive oil
⅓ cup safflower oil
⅓ cup fresh lemon juice
2 tablespoons white wine
  vinegar
2 teaspoons sugar

1½ teaspoons salt
1 teaspoon finely chopped
  fresh chives
½ teaspoon dry mustard
¼ teaspoon pepper

Combine all ingredients in container of an electric blender; top with cover, and blend well. Cover and chill dressing thoroughly. Serve vinaigrette over salad greens. Yield: 1 cup.

Cornsilk
The Junior League of Sioux City, Iowa

Sauces & Condiments

Saguaro Cacti are a familiar sight in the Santa Catalina Mountains, a small range in the northeastern corner of Arizona. The tall, columnar and sparsely branched trunk of the cacti may look stark and barren, but the Saguaro actually bear white flowers and edible fruit.

☆☆☆

Maple Butterscotch Sauce

¼ cup butter or margarine,
softened
1 cup firmly packed brown
sugar
2 egg yolks, beaten

½ cup whipping cream
⅛ teaspoon salt
½ teaspoon maple extract
½ cup chopped walnuts

Cream butter; gradually add sugar, beating well. Add egg yolks, cream, and salt. Mix well.

Pour mixture in top of a double boiler; bring water to a boil. Reduce heat to low; cook until mixture is thickened and creamy. Remove from heat, and cool slightly. Add maple extract and chopped walnuts. Serve sauce warm or cold over ice cream, pudding, or cake. Yield: 2 cups.   Jo Gross Huffman

Temptations
The Junior Service League of Rome, Georgia

Chantilly-Rum Sauce for Fresh Fruit

½ teaspoon unflavored gelatin
5 tablespoons cold water,
divided
1 cup sugar
2 egg whites
¼ teaspoon cream of tartar

⅛ teaspoon salt
½ teaspoon vanilla extract
2 tablespoons dark rum
1 cup whipping cream,
whipped

Soften gelatin in 2 tablespoons cold water; set aside. Combine remaining 3 tablespoons cold water, sugar, egg whites, cream of tartar, salt, and vanilla in top of a double boiler, mixing well. Bring water to a boil; reduce heat to low. Beat at medium speed of an electric mixer until mixture is thickened. Remove top of boiler from water; set aside.

Place softened gelatin in a heat-proof dish. Place dish in simmering water, stirring until gelatin dissolves. Add rum; mix well. Remove dish from water. Gradually add rum mixture to egg white mixture, beating well. Chill 1 to 1½ hours or until slightly thickened.

Fold whipped cream into chilled mixture. Serve with fresh strawberries or other fresh fruit. Yield: 5 cups.

Winning at the Table
The Junior League of Las Vegas, Nevada

Hot Fudge Sauce

½ cup sugar
¼ cup cocoa
½ cup light corn syrup
¼ cup half-and-half

2 tablespoons butter or
  margarine, melted
½ teaspoon vanilla extract

Combine sugar and cocoa in a small saucepan. Stir in corn syrup, and half-and-half. Cook over medium heat, stirring constantly, until mixture boils. Reduce heat, and simmer 3 minutes, stirring constantly. Remove from heat; stir in butter and vanilla. Serve hot over ice cream. Yield: 1⅓ cups.

Necessities and Temptations
The Junior League of Austin, Texas

Broussard Sauce

1 (8-ounce) package cream
  cheese
1¼ cups sugar
¾ cup half-and-half

3 to 4 tablespoons vanilla
  extract
1 to 2 teaspoons ground
  nutmeg

Position knife blade in food processor bowl; add all ingredients. Top with cover, and process until mixture is smooth. Chill sauce until serving time. Serve Broussard Sauce with assorted fresh fruit. Yield: 2 cups.

Sara Blough

Taste of the South
The Symphony League of Jackson, Mississippi

Pulliam's Barbecue Sauce

2 (14-ounce) bottles catsup
1 (12-ounce) bottle chili sauce
1 (12-ounce) can beer
1 (5-ounce) bottle steak sauce
1 medium onion, chopped
½ cup lemon juice
½ cup vinegar
½ cup firmly packed brown
  sugar
⅓ cup prepared mustard

¼ cup Worcestershire sauce
2 tablespoons dry mustard
2 tablespoons coarsely
  ground pepper
2 tablespoons vegetable oil
1 tablespoon red pepper
1 tablespoon soy sauce
4 whole cloves
1 clove garlic, minced

Combine all ingredients in a large Dutch oven. Cook over medium heat for 10 minutes, stirring occasionally. Reduce heat, and simmer, stirring occasionally, 15 minutes. Use as a basting sauce for beef, pork, or chicken. Store in an airtight container in the refrigerator. Yield: 2 quarts.   Janyce Shorbe Coffeen

Superlatives
The Junior League of Oklahoma City, Oklahoma

Garlic Butter Steak Sauce

½ cup butter or margarine,
  softened
2 large cloves garlic,
  crushed
1 tablespoon prepared
  horseradish

1 tablespoon Worcestershire
  sauce
6 drops hot sauce

Combine all ingredients in a medium mixing bowl. Beat at medium speed of an electric mixer until mixture is creamy. Serve with broiled steak. Yield: ¾ cup.

Note: Garlic Butter Steak Sauce can be used to prepare garlic bread. Spread on both sides of French bread slices. Broil 6 inches from heat until bread is toasted.   Phyllis Conrad

Our Country Cookin'
The Junior Social Workers of Chickasha, Oklahoma

Fluffy Mustard Sauce

2 eggs, beaten
3 tablespoons prepared
  mustard
2 tablespoons sugar
2 tablespoons cider vinegar
1 tablespoon water
½ teaspoon salt

1 tablespoon butter or
  margarine
2 teaspoons prepared
  horseradish
⅓ cup whipping cream,
  whipped

Combine eggs, mustard, sugar, vinegar, water, and salt in top of a double boiler. Cook over hot, not boiling, water 5 minutes or until mixture is thickened and smooth, stirring constantly, using a wire whisk. Remove from heat; add butter and horseradish, stirring until butter melts. Cool thoroughly, and fold in whipped cream. Cover and store in refrigerator. Serve with beef or ham. Yield: 1 cup.

According to Taste
The Service League of Lufkin, Texas

Stir-Fry Sauce

½ cup soy sauce
½ cup dry sherry
⅓ cup cornstarch
4 cloves garlic, chopped
3 tablespoons red wine
  vinegar
3 tablespoons dark brown
  sugar

2 teaspoons minced fresh
  gingerroot
¼ teaspoon hot sauce
2½ cups diluted canned beef
  or chicken broth

Combine all ingredients, except broth, in container of an electric blender; process on medium speed 1 minute or until smooth. Add broth, and process until well blended. Cover and store in refrigerator up to 10 days or freeze up to 3 months. If frozen, thaw at room temperature for 2 hours before use. Shake well before each use. Yield: 4 cups.

Peggy Chamberlin

Feast and Fellowship
The St. Frances Guild
Atlanta, Georgia

Good Mayonnaise

2 eggs
1 tablespoon vinegar
2 teaspoons lemon juice

1 teaspoon prepared mustard
½ teaspoon salt
2 cups safflower oil

Position knife blade in food processor bowl; add eggs, vinegar, lemon juice, mustard, and salt. Top with cover, and process 15 seconds or until smooth. With processor running, pour oil through food chute in a slow steady stream; process until thickened and smooth. Spoon mayonnaise into a glass or plastic container (do not store mayonnaise in a metal container); cover tightly, and store in refrigerator. Yield: 2¼ cups.   Mary Frances Cook

What's Cooking at Woodlawn?
United Methodist Women, Woodlawn United Methodist Church
Birmingham, Alabama

Green Mayonnaise

1 cup coarsely chopped fresh
   parsley
5 green onions, cut into
   1-inch pieces
¼ cup coarsely chopped
   fresh chives
2 cloves garlic

3 egg yolks
3 tablespoons lemon juice
1 tablespoon Dijon mustard
½ teaspoon salt
⅛ teaspoon freshly ground
   pepper
1½ cups vegetable oil

Combine first four ingredients in container of an electric blender or food processor; top with cover, and process 5 seconds or until minced. Add egg yolks, lemon juice, mustard, salt, and pepper; process 10 seconds, scraping sides of container occasionally. With machine running, gradually add oil in a slow steady stream, and process 10 seconds or until mixture is creamy. Spoon mayonnaise into a glass or plastic container (do not store mayonnaise in metal container). Cover and store in refrigerator. Yield: 2½ cups.

A Taste of Aloha
The Junior League of Honolulu, Hawaii

Sweet and Hot Mustard

2 (2-ounce) cans dry mustard   3 eggs
1 cup vinegar   1 cup sugar

Combine dry mustard and vinegar in a small bowl. Cover and refrigerate 8 hours.

Beat eggs and sugar, using a wire whisk. Add to cold mustard mixture. Pour into top of a double boiler; bring water to a boil. Reduce heat to low; cook, stirring constantly, 7 minutes or until mixture is thickened and smooth. Store in an airtight container in refrigerator. Yield: 2¼ cups.   Susan Wilson Jarrett

A Dash of Down East
The Junior Guild of Rocky Mount, North Carolina

Spiced Green Onions

1 pound green onions, thinly   ½ teaspoon paprika
  sliced   ⅛ teaspoon ground cinnamon
1 cup sugar   ⅛ teaspoon ground nutmeg
1 cup golden raisins   ⅛ teaspoon coarsely ground
1 cup white wine vinegar   pepper

Combine all ingredients in a saucepan. Bring to a boil; reduce heat, and simmer, uncovered, 20 minutes or until thickened. Chill before serving. Yield: 2 cups.   Patricia Braun

Our Special Blend
The Rehabilitation Center of Eastern Fairfield County
Bridgeport, Connecticut

Squash Relish

3 pounds yellow squash,   ¼ cup plus 1 tablespoon salt
  shredded (12 cups)   2 tablespoons pickling spices
4 large yellow onions,   2½ cups cider vinegar (5%
  chopped   acidity)
4 sweet red or green peppers,   1 teaspoon ground turmeric
  finely chopped   6 cups sugar

Combine squash, onions, and peppers in a large bowl; toss gently. Sprinkle salt over vegetables. Cover and let stand 8 hours. Drain.

Return vegetables to large bowl. Cover with cold water. Let stand 20 minutes. Drain vegetables well.

Tie pickling spices in a cheesecloth bag. Combine pickling spices, vinegar, and turmeric in a medium saucepan. Bring to a boil. Place sugar in a large Dutch oven. Pour boiling mixture over sugar, stirring well. Stir in vegetables. Cook over medium-high heat for 10 minutes. Remove spice bag. Ladle relish into hot sterilized jars, leaving ¼-inch headspace. Remove air bubbles; wipe jar rims. Cover at once with metal lids, and screw on bands. Store in refrigerator. Yield: 6 pints.   Nancy Mosley

Temptations
Presbyterian Day School
Cleveland, Mississippi

Rosy Relish

4 cups peeled and chopped tomatoes	1 (3-inch) stick cinnamon
2 cups peeled and chopped cooking apples	2 tablespoons mustard seeds
1 cup chopped green pepper	2 tablespoons chopped sweet red pepper
1 cup chopped celery	1 tablespoon salt
2¼ cups sugar	10 whole cloves, crushed
1½ cups cider vinegar (5% acidity)	

Combine all ingredients in a Dutch oven. Bring mixture to a boil; reduce heat, and simmer, uncovered, 4½ hours, stirring every 15 minutes. Let cool.

Spoon relish into hot sterilized jars, leaving ¼-inch headspace. Remove air bubbles; wipe jar rims. Cover at once with metal lids, and screw on bands. Store in refrigerator. Yield: 4 half pints.

Cabell West

Virginia Seasons
The Junior League of Richmond, Virginia

Pottsfield Relish

3 pints ripe tomatoes,
chopped
3 pints green tomatoes,
chopped
1 medium cabbage, cored and
chopped
1 bunch celery, chopped
4 onions, chopped

4 sweet red peppers, chopped
½ cup salt
6 cups vinegar (5% acidity)
6 cups sugar
¼ cup whole mustard seeds
¼ cup celery seeds
1 teaspoon ground cinnamon
½ teaspoon ground cloves

Combine first 7 ingredients. Cover and let stand overnight. Drain.
Add vinegar, sugar, mustard seeds, celery seeds, cinnamon, and
cloves; bring to a rolling boil. Ladle relish into hot sterilized jars,
leaving ¼-inch headspace. Remove air bubbles; wipe jar rims. Cover
with metal lids, and screw on bands. Process in boiling-water bath 15
minutes. Yield: 5 quarts.   Ora Ellen Lawrence

Angel Food
St. Anne's Church
Annapolis, Maryland

Jalapeño Corn Relish

1 (17-ounce) can whole kernel
corn, drained
3 cups chopped cabbage
2 jalapeño peppers, seeded
and minced
2 small sweet red peppers,
chopped

1 medium onion, chopped
½ cup sugar
2 teaspoons salt
2 teaspoons all-purpose flour
2 teaspoons dry mustard
¼ teaspoon ground turmeric
1 cup white wine vinegar

Combine first 5 ingredients. Combine sugar, salt, flour, mustard,
and turmeric in a saucepan. Stir in vinegar. Bring to a boil. Add
vegetables; stir well. Reduce heat; simmer 15 minutes, stirring often.
Spoon relish into hot sterilized jars, leaving ¼-inch headspace.
Remove air bubbles; wipe jar rims. Cover with metal lids, and screw
on bands. Process in boiling-water bath 10 minutes. Yield: 2 pints.

A Taste of California
The San Francisco Home Economists in Business
San Francisco, California

Brandied Cranberries

3 cups fresh cranberries   ⅓ cup brandy
1½ cups sugar

Combine all ingredients in a large bowl; stir well. Spoon mixture into a 13- x 9- x 2-inch baking dish. Cover and bake at 300° for 1 hour. Remove from oven. Serve cranberries warm or cold with poultry or pork. Yield: 2 cups.   Ann Miller

Just What the Doctor Ordered
The Peoria Medical Society Auxiliary, Inc.
Peoria, Illinois

Spiced Blueberry-Peach Jam

4 cups peeled, chopped   5½ cups sugar
  peaches (about 2 pounds)   ½ teaspoon salt
4 cups fresh blueberries   1 (3-inch) stick cinnamon
½ cup water   ½ teaspoon whole cloves
2 tablespoons lemon juice   ¼ teaspoon whole allspice

Place peaches and blueberries in a large Dutch oven. Add water and lemon juice. Cover and bring to a boil over medium-high heat. Reduce heat, and simmer 10 minutes, stirring occasionally. Stir in sugar and salt.

Tie cinnamon, cloves, and allspice in a cheesecloth bag; add to fruit mixture. Return to a rolling boil; reduce heat, and simmer, uncovered, 30 minutes or until thickened, stirring frequently. Remove from heat. Discard spice bag; skim off foam.

Ladle hot jam into hot sterilized jars, leaving ¼-inch headspace; wipe jar rims. Cover at once with metal lids, and screw on bands. Process in boiling-water bath 10 minutes. Yield: 7 half pints.

Putting on the Grits
The Junior League of Columbia, South Carolina

Cranberry Marmalade

2 medium oranges
1 medium lemon
3 cups water
1 pound fresh cranberries, chopped

1 (1¾-ounce) package powdered fruit pectin
7 cups sugar

Peel oranges and lemon, reserving rind and half of The white pith. Reserve pulp, and set aside.

Position knife blade in food processor bowl; add orange and lemon rind and pith, and process until finely chopped.

Combine chopped mixture and water in a large Dutch oven; bring to a boil over high heat. Reduce heat; boil 20 minutes, uncovered, stirring frequently.

Cut orange and lemon pulp into quarters; remove and discard seeds. Place pulp in food processor bowl, and chop. Combine pulp and cranberries, and add to rind mixture in Dutch oven; simmer 10 minutes, stirring frequently.

Add powdered pectin to fruit mixture in Dutch oven; bring to a boil, stirring constantly. Gradually add sugar; return mixture to a boil, and cook, stirring constantly, until temperature registers 220° on a candy thermometer. Remove from heat, and skim off foam, using a metal spoon. Pour marmalade into hot sterilized jars, leaving ¼-inch headspace; wipe jar rims. Cover jars at once with metal lids, and screw on bands. Process marmalade in boiling-water bath 10 minutes. Yield: 4 pints.   Maureen Buckmiller

"delicious"
The Elisabeth Morrow School Parents Association
Englewood, New Jersey

Soups & Stews

Maryland is diverse in its landscapes and ways of life from the water-oriented Eastern shore to the forested Appalachian foothills. Once a neglected waterfront area, metropolitan Baltimore has undergone a major restoration process. Specialties of the bustling, 207-year-old Lexington Market include homemade Polish sausage, steamed crabs, and hot oyster stew.

☆☆☆

Cold Peach Soup

1½ pounds peeled, sliced
   fresh peaches
2 (8-ounce) cartons
   commercial sour cream
1 cup fresh orange juice

1 cup pineapple juice
½ cup dry sherry
1 tablespoon fresh lemon
   juice
2 tablespoons sugar

Position knife blade in food processor bowl; add peaches, and top with cover. Process until smooth. Add sour cream, orange juice, pineapple juice, sherry, and lemon juice; process until smooth.

Press peach mixture through a sieve; pour soup into a large bowl. Add sugar, stirring well. Chill thoroughly. Ladle soup into individual serving bowls. Yield: 5½ cups.   Bill Rodgers

Treat Yourself to the Best
The Junior League of Wheeling, West Virginia

Fresh Strawberry Soup

2 pints strawberries, washed,
   hulled, and halved
1 cup orange juice, divided
1 tablespoon cornstarch
1 cup Burgundy or other dry
   red wine

½ cup sugar
Commercial sour cream
Additional whole
   strawberries

Place halved strawberries in container of an electric blender or food processor. Cover and process until pureed. Set aside.

Combine ¼ cup orange juice and cornstarch in a medium saucepan, stirring well. Add remaining orange juice, wine, and sugar. Bring mixture to a boil. Remove from heat.

Combine orange juice mixture and pureed strawberries in a large bowl. Chill thoroughly. Ladle into individual soup bowls. Top each serving with a dollop of sour cream and a whole strawberry. Yield: 6 servings.   Marsha Lewis

Beyond the Bay
The Junior Service League of Panama City, Florida

Chilled Avocado Soup

2 large ripe avocados
2 tablespoons lemon juice,
  divided
1½ cups diluted canned
  chicken broth
1 teaspoon grated onion

½ teaspoon salt
2 to 3 drops of hot sauce
1½ cups half-and-half
Chopped fresh chives
  (optional)
Paprika (optional)

Cut avocados in half lengthwise; remove seeds. Peel avocado, and cut into thin slices. Sprinkle with 1 or 2 teaspoons lemon juice, and set aside several slices for garnish, if desired. Cube remaining avocado, and place in container of an electric blender. Add remaining lemon juice, chicken broth, onion, salt, and hot sauce; top with cover, and process until smooth. Pour into a large bowl; add half-and-half, and stir well. Chill 1 hour.

Pour soup into chilled wine glasses; garnish with avocado slices, chives, and paprika, if desired. Yield: 4 cups.

Gulfshore Delights
The Junior League of Fort Myers, Florida

Clear Gazpacho

1 quart chicken broth,
  strained
2 cups Chablis or other dry
  white wine
½ cup lemon juice
3 small cucumbers, thinly
  sliced
3 medium tomatoes, peeled,
  seeded, and coarsely
  chopped

¾ cup thinly sliced green
  onions
½ cup minced fresh
  parsley
¼ teaspoon salt
¼ teaspoon pepper
¼ teaspoon hot sauce

Combine chicken broth, wine, and lemon juice in a large Dutch oven; bring to a boil. Remove from heat; cover and chill at least 8 hours. Add cucumbers and remaining ingredients to broth; stir well. Ladle into individual serving bowls. Yield: 2½ quarts.

Gallery Buffet Soup Cookbook
The Dallas Museum of Art League
Dallas, Texas

French Onion Soup with Applejack

4 large onions, diced
½ cup butter or margarine, melted
1 cup Chablis or other dry white wine
2 (10½-ounce) cans beef broth, diluted
⅓ cup applejack brandy
1 teaspoon Worcestershire sauce

½ teaspoon dried whole thyme
1 bay leaf
1 clove garlic, crushed
Croutons
1 cup (4 ounces) grated Gruyère cheese

Sauté onion in butter in a Dutch oven until tender. Add wine; cook over high heat 10 minutes or until liquid evaporates, stirring frequently.

Stir in beef broth, brandy, Worcestershire sauce, thyme, bay leaf, and garlic. Cook over medium heat 30 minutes. Remove and discard bay leaf.

Place 8 ovenproof serving bowls on a baking sheet. Ladle soup into bowls. Top each serving with croutons, and sprinkle with cheese. Broil 6 inches from heat 3 minutes or until cheese melts. Serve immediately. Yield: 8 cups.   Jane Wolf

"delicious"
The Elisabeth Morrow School Parents Association
Englewood, New Jersey

Six Lily Soup

½ cup unsalted butter
5 large onions, chopped
6 shallots, minced
3 leeks, chopped
3 cloves garlic, minced
4 cups diluted canned
  chicken broth
3 cups diluted canned beef
  broth

2 cups whipping cream
¼ teaspoon salt
⅛ teaspoon red pepper
3 tablespoons cornstarch
3 tablespoons water
3 tablespoons chopped fresh
  chives
3 green onions, chopped

Melt butter in a large Dutch oven. Add onion, shallots, leeks, and garlic. Simmer 20 minutes, stirring occasionally. Add broths. Bring to a boil; reduce heat, and simmer, uncovered, 45 minutes.

Transfer mixture in 4 batches to container of an electric blender or food processor. Cover and process until smooth. Return pureed mixture to Dutch oven. Repeat procedure with remaining onion mixture. Stir in whipping cream. Cook until thoroughly heated. (Do not boil.) Add salt and red pepper. Combine cornstarch and water, stirring well. Add to soup. Cook until soup is thickened. Top each serving with chives and green onions. Yield: 8 to 10 servings.

Noteworthy
The Ravinia Festival
Highland Park, Illinois

Cheese Soup

¼ cup butter or margarine
¼ cup all-purpose flour
2 cups half-and-half
2 cups milk
2 cups (8 ounces) shredded
  Gouda cheese
1 teaspoon Worcestershire
  sauce

¼ teaspoon red pepper
  (optional)
2 to 3 drops hot sauce
Salt to taste
Paprika (optional)

Melt butter in a large saucepan over medium-low heat. Stir in flour. Cook for 1 minute, stirring constantly. Gradually add half-and-half and milk, stirring constantly. Cook over medium-low heat until slightly thickened.

Pour milk mixture into container of an electric blender; add cheese. Top with cover, and process until foamy.

Return mixture to saucepan. Cook over medium-low heat until thoroughly heated. Stir in Worcestershire sauce, red pepper, if desired, hot sauce, and salt. Ladle into soup bowls. Sprinkle with paprika, if desired. Yield: 5 cups.

Temptations
The Junior League of Lansing, Michigan

Cream of Wild Rice Soup

2 large onions, chopped
1½ cups butter or margarine, divided
6 cups chopped celery with leaves
1 pound fresh mushrooms, sliced

½ cup all-purpose flour
2 teaspoons salt
1 teaspoon pepper
2 quarts milk
3½ cups cooked wild rice

Sauté onion in 1 cup butter in a large skillet 5 minutes or until tender. Add celery and mushrooms, and sauté until vegetables are tender; set aside.

Melt remaining ½ cup butter in a large Dutch oven. Add flour, salt, and pepper, stirring until smooth. Cook 1 minute, stirring constantly. Reduce heat to medium; gradually add milk, and cook, stirring constantly, until mixture is thickened and bubbly.

Stir in sautéed vegetables and rice; reduce heat to low, and simmer 15 minutes. Yield: 12 cups.

Sassafras!
The Junior League of Springfield, Missouri

Cream of Peanut Soup

1 small onion, chopped
½ cup chopped celery
¼ cup butter or margarine
2 tablespoons all-purpose
  flour
2 cups diluted canned
  chicken broth

1 cup milk
1 cup half-and-half
1 cup creamy peanut butter
⅛ teaspoon salt
⅛ teaspoon pepper
⅛ teaspoon paprika

Sauté onion and celery in butter in a Dutch oven until tender; add flour, stirring until smooth. Gradually add chicken broth; bring mixture to a boil. Add milk and half-and-half.

Remove from heat; strain soup, and discard vegetables. Add peanut butter, and stir well. Simmer 5 minutes. Stir in salt, pepper, and paprika. Yield: 4 cups.

Down Home in High Style
The Houston Academy
Dothan, Alabama

Soupe de Tomates en Croûte

1 pound onions, chopped
2 tablespoons butter or
  margarine
2 pounds tomatoes, quartered
6 cloves garlic
1 bay leaf
Pinch of dried whole thyme
1 cup whipping cream
¼ teaspoon salt

⅛ teaspoon white pepper
1 carrot, scraped and cut into
  julienne strips (optional)
1 leek, cut into julienne
  strips (optional)
1 (17¼-ounce) package frozen
  puff pastry, thawed
1 egg, beaten
1 tablespoon water

Sauté chopped onion in butter in a large Dutch oven until tender. Add tomatoes, garlic, bay leaf, and thyme. Cook, uncovered, over low heat for 1½ hours. Remove and discard bay leaf. Transfer mixture to container of an electric blender or food processor. Top with cover, and process until mixture is smooth. Stir in whipping cream, salt, and pepper. Ladle soup into 6 individual crocks or ovenproof bowls.

If desired, blanch carrot and leek strips in a small amount of boiling water for 30 seconds. Add to soup in crocks.

Roll puff pastry sheets to about ⅛-inch thickness. Cut 6 circles of pastry, 2 inches larger than individual crocks. Combine egg and water, stirring well. Brush one side of each circle with egg mixture. Place pastry circles, brushed side down, over each crock, pressing firmly to sides of crock to seal edges. Refrigerate for 1 hour. Brush top of each pastry circle with remaining half of egg mixture. Bake at 450° for 20 minutes. Serve immediately. Yield: 6 servings.

San Francisco Encore
The Junior League of San Francisco, California

Sopa de Lima

1 lime
1 large sweet red pepper, chopped
1 onion, minced
1 clove garlic, minced
¼ cup plus 1 tablespoon vegetable oil, divided
2 tomatoes peeled, seeded, and chopped
2 (10¾-ounce) cans chicken broth, diluted

3 jalapeño peppers, seeded and chopped
6 (6-inch) flour tortillas, halved
1½ cups chopped cooked chicken
¼ teaspoon salt
¼ teaspoon pepper
6 lime slices

Cut lime in half crosswise. Juice lime, reserving juice and shells; set aside.

Sauté red pepper, onion, and garlic in 2 tablespoons oil until tender. Add tomatoes, and cook 2 minutes, stirring constantly. Add chicken broth, jalapeño peppers, lime juice, and lime shells. Bring mixture to a boil, reduce heat, and simmer 5 minutes. Remove and discard lime shells.

Cut tortilla halves into ½-inch strips. Heat remaining oil in a large skillet over medium heat. Add tortilla strips, and cook until golden brown. Drain well on paper towels. Set aside.

Add chicken to broth mixture. Simmer over low heat until thoroughly heated. Add salt and pepper. Garnish each serving with tortilla strips and a lime slice. Yield: 6 cups.

Purple Sage and Other Pleasures
The Junior League of Tucson, Arizona

Tostada Soup with Fresh Salsa

3 medium tomatoes, peeled
and finely chopped
¾ cup chopped green onions
3 tablespoons chopped green
chiles
½ teaspoon ground coriander
¼ teaspoon salt, divided
¼ teaspoon pepper, divided
3 pounds beef stew meat, cut
into 1-inch cubes
3 cups undiluted canned beef
broth
2 large onions, thinly sliced

1 sweet red pepper, chopped
1 (4-ounce) can chopped
green chiles, drained
1 (28-ounce) can tomatoes,
undrained
1½ cups fresh corn
Shredded lettuce
Shredded Cheddar cheese
Chopped tomatoes
Sour cream
Sliced avocado
Tortilla chips

Combine finely chopped tomatoes, green onions, 3 tablespoons chopped green chiles, coriander, ⅛ teaspoon salt, and ⅛ teaspoon pepper; mix well. Cover salsa, and refrigerate 3 to 4 hours.

Combine beef, broth, onion slices, red pepper, and 1 can chopped green chiles in a large Dutch oven. Bring to a boil; cover, reduce heat, and simmer 1½ hours. Stir in tomatoes; cover and simmer 1 hour or until beef is tender.

Add corn, ⅛ teaspoon salt, ⅛ teaspoon pepper, and one tablespoon chilled salsa; stir well. Simmer, uncovered, 5 minutes.

Top soup with remaining salsa, lettuce, cheese, tomatoes, sour cream, and avocado. Serve with tortilla chips. Yield: 10 cups.

Taste the Seasons
Woodside-Atherton Auxiliary to Children's Hospital at Stanford
Menlo Park, California

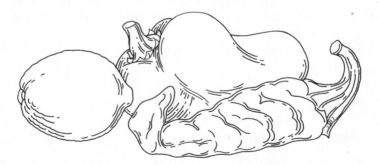

Oysters Rockefeller Soup

1 (10-ounce) package frozen
  chopped spinach, thawed
½ cup coarsely chopped
  onion
2 green onions, coarsely
  chopped
½ cup coarsely chopped
  lettuce
¼ cup coarsely chopped
  fresh parsley
2 stalks celery with leaves,
  coarsely chopped
¼ cup butter or margarine
3 tablespoons all-purpose
  flour
1 teaspoon seasoned salt

½ teaspoon pepper
2 tablespoons anchovy paste
1 tablespoon lemon juice
3 dozen fresh Standard
  oysters, undrained
1 (10¾-ounce) can chicken
  broth, undiluted
2 teaspoons Worcestershire
  sauce
2 cups half-and-half
2 tablespoons grated
  Parmesan cheese
2 tablespoons Italian-style
  breadcrumbs
1 tablespoon aromatic bitters

Drain spinach well, pressing between layers of paper towels. Combine spinach, onion, green onions, lettuce, parsley, and celery in container of an electric blender or food processor. Top with cover, and process until smooth.

Melt butter in a Dutch oven over medium heat. Add vegetable mixture, and cook 8 minutes, stirring occasionally. Stir in flour, salt, pepper, anchovy paste, and lemon juice.

Drain oysters, reserving ½ cup liquid. Add oysters and ½ cup liquid to vegetable mixture in Dutch oven; simmer 3 minutes. Gradually add chicken broth and Worcestershire sauce, stirring until blended. Bring mixture to a boil, reduce heat, and simmer 2 minutes. Stir in half-and-half; cook over low heat until soup is thoroughly heated, stirring occasionally. Ladle into soup bowls, and sprinkle with Parmesan cheese and breadcrumbs. Add aromatic bitters just before serving. Yield: 8½ cups.

Artist's Palate Cookbook
Women's Volunteer Committee, New Orleans Museum of Art
New Orleans, Louisiana

Sweet Italian Sausage Soup

2 pounds Italian sausage
links, cut into ¾-inch
pieces
1 (28-ounce) can tomatoes,
undrained and chopped
2 (14½-ounce) cans beef
broth, undiluted
2 cups water
2 medium onions, chopped
1 medium eggplant, peeled
and cut into 1-inch cubes

1 medium-size green pepper,
chopped
3 cloves garlic, minced
2 tablespoons chopped fresh
parsley
1 teaspoon dried whole basil
1 teaspoon dried whole
oregano
Grated Parmesan cheese

Brown sausage in a large skillet over medium heat; remove sausage, and drain well. Combine sausage and remaining ingredients, except cheese, in a large Dutch oven. Bring to a boil; cover, reduce heat, and simmer 4 to 6 hours. Sprinkle with cheese, and serve immediately. Yield: 6 cups.   Phyllis R. Hamilton

Cooking with Class
Frederick Community College
Frederick, Maryland

Chicken Minestrone

1 large onion, chopped
3 cloves garlic, minced
¼ cup vegetable oil
2 large potatoes, peeled and
diced
3 medium carrots, scraped
and diced
2 stalks celery, sliced
2 medium zucchini, diced
2 leeks, thinly sliced
¼ pound diced cooked ham
2 quarts diluted canned
chicken broth

1 (16-ounce) can Italian plum
tomatoes, undrained
1 tablespoon dried whole
basil
2 teaspoons salt
½ teaspoon pepper
3 cups diced cooked chicken
1 cup cooked Great Northern
beans or garbanzo beans
½ cup uncooked macaroni
Grated Parmesan cheese

Sauté onion and garlic in oil in a large Dutch oven until tender. Add potatoes, carrots, celery, zucchini, leeks, and ham. Sauté over medium heat 5 minutes. Add broth, tomatoes, basil, salt, and pepper. Bring to a boil; reduce heat, and simmer, uncovered, 2½ to 3 hours. Stir in chicken, beans, and macaroni. Simmer 10 minutes. Sprinkle each serving with cheese. Yield: 10 cups.

First There Must Be Food
Northwestern Memorial Hospital
Chicago, Illinois

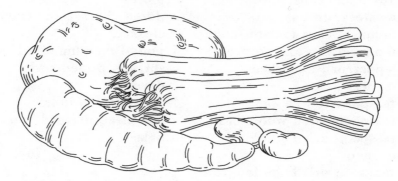

Illini Corn Chowder

½ cup chopped salt pork
1 medium onion, chopped
2 cups diced potato
2 cups water
1 medium green pepper, diced
½ cup chopped celery

1 teaspoon salt
1 bay leaf
2 cups milk, divided
¼ cup all-purpose flour
2 cups fresh corn
½ cup half-and-half

Sauté pork in a large Dutch oven until crisp. Add onion. Sauté until onion is tender. Add diced potato, water, green pepper, celery, salt, and bay leaf. Simmer, uncovered, 15 minutes or until potatoes are tender.

Combine ¼ cup milk and flour, stirring well. Add to potato mixture. Stir in remaining 1¾ cups milk. Cook, stirring constantly, until thickened. Add corn and half-and-half. Cook, stirring constantly, until thoroughly heated. Remove and discard bay leaf. Yield: 8 cups.

Fest of All Worlds
The American Lebanese Christian Women's Society of Illinois
Chicago, Illinois

Oregon Bouillabaisse

2 medium onions, chopped
2 green peppers, diced
1 leek, sliced
4 cloves garlic, minced
1 cup butter or margarine
¼ cup olive oil
3 (16-ounce) cans whole tomatoes, undrained
2 (8-ounce) cans tomato sauce
1 (6-ounce) can tomato paste
6 peppercorns, crushed
1 bay leaf
½ teaspoon red pepper
½ teaspoon dried whole basil
½ teaspoon dried whole oregano
½ teaspoon dried whole thyme

2 cups Chablis or other dry white wine
1 cup clam juice
¼ pound scallops
2 pounds red snapper, skinned and cut into 2-inch pieces
2 dozen cherrystone clams, cleaned
1 pound medium-size fresh shrimp, peeled and deveined
1 pound fresh lump crabmeat, drained and flaked

Sauté onion, peppers, leek, and garlic in butter and oil in a Dutch oven until tender. Add tomatoes and next 8 ingredients. Cook over low heat for 15 minutes. Add wine and clam juice. Cook 10 minutes. Add scallops, snapper, and clams. Simmer 20 minutes. Add shrimp and crabmeat. Cook 10 minutes or until thoroughly heated. Remove and discard bay leaf. Yield: 5 quarts.

Oregon Sampler: Resorts & Recipes
The Assistance League of Corvallis, Oregon

Bayou Bouillabaisse

2 medium onions, sliced and separated into rings
⅓ cup olive oil
3 medium tomatoes, peeled and chopped, or 1 (16-ounce) can whole tomatoes, drained and chopped
½ cup Chablis or other dry white wine
6 cups fish stock
3 cloves garlic, minced
1 bay leaf
¼ teaspoon dried whole thyme
⅛ teaspoon anise seeds
3½ pounds red snapper fillets, cut into 1-inch cubes
1 pound uncooked medium-size shrimp, peeled and deveined
1 cup fresh lump crabmeat, drained and flaked
1 (16-ounce) container Standard oysters, drained
¼ teaspoon ground saffron
½ teaspoon salt
½ teaspoon red pepper
½ teaspoon pepper
Garlic toast (optional)

Sauté onion in olive oil in a Dutch oven until tender. Add tomatoes, wine, fish stock, garlic, bay leaf, thyme, and anise seeds. Bring to a boil. Reduce heat; cover and simmer 15 minutes. Add seafood, saffron, salt, and peppers. Simmer 15 to 20 minutes or until fish flakes easily when tested with a fork. (Do not overcook fillets.) Remove and discard bay leaf.

Ladle into individual serving bowls. Serve hot with garlic toast, if desired. Yield: 4 quarts.   Tanya B. Ditto

Down the Bayou
The Bayou Civic Club
Larose, Louisiana

Cioppino

2 medium onions, chopped
6 cloves garlic, minced
3 tablespoons olive oil
4 (15-ounce) cans tomato
  sauce
1 (28-ounce) can tomato
  puree
1 cup chopped fresh celery
  leaves
2 tablespoons Worcestershire
  sauce
¼ teaspoon hot sauce
6 bay leaves
2 teaspoons dry mustard
1 teaspoon dried whole basil
1 teaspoon dried whole
  oregano

1 teaspoon dried whole
  thyme
1 teaspoon rubbed sage
1 teaspoon ground savory
⅛ teaspoon red pepper
3 dozen littleneck clams
1 cup water
2 cups Sauterne wine
3 pounds sea bass, cut into
  2-inch pieces
1½ pounds medium-size fresh
  shrimp, peeled and
  deveined
1 pound fresh lump
  crabmeat, drained and
  flaked

Sauté chopped onion and minced garlic in oil in a large Dutch oven until tender. Stir in tomato sauce, tomato puree, chopped celery leaves, Worcestershire sauce, hot sauce, and seasonings. Simmer, uncovered, over low heat 1 hour.

Scrub clams thoroughly, discarding any shells that are cracked or opened. Place water in a large Dutch oven. Bring water to a boil; add clams. Cover, reduce heat, and steam 8 to 10 minutes or until shells open wide. Remove clams, using a slotted spoon. Set clams aside.

Add wine, clams, and remaining seafood to tomato sauce; simmer 15 minutes or until fish flakes easily when tested with a fork. Remove and discard bay leaves. Yield: 32 cups.

Virginia D'Alfonso

Santa Barbara: 200 Years of Good Taste
The Santa Barbara Historical Society—Docent Council
Santa Barbara, California

Oyster Stew

2 (12-ounce) containers fresh
  Standard oysters
2 stalks celery, diced
1 medium onion, diced
1 (4-ounce) can sliced
  mushrooms, drained
¼ cup butter or margarine
¼ cup all-purpose flour
1 cup Chablis or other dry
  white wine
2 teaspoons chicken-flavored
  bouillon granules

½ cup whipping cream
2 tablespoons grated
  Parmesan cheese
2 tablespoons chopped fresh
  parsley
1 tablespoon fresh lemon
  juice
⅛ teaspoon ground nutmeg
⅛ teaspoon pepper
⅛ teaspoon dried whole
  thyme

Drain oysters, reserving 1 cup liquid. Set aside. Sauté celery, onion, and mushrooms in butter in a Dutch oven until tender. Stir in flour. Cook 1 minute, stirring constantly. Gradually add oyster liquid, wine, and bouillon granules. Bring to a boil; reduce heat, and add cream and next 6 ingredients. Stir in oysters. Cook until edges of oysters begin to curl. Yield: 5 cups.

Tidewater on the Half Shell
The Junior League of Norfolk-Virgina Beach, Virginia

New Mexico Green Chile Stew

1½ pounds lean boneless
  beef, cut into 1-inch cubes
1 tablespoon vegetable oil
3 cups hot water
3 (4-ounce) cans chopped
  green chiles, drained
1 cup canned pinto beans,
  drained

1 (14½-ounce) can stewed
  tomatoes
2 small onions, chopped
1 clove garlic, minced
1 teaspoon salt
¼ teaspoon ground cumin
¼ teaspoon, dried whole
  oregano

Cook meat in hot oil in a Dutch oven until browned; add water. Cover, reduce heat, and simmer 1 hour. Add chiles and remaining ingredients; cover and simmer 30 minutes. Yield: about 6 cups.

Savoring the Southwest
Roswell Symphony Guild Publications
Roswell, New Mexico

Kentucky Burgoo

1 (4- to 5-pound) hen
1 pound beef stew meat
1 pound veal stew meat
1½ to 2 pounds beef bones
1 stalk celery
1 carrot, scraped
1 small onion, peeled
2 tablespoons chopped fresh
parsley
1 red pepper pod
1 (10½-ounce) can tomato
puree
4 quarts water
¼ cup salt
1 tablespoon sugar
1½ teaspoons pepper
½ teaspoon red pepper
1 tablespoon lemon juice

1 tablespoon Worcestershire
sauce
6 onions, finely chopped
8 to 10 tomatoes, peeled and
chopped
1 turnip, peeled and finely
chopped
2 green peppers, finely
chopped
2 cups fresh lima beans
2 cups thinly sliced celery
2 cups finely chopped
cabbage
2 cups sliced fresh okra
2 cups fresh corn, cut from
cob
½ lemon, seeded

Combine first 17 ingredients in a large Dutch oven. Bring to a boil; cover, reduce heat, and simmer 4 hours. Cool. Strain meat mixture, reserving meat and liquid; discard vegetables. Remove skin, bone, and gristle from meat; finely chop meat. Return meat to liquid, and refrigerate 8 hours.

Skim fat layer from mixture. Add chopped onions, tomatoes, turnip, green peppers, beans, celery, cabbage, okra, corn, and lemon. Bring mixture to a boil; cover, reduce heat, and simmer 1 hour. Uncover and simmer 2 hours or to desired consistency, stirring frequently. Remove and discard lemon before serving. Yield: 32 cups.

To Market, To Market
The Junior League of Owensboro, Kentucky

Vegetables

A harrow is used in the spring for pulverizing and smoothing the soil, mulching, and covering seed on a farm near Newport, New Hampshire. Hard work in the spring makes possible a fall harvest of fresh-from-the-garden vegetables.

☆☆☆

Artichokes with Crumb Topping

6 large artichokes
1 teaspoon salt
3 tablespoons butter or
  margarine
3 tablespoons all-purpose
  flour
1½ cups milk

½ teaspoon salt
¾ cup (3 ounces) shredded
  Cheddar cheese
½ cup mayonnaise
¾ cup soft breadcrumbs
2 tablespoons butter or
  margarine, melted

Wash artichokes by plunging up and down in cold water. Cut off stem ends. Place artichokes in a large Dutch oven. Add water to cover and 1 teaspoon salt. Bring water to a boil. Cover and boil gently 40 to 45 minutes or until tender. Drain; let cool.

Spread artichoke leaves apart. Scrape meat from each leaf, using a stainless steel spoon; reserve meat. Discard leaves. Scrape out fuzzy thistle (choke) with spoon. Coarsely chop hearts. Set aside.

Melt 3 tablespoons butter in a heavy saucepan over low heat; add flour, stirring until smooth. Cook 1 minute, stirring constantly. Gradually add milk; cook over medium heat, stirring constantly, until mixture is thickened and bubbly. Stir in ½ teaspoon salt. Remove from heat. Add artichoke meat, and stir in Cheddar cheese and mayonnaise.

Spoon mixture into a 1-quart casserole. Combine breadcrumbs and melted butter, stirring well. Sprinkle over casserole. Bake at 350° for 35 to 40 minutes. Serve immediately. Yield: 6 servings.

California Fresh
The Junior League of Oakland-East Bay, California

Asparagus with Toasted Pine Nuts and Lemon Vinaigrette

1 pound fresh asparagus spears
3 tablespoons pine nuts
¼ cup olive oil
1 tablespoon fresh lemon juice
1 clove garlic, crushed
½ teaspoon salt
½ teaspoon dried whole basil
½ teaspoon dried whole oregano
Freshly ground pepper

Snap off tough ends of asparagus. Remove scales from stalks with a knife or vegetable peeler, if desired. Place spears in a steaming rack over boiling water; cover and steam 4 to 5 minutes or until asparagus spears are crisp-tender. Transfer steamed asparagus to a serving platter.

Sauté pine nuts in a small skillet over medium heat 2 to 3 minutes or until browned. Set aside.

Combine olive oil and remaining ingredients in a medium saucepan; stir using a wire whisk to blend. Cook over medium heat 2 to 3 minutes or until thoroughly heated, stirring constantly. Pour over asparagus. Sprinkle with pine nuts. Let stand to room temperature before serving. Yield: 4 servings.　　　　　James R. Lenney

Victuals and Vignettes
The Herkimer County Historical Society
Herkimer, New York

Asparagus-Orange Spears

1½ pounds fresh asparagus spears
3 tablespoons butter or margarine
1 clove garlic, crushed
2 tablespoons grated orange rind
¼ cup fresh orange juice
¼ teaspoon salt
⅛ teaspoon pepper
1 medium-size orange

Snap off tough ends of asparagus. Remove scales from stalks with a knife or vegetable peeler, if desired. Cook asparagus, uncovered, in boiling water to cover 5 minutes or until crisp-tender. Drain and set asparagus aside.

Melt butter in a large skillet over medium heat. Add garlic, and sauté 1 minute. Remove garlic. Add orange rind and orange juice to butter in skillet. Add asparagus, and cook until asparagus is thoroughly heated.

Transfer asparagus spears to a serving platter. Spoon orange juice mixture over asparagus. Sprinkle with salt and pepper.

Peel orange, removing white pith. Cut orange into 6 thin slices. Cut each orange slice in half. Arrange on platter with asparagus. Serve immediately. Yield: 6 servings.

San Francisco Encore
The Junior League of San Francisco, California

Black Beans

1 pound dried black beans
2 quarts water
1 green pepper, finely
   chopped
2 medium onions, finely
   chopped
3 cloves garlic, minced
¼ cup olive oil
1 tablespoon wine vinegar
2 teaspoons dried whole
   oregano

½ teaspoon salt
¼ teaspoon pepper
3 bay leaves
Hot cooked yellow rice
1 (2-ounce) jar diced
   pimiento, drained
Chopped onion (optional)
Diced avocado (optional)

Sort and wash beans. Place beans in a large Dutch oven with water to cover, and let soak overnight. Drain beans; combine beans and 2 quarts water in Dutch oven. Simmer, uncovered, 1 hour.

Sauté green pepper, 2 finely chopped onion, and garlic in olive oil in a large skillet over medium heat until vegetables are tender. Add to beans in Dutch oven. Stir in vinegar, oregano, salt, pepper, and bay leaves. Cook, uncovered, over low heat 3 to 4 hours or until thickened and creamy, stirring frequently.

Remove and discard bay leaves. Serve over rice. Garnish with pimiento and, if desired, onion and avocado. Yield: 6 servings.

Gulfshore Delights
The Junior League of Fort Myers, Florida

Down South Beans

1 pound dried pinto beans	¼ teaspoon pepper
1 tablespoon salt	2 cloves garlic, minced
1 tablespoon chili powder	1 large ham hock
¼ teaspoon red pepper	Green onions, sliced

Sort and wash beans; place in a Dutch oven. Cover with 4 inches of water. Add salt and next 5 ingredients; bring to a boil. Reduce heat, and simmer 8 hours, adding water as needed. Remove meat from bone; return meat to beans. Top with green onions. Yield: 6 servings.   Sarah Grimes Butts

Perennials
The Junior Service League of Gainesville, Georgia

Vegetable Chili

1 pound dried red kidney beans	¼ cup Burgundy or other dry red wine
8 cups water, divided	¼ cup chopped fresh parsley
1½ to 2 teaspoons salt	2 tablespoons tomato paste
2 medium onions, chopped	2 tablespoons lemon juice
4 cloves garlic, minced	2 teaspoons chili powder
3 tablespoons vegetable oil	½ teaspoon ground cumin
2 (16-ounce) cans Italian plum tomatoes	¼ teaspoon salt
2 stalks celery, diced	¼ teaspoon pepper
2 medium carrots, scraped and diced	⅛ teaspoon hot sauce
	Shredded Cheddar cheese
2 small green peppers, diced	Sour cream
	Diced green onions

Sort and wash beans; place in a Dutch oven. Add 6 cups water; let beans soak 3 hours. Add 2 cups water and 1½ to 2 teaspoons salt; bring to a boil. Reduce heat; cook 1 hour or until tender.

Sauté onion and garlic in oil in a skillet. Drain tomatoes, reserving liquid. Dice tomatoes, and add to onion mixture. Add celery and next 11 ingredients, stirring well. Cook, uncovered, 20 minutes, stirring occasionally. Add vegetable mixture and tomato liquid to beans. Cook over medium heat until thoroughly heated. Serve with cheese, sour cream, and green onions. Yield: about 8 cups.

California Cooking
The Art Council, Los Angeles County Museum of Art
Los Angeles, California

Beets in Orange Sauce

5 medium beets, or 2
   (16-ounce) cans sliced beets,
   drained
1½ quarts water
1 teaspoon salt
1 tablespoon brown sugar

2 teaspoons cornstarch
½ teaspoon salt
½ teaspoon pepper
¾ cup orange juice
2 teaspoons vinegar

Leave root and 1-inch stem on beets; scrub with a vegetable brush. Place beets in a 3-quart saucepan; add water and 1 teaspoon salt. Bring to a boil; cover, reduce heat, and simmer 35 minutes or until tender. Drain; pour cold water over beets, and drain. Trim off stems and roots, and rub off skins; slice beets, and set aside.

Combine sugar, cornstarch, ½ teaspoon salt, and pepper in a 2-quart saucepan; gradually stir in orange juice and vinegar. Cook over medium heat, stirring constantly, until thickened and bubbly.

Add beets to sauce, and cook over medium heat until thoroughly heated. Serve immediately. Yield: 6 servings.

Sassafras!
The Junior League of Springfield, Missouri

Broccoli Flowerets with Orzo

2½ quarts water
1⅓ cups uncooked orzo
1 teaspoon salt
3 tablespoons olive oil
2 cloves garlic, minced

3 cups broccoli flowerets
½ cup diluted canned
   chicken broth
½ teaspoon salt
¼ teaspoon pepper

Bring water to a boil; add orzo and 1 teaspoon salt. Cook 10 to 12 minutes or until tender; drain and set aside.

Heat oil in a large skillet; sauté garlic in oil 1 minute. Stir in broccoli, and coat well. Add broth, ½ teaspoon salt, and pepper; cover and cook 3 to 5 minutes or until broccoli is crisp-tender. Add orzo; toss well. Yield: 6 servings.

First There Must Be Food
Northwestern Memorial Hospital
Chicago, Illinois

Tender-Crisp Broccoli and Carrots

⅓ cup light corn syrup
3 tablespoons cider vinegar
2 tablespoons cornstarch
2 tablespoons soy sauce
½ teaspoon ground ginger
1 pound fresh broccoli
2 tablespoons vegetable oil
2 medium carrots, scraped
    and cut into julienne strips

2 medium onions, cut into
    wedges
1 (8-ounce) can water
    chestnuts, drained and
    sliced
¼ cup roasted cashews,
    chopped

Combine corn syrup, vinegar, cornstarch, soy sauce, and ginger; mix well. Set aside.

Trim off large leaves of broccoli, and remove tough ends of lower stalks. Wash broccoli thoroughly. Cut off flowerets, and set aside; cut stalks into ¼-inch slices; set aside.

Heat electric wok or skillet to 325° for 2 to 3 minutes. Pour oil around top of preheated wok, coating sides; allow to heat 1 minute. Add broccoli stems, carrot strips, and onion wedges; stir-fry 2 minutes or until vegetables are crisp-tender. Add broccoli flowerets and water chestnuts; stir-fry 1 minute or until crisp-tender. Pour soy sauce mixture over vegetables, stirring well. Cook 1 to 2 minutes or until sauce is thickened. Sprinkle with cashews. Serve immediately. Yield: 4 to 6 servings.

Look What's Cooking Now! Minnesota Heritage Cookbook Volume II
The American Cancer Society, Minnesota Division
Minneapolis, Minnesota

Hanna's Martini Sauerkraut

2 quarts water
1 (½-pound) slab of bacon
¼ cup butter or margarine
1 cup sliced onion
½ cup sliced carrot
2 (14-ounce) cans sauerkraut,
    drained
6 peppercorns

4 parsley sprigs
1 bay leaf
2 cups diluted canned beef
    broth
1 cup vermouth
¼ cup gin
Salt and pepper to taste

Bring water to a boil in a large Dutch oven; reduce heat, add bacon, and simmer 10 minutes. Drain; chop bacon, and set aside.

Melt butter in Dutch oven; add chopped bacon, onion, and carrot. Cook over low heat 10 minutes, stirring occasionally. Stir in sauerkraut; cover and simmer 10 minutes.

Tie peppercorns, parsley sprigs, and bay leaf in a cheesecloth bag. Bury herb bag in sauerkraut mixture. Pour beef broth, vermouth, and gin over sauerkraut mixture. Season with salt and pepper. Cover and bake at 325° for 4 hours or until liquid is absorbed. Remove and discard cheesecloth bag. Yield: 6 servings.

Vicky Strohl Parish

America Discovers Columbus
The Junior League of Columbus, Ohio

Carrot Tart

4 **large carrots, scraped and thinly sliced**	**¼ cup commercial sour cream**
1 **tablespoon butter or margarine, melted**	1 **teaspoon grated orange rind**
3 **cups shredded carrots**	**¼ teaspoon salt**
1 **potato, peeled and cubed**	**⅛ teaspoon ground turmeric**
2 **eggs**	**⅛ teaspoon white pepper**

Cook sliced carrots in a small amount of boiling water 5 minutes or until crisp-tender; drain. Brush an 8-inch round cakepan with butter. Arrange carrot slices in cakepan, overlapping to cover bottom and sides of pan. Set aside.

Cook shredded carrots and potato in a small amount of boiling water 15 minutes or until tender; drain. Position knife blade in food processor bowl. Combine half of potato mixture and remaining ingredients in food processor bowl. Top with cover, and process until smooth. Add remaining potato mixture; process until smooth.

Spoon puree into prepared pan. Bake at 350° for 30 to 35 minutes, or until set. Let stand 5 minutes. Loosen tart from sides of pan, using a narrow metal spatula; invert onto a serving platter. Yield: 8 servings.   Kay Forde

Philadelphia Homestyle Cookbook
The Norwood-Fontbonne Academy Home and School
Philadelphia, Pennsylvania

Carrots with Pistachios and Cointreau

¼ cup plus 1 tablespoon
  butter or margarine,
  divided
½ cup pistachio nuts
1 pound carrots, scraped and
  diagonally sliced

3 tablespoons water
1 teaspoon salt
¼ cup Cointreau or other
  orange-flavored liqueur

Melt 2 tablespoons butter in a small skillet over medium heat. Add pistachios, and sauté 1 minute. Remove from heat, and set aside.

Combine carrots, remaining 3 tablespoons butter, water, and salt in a large saucepan. Bring to a boil over medium-high heat. Reduce heat to medium-low; cover and cook 5 minutes or until carrots are tender. Transfer carrots to a serving bowl, using a slotted spoon; reserve liquid.

Bring liquid to a boil, and boil until liquid is reduced to 2 tablespoons. Pour liquid over carrots. Add pistachios and Cointreau. Toss gently, and serve, using a slotted spoon. Yield: 6 servings.

Clock Wise Cuisine
The Junior League of Detroit, Michigan

Glazed Carrots with Grapes

2 pounds carrots, scraped
  and diagonally sliced
½ cup water
3 tablespoons cornstarch
2 cups orange juice

½ cup sugar
¼ cup Chablis or other dry
  white wine
1 pound seedless green
  grapes

Cook carrots in a small amount of boiling water 12 to 15 minutes or until crisp-tender; drain and set aside.

Stir ½ cup water into cornstarch, and set aside.

Combine orange juice, sugar, and wine in a saucepan; bring to a boil. Add cornstarch mixture, and cook, stirring constantly, until thickened and smooth. Remove from heat, and stir in carrots and grapes. Serve immediately. Yield: 8 servings.

Concertos for Cooks
The North Group, Symphony Women's Committee
Indiana State Symphony Society, Inc.
Indianapolis, Indiana

Cauliflower with Topping

1 large head cauliflower
¼ cup olive oil
3 cloves garlic, minced
1 tablespoon chopped fresh
  parsley
¼ teaspoon salt
⅛ teaspoon pepper
1 tablespoon sesame seeds,
  toasted

Remove large outer leaves and stalk of cauliflower; wash. Leave head whole. Cover and cook in a small amount of boiling water 15 minutes or until tender; drain. Place on a plate; keep warm.

Heat oil in a saucepan over medium heat. Add garlic and parsley; cook until crisp. Stir in salt and pepper. Pour over cauliflower. Sprinkle with toasted sesame seeds. Yield: 6 to 8 servings.

Savoring the Southwest
Roswell Symphony Guild Publications
Roswell, New Mexico

Terrific Cauliflower

1 medium head cauliflower
¼ teaspoon salt
⅛ teaspoon pepper
1 (8-ounce) carton
  commercial sour cream
1 cup (4 ounces) shredded
  sharp Cheddar cheese
1 tablespoon sesame seeds,
  toasted

Remove large outer leaves of cauliflower. Break cauliflower into flowerets. Bring a small amount of water, ¼ teaspoon salt, and ⅛ teaspoon pepper to a boil in a large saucepan; add cauliflower. Cover and cook 8 to 10 minutes or until tender; drain.

Arrange half of cauliflower in a 1-quart baking dish. Spread ½ cup sour cream over cauliflower. Sprinkle with ½ cup cheese and 1½ teaspoons sesame seeds. Repeat layers. Bake at 350° for 10 to 15 minutes. Yield: 4 to 6 servings.   Christie Key

Deep in the Heart
The Junior Forum of Dallas, Texas

Celery and Corn

¼ cup butter or margarine
2 cups diagonally sliced
celery
1 (10-ounce) package frozen
whole kernel corn

2 tablespoons sliced pimiento
½ teaspoon salt

Melt butter in a large skillet over medium heat. Add celery; cover and cook 5 minutes.

Cook corn according to package directions; drain. Add to celery in skillet. Stir in pimiento and salt. Cook until thoroughly heated. Yield: 4 servings.

Celebrate San Antonio
The Junior Forum of San Antonio, Texas

Choctaw Corn Pudding

4 eggs, beaten
½ cup half-and-half
1½ teaspoons baking powder
¼ cup plus 2 tablespoons
butter or margarine
2 tablespoons sugar
2 tablespoons all-purpose
flour

3 cups fresh corn
2 tablespoons butter or
margarine, melted
2 tablespoons firmly packed
brown sugar
¼ teaspoon ground cinnamon

Combine beaten eggs, half-and-half, and baking powder, stirring well. Set aside.

Melt ¼ cup plus 2 tablespoons butter in a large saucepan over low heat; add 2 tablespoons sugar and flour, stirring until smooth. Remove from heat; gradually add egg mixture, stirring constantly with a wire whisk until smooth. Add corn, and stir well.

Pour corn mixture into a greased 1½-quart casserole. Bake, uncovered, at 350° for 30 to 40 minutes or until pudding is set. Remove from oven, and drizzle 2 tablespoons melted butter over pudding. Combine brown sugar and cinnamon, and sprinkle over pudding. Bake an additional 3 to 5 minutes or until sugar melts. Yield: 6 servings.   Sally Simpson

Sugar Beach
The Junior League of Ft. Walton Beach, Florida

Calabacitas con Chili Verde

1 (17-ounce) can whole kernel
corn, drained
¼ cup butter or
margarine
½ cup chopped onion
1 clove garlic, minced
4 medium zucchini, unpeeled
and diced

4 (4-ounce) cans chopped
green chiles
½ cup water
1 teaspoon salt
¼ teaspoon pepper
¾ cup (3 ounces) shredded
Monterey Jack or Cheddar
cheese

Sauté corn in butter in a skillet over medium heat 2 minutes. Add onion and garlic; cook until tender. Stir in zucchini and next 4 ingredients. Cook, uncovered, 15 minutes or until zucchini is tender. Top with cheese; serve immediately. Yield: 8 to 10 servings.

Cooking with the Santa Fe Opera
The Santa Fe Opera Guild
Santa Fe, New Mexico

Escalloped Eggplant Pyramids

1 large eggplant, cut into 12
slices
2 medium tomatoes, cut into
12 slices
1 large onion, cut into 12
slices
½ cup butter or margarine,
melted and divided

½ teaspoon salt
½ teaspoon dried whole basil
1 (8-ounce) package
mozzarella cheese, sliced
½ cup seasoned, dry
breadcrumbs
2 tablespoons grated
Parmesan cheese

Arrange eggplant slices in an 18- x 12- x 1-inch jellyroll pan. Place a tomato slice then an onion slice on top of each eggplant slice. Drizzle with ¼ cup melted butter. Combine salt and basil; sprinkle over vegetables. Bake, uncovered, at 450° for 20 minutes. Remove from oven; layer cheese slices over vegetables. Combine remaining melted butter and breadcrumbs; sprinkle over cheese. Sprinkle Parmesan cheese over breadcrumbs. Bake, uncovered, 5 minutes or until cheese melts. Yield: 8 to 10 servings.   Myrtis Tabb

Temptations
Presbyterian Day School
Cleveland, Mississippi

Eggplant Monreale

1 (14½-ounce) can whole tomatoes, undrained and chopped
1 (8-ounce) can tomato sauce
2 tablespoons onion flakes
1 teaspoon dried whole basil
1 teaspoon dried whole oregano
¼ teaspoon garlic powder
1 tablespoon Chablis or other dry white wine
1 medium eggplant, peeled

2 eggs, beaten
½ teaspoon salt
1 cup fine, dry breadcrumbs
¼ cup plus 1 tablespoon olive oil
¼ cup plus 1 tablespoon vegetable oil
1 cup (4 ounces) shredded mozzarella cheese
¼ cup grated Parmesan cheese

Combine tomatoes, tomato sauce, onion flakes, basil, oregano, garlic powder, and wine in a medium saucepan. Bring to a boil; reduce heat, and simmer 20 minutes.

Cut eggplant into ¼-inch slices. Combine eggs and salt. Dip each eggplant slice in egg mixture, and coat with breadcrumbs. Combine oils in a skillet; fry eggplant slices in hot oil until golden brown. Drain well on paper towels.

Place half of eggplant slices in a 12- x 8- x 2-inch baking dish; spread half of tomato mixture over eggplant. Repeat layers. Sprinkle with cheeses. Bake at 325° for 15 to 20 minutes. Yield: 8 servings.

Necessities and Temptations
The Junior League of Austin, Texas

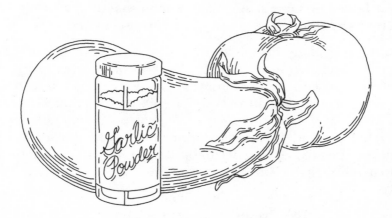

French Fried Mushrooms

½ cup all-purpose flour
1 teaspoon salt
½ teaspoon baking powder
⅛ teaspoon pepper
⅓ cup milk
1 egg, separated

1 teaspoon sugar
1 pound small fresh
  mushrooms
1⅔ cups corn flakes, crushed
Vegetable oil

Combine flour, salt, baking powder, and pepper. Combine milk and egg yolk; add to flour mixture.

Beat egg white (at room temperature) until soft peaks form; add sugar, and beat until stiff peaks form. Fold into flour mixture.

Dip mushrooms in batter; roll in corn flake crumbs. Deep fry in hot oil (375°) until golden brown. Drain well on paper towels. Yield: 8 servings.   Mrs. William Flowers

Simply Southern
The DeSoto School, Inc. Parents-Teachers Club
West Helena, Arkansas

Creole Okra and Tomatoes

1 large onion, chopped
½ cup butter or margarine
⅓ cup diced green pepper
4 ripe tomatoes, chopped

2 pounds fresh okra, sliced
½ teaspoon salt
¼ teaspoon pepper

Sauté onion in butter in a large skillet until tender; add green pepper and remaining ingredients. Cover and simmer 40 minutes, stirring occasionally. Yield: 8 servings.   Bobbie Boyd

Best Kept Secrets of Enon Baptist Church
Enon Baptist Church
Tylertown, Mississippi

Peas with Prosciutto

2 large cloves garlic
2 tablespoons olive oil
2 ounces prosciutto, chopped
2 (10-ounce) packages frozen
  green peas, thawed and
  drained

¼ cup minced fresh
  parsley
¼ teaspoon salt
⅛ teaspoon freshly ground
  pepper

Sauté garlic in oil in a saucepan until golden; remove and discard garlic. Add prosciutto to oil; sauté over medium heat 1 minute. Add peas, parsley, salt, and pepper; cover and cook 5 minutes or until peas are tender, stirring occasionally. Yield: 6 servings.

California Heritage Continues
The Junior League of Pasadena, California

Company Peas

2 medium onions, chopped
¼ cup olive oil
2 (10-ounce) packages frozen
  green peas
½ teaspoon dried whole
  thyme

1 (14-ounce) can artichoke
  hearts, drained and
  quartered
1 (8-ounce) can sliced water
  chestnuts, drained
Salt and pepper to taste

Sauté onion in hot oil in a skillet until tender. Add peas and thyme; cover and simmer 5 minutes or until peas are thawed. Stir in artichoke hearts, water chestnuts, salt, and pepper. Cook 2 minutes or until mixture is thoroughly heated. Yield: 8 servings.

Rare Collection
The Junior League of Galveston County, Texas

Roesti

2½ pounds red potatoes
1 teaspoon salt
¼ teaspoon pepper
¼ cup unsalted butter or
  margarine, divided

2 tablespoons olive oil,
  divided

Cook potatoes, covered, in boiling water for 10 minutes. Drain; cool and chill at least 2 hours.

Peel and shred potatoes; stir in salt and pepper.

Heat 2 tablespoons butter and 1 tablespoon olive oil in a 10-inch nonstick skillet. Add potatoes; spread evenly, and press firmly with a metal spatula. Cook, uncovered, 10 to 12 minutes or until browned. Invert onto a serving platter.

Heat remaining butter and olive oil in skillet. Slide potato cake, uncooked side down, into skillet; cook 10 to 12 minutes or until brown. Slide onto platter; cut into wedges, and serve immediately. Yield: 6 to 8 servings.

Temptations
The Junior League of Lansing, Michigan

Grilled New Potatoes with Onions and Peppers

3 **large banana peppers**
1 **large green or sweet red pepper, sliced**
1 **large onion, sliced**
½ **cup unsalted butter or margarine, divided**
2 **pounds new potatoes, cleaned and halved**
1 **teaspoon salt**
½ **teaspoon freshly ground pepper**
½ **teaspoon dried whole rosemary**
½ **teaspoon dried whole marjoram**
½ **teaspoon dried whole thyme**

Slit each banana pepper lengthwise, and carefully remove and discard seeds; wash peppers.

Sauté banana peppers, green pepper, and onion, in 3 tablespoons butter until crisp-tender. Set aside. Cut 3 pieces of aluminum foil 30 inches long. Stack aluminum foil. Place half of the potatoes in center of aluminum foil; top with half of the onion mixture and half of the remaining butter. Sprinkle with half each of salt, pepper, rosemary, marjoram, and thyme. Repeat layers with remaining ingredients. Secure foil.

Grill over hot coals 15 to 20 minutes or until potatoes are tender. Serve immediately. Yield: 6 servings.

Even More Special
The Junior League of Durham and Orange Counties,
North Carolina

Greek Spinach Casserole

⅔ cup chopped onion
1 tablespoon butter or
    margarine
2 (10-ounce) packages frozen
    chopped spinach, thawed
    and drained

3 eggs
1 (12-ounce) carton
    cream-style cottage cheese
⅔ cup crumbled feta cheese
½ teaspoon salt
½ teaspoon pepper

Sauté onion in butter in a large skillet until tender. Add spinach, and cook 5 minutes, stirring frequently. Combine eggs and remaining ingredients; add to spinach mixture. Pour mixture into a greased 8-inch square baking pan. Bake at 350° for 25 to 30 minutes or until set. Yield: 6 servings.   Helen Adamthwaite

Culinary Arts & Crafts
The Park Maitland School
Maitland, Florida

Baked Spaghetti Squash with Goat Cheese

1 large spaghetti squash
1 cup minced fresh parsley
2 cloves garlic, minced
1 (3-ounce) package sun-dried
    tomatoes, chopped
¼ cup freshly grated
    Parmesan cheese

½ teaspoon salt
Freshly ground pepper to
    taste
¾ cup (3 ounces) shredded
    Swiss cheese
3 ounces soft goat cheese,
    crumbled

Place squash in boiling water to cover in a Dutch oven; cover and cook over medium heat 25 minutes or until tender. Drain and cool. Cut in half lengthwise, and discard seeds. Using a fork, remove spaghetti-like strands, and reserve shells. Combine squash and next 6 ingredients. Return mixture to squash shells. Combine Swiss and goat cheeses; sprinkle over squash. Bake, uncovered, at 350° for 25 minutes or until cheese is lightly browned. Yield: 6 servings.

Taste of Today
BUNWC, North Shore Illinois Chapter
Northfield, Illinois

Neapolitan Vegetable Cheesecake

3 cups packed coarsely grated
  zucchini
1 teaspoon salt, divided
1 onion, chopped
1 tablespoon butter or
  margarine
1 cup coarsely grated carrots
3 tablespoons all-purpose
  flour
3 cloves garlic, finely minced
½ teaspoon dried whole basil
½ teaspoon dried whole
  oregano
¼ cup packed chopped fresh
  parsley

1½ tablespoons lemon juice
4 eggs, slightly beaten
3 cups ricotta cheese
1 (8-ounce) package
  mozzarella cheese, grated
¾ cup grated Parmesan
  cheese, divided
Salt and freshly ground
  pepper to taste
⅓ cup fine, dry breadcrumbs,
  divided
4 plum tomatoes, thinly
  sliced
1 (2-ounce) can anchovy
  fillets, drained and rolled

Combine zucchini and ½ teaspoon salt; stir well. Let stand 15 minutes; drain. Roll zucchini in paper towels to squeeze out excess moisture; place in a bowl, and set aside.

Combine ½ teaspoon salt, onion, and butter in a large skillet; sauté 3 to 4 minutes. Add zucchini, carrots, flour, garlic, basil, and oregano. Cook over medium heat 5 to 6 minutes. Remove from heat; add parsley and lemon juice.

Combine eggs, ricotta cheese, mozzarella cheese, and ⅔ cup Parmesan cheese in a large mixing bowl; beat well. Add vegetable mixture and salt and pepper to taste; stir until well blended.

Sprinkle 1 tablespoon breadcrumbs over the bottom of a greased 10-inch springform pan. Pour vegetable mixture into pan. Bake at 375° for 30 minutes. Remove from oven.

Dredge plum tomato slices in remaining breadcrumbs. Garnish cheesecake with tomato slices and rolled anchovies. Sprinkle with remaining Parmesan cheese. Reduce heat to 350°, and bake 30 minutes. Turn off oven, and open door; let cheesecake cool in oven 15 minutes. Remove from oven; cool on a wire rack 10 minutes. Yield: one 10-inch cheesecake.

Noteworthy
The Ravinia Festival
Highland Park, Illinois

Acknowledgments

Special thanks to Dot Gibson and Ellen Rolfes for their support of this project and to the
fund-raising groups who participated in this celebration of American cooking.
America's best recipes have been selected and adapted from the following community
cookbooks. The copyright for each of these is held by the sponsoring organization
unless otherwise noted.

According to Taste, Lufkin Service League, P.O. Box 1311, Lufkin, TX 75902-1311
Acornucopia, Valley Hospital Auxiliary, Linwood and N. Van Dien Ave., Ridgewood, NJ 07451
Almost Heaven, Junior League of Huntington, 617 9th Ave., Huntington, WV 25701
America Discovers Columbus, Junior League of Columbus Publications, 586 East Town St.,
    Columbus, OH 43215
Angel Food, St. Anne's Episcopal Church, 199 Duke of Gloucester St., Annapolis, MD 21401
Appetizers, Entrées 'n More, Winona Memorial Foundation Auxiliary, 3202 N. Meridian St.,
    Indianapolis, IN 46208
Armour Centennial Cookbook, Armour Centennial Committee, P.O. Box 424, Armour, SD 57313
Artist's Palate Cookbook, Women's Volunteer Committee, New Orleans Museum of Art,
    P.O. Box 19123, City Park, New Orleans, LA 70179
Best Kept Secrets of Enon Baptist Church, Route 3, Box 90C, Tylertown, MS 39667
Best of Friends, Friends of the Maitland Public Library, 501 S. Maitland Ave., Maitland, FL 32751
Best of Mississippi's Old and New Recipes, Grand Chapter of Mississippi, Order of the
    Eastern Star, P.O. Box 892, Woodville, MS 39669
Between Greene Leaves, Greene County Homemakers Extension, Kathy Harms, RR 1, Box
    216, Carrollton, IL 62016
Beyond Parsley, Junior League of Kansas City, 4651 Roanoke Parkway, Kansas City, MO 64112
Beyond the Bay, Junior Service League of Panama City, P.O. Box 404, Panama City, FL 32402
Bienvenue! La Cuisine de la Maison Destrehan, River Road Historical Society, P.O. Box 5,
    Destrehan, LA 70047
Bluegrass Winners, Garden Club of Lexington, Inc., P.O. Box 22091, Lexington, KY 40522
A Book of Favorite Recipes, Missionary Society of Victory Chapel, RD 2, Box 327, Dover,
    DE 19901. ©1968-1982 by Circulation Service.
Bound to Please, Junior League of Boise, P.O. Box 6126, Boise, ID 83707
Bravo, Greensboro Symphony Guild, P.O. Box 29224, Greensboro, NC 27408
Brunch Basket, Junior League of Rockford, 4118 Pinecrest Rd., Rockford, IL 61107
Bytes, Colorado's Family-Friendly Cookbook, Graland Country Day School, 30 Birch St.,
    Denver, CO 80220
California Cooking, Art Council, Los Angeles County Museum of Art, 5905 Wilshire Blvd.,
    Los Angeles, CA 90036. Recipes used by permission of Clarkson N. Potter, Inc.
California Fresh, Junior League of Oakland-East Bay, 3730 Mt. Diablo Blvd., Suite 310,
    Lafayette, CA 94549
California Heritage Continues, Junior League of Pasadena, 149 South Madison Ave.,
    Pasadena, CA 91101. Recipe used by permission of Doubleday, a division of Bantam,
    Doubleday, Dell Publishing Group, Inc.
Carnegie Treasures Cookbook, Women's Committee, Carnegie Museum of Art, 4400 Forbes
    Ave., Pittsburgh, PA 15213
Celebrate San Antonio—A Cookbook, San Antonio Junior Forum, P.O. Box 791186, San
    Antonio, TX 78279
Celebration: A Taste of Arkansas, Sevier County Cookbook Committee, P.O. Box 66,
    Lockesburg, AR 71846
Centennial Cookbook: 100 Years of Free Masonry in North Dakota, Masonic Grand Lodge, 201
    14th Ave. North, Fargo, ND 58102
Charleston Receipts Repeats, Junior League of Charleston, P.O. Box 177, Charleston, SC 29402

Chord en Bleu, Orchestra of Illinois Guild, 148 Shermer, Glenview, IL 60025
Christmas Memories Cookbook, Mystic Seaport Museum Stores, 39 Greenmanville Ave.,
    Mystic, CT 06355
Clock Wise Cuisine, Junior League of Detroit, 32 Lake Shore Rd., Grosse Pointe Farms, MI 48236
Colorado WIFE, Colorado Women Involved in Farm Economics, Route 1, Box 91,
    Brandon, CO 81026
Concertos for Cooks, North Group, Symphony Women's Committee, Indiana State
    Symphony Society, Inc., 45 Monument Circle, Indianapolis, IN 46204
Cooking with Class, Frederick Community College, 7932 Oppossumtown Pike, Frederick, MD 21701
Cooking with the Santa Fe Opera, Santa Fe Opera Guild, P.O. Box 2371, Santa Fe, NM 87504
Cornsilk, Junior League of Sioux City, P.O. Box 2166, Northside Station, Sioux City, IA 51104
The Cove Cookery, Ladies Aid Society, St. John's Lutheran Church, Route 2, Box 15,
    Accident, MD 21520
Culinary Arts & Crafts, Park Maitland School, 1450 South Orlando Ave., Maitland, FL 32751
A Dash of Down East, Junior Guild of Rocky Mount, P.O. Box 7912, Rocky Mount, NC 27804
Deep in the Heart, Dallas Junior Forum, 2116 East Arapaho, Suite 721, Richardson, TX 75081
"delicious," Elisabeth Morrow School Parents Association, EMS Publications, P.O. Box 672,
    Englewood, NJ 07631
Down Home in High Style, Houston Academy Library Committee, Route 5, Box 120,
    Dothan, AL 36301
Down the Bayou, Bayou Civic Club, P.O. Box 602, Larose, LA 70373
Even More Special, Junior League of Durham and Orange Counties, 900 South Duke St.,
    Durham, NC 27707
Feast and Fellowship, St. Frances Guild, Cathedral Bookstore, 2744 Peachtree Rd., NW,
    Atlanta, GA 30363
Fest of All Worlds, American Lebanese Christian Women's Society of Illinois, P.O. Box
    3874, Oak Brook, IL 60521
First There Must Be Food, Northwestern Memorial Hospital, 303 East Superior, Chicago, IL 60611
Flavors of Cape Cod, Thornton W. Burgess Society, 6 Discovery Hill Rd., East Sandwich, MA 02537
From Palette to Palate, Cincinnati Art Museum, Eden Park, Cincinnati, OH 45202
Gallery Buffet Soup Cookbook, Dallas Museum of Art League, 1717 North Harwood, Dallas, TX 75201
The Gardner Museum Café Cookbook, by Lois McKitchen Conroy, Isabella Stewart Gardner
    Museum, ©1985 by The Harvard Common Press, Inc., 535 Albany St., Boston, MA 02118
The Grace Cathedral Cookbook, Women's Evening Organization, 1051 Taylor St., San
    Francisco, CA 94108
The Great Entertainer Cookbook, Buffalo Bill Historical Center, P.O. Box 2630C, Cody, WY 82414
A Great Taste of Arkansas, Spice of the South, Inc., P.O. Box 1683, Pine Bluff, AR 71613
The Grecian Plate, Hellenic Ladies Society, St. Barbara Greek Orthodox Church, P.O. Box
    1149, Durham, NC 27702
Gulfshore Delights, Junior League of Fort Myers, P.O. Box 6774, Fort Myers, FL 33911
Home at the Range, Chapter EX-P.E.O., 429 Smokyhill, Oakley, KS 67748
Just What the Doctor Ordered, Peoria Medical Society Auxiliary, Inc., P.O. Box 9094, Peoria, IL 61614
Kitchen Sampler, Junior Service League of Bessemer, P.O. Box 928, Bessemer, AL 35021
The Little Red Cookbook, Allen-Wells Chapter, American Red Cross, 1212 East California
    Rd., Fort Wayne, IN 46825
Lone Star Legacy II, Austin Junior Forum, P.O. Box 26628, Austin, TX 78755
Look What's Cooking Now! Minnesota Heritage Cookbook Volume II, American Cancer Society,
    Minnesota Division, 3316 West 66th St., Minneapolis, MN 55435
The Maine Ingredient, Southern Coastal Family Planning, Inc., 500 Forest Ave., Portland ME 04101
The Market Place, Augusta Junior Woman's Club, P.O. Box 3133, Augusta, GA 30904
Maui Cooks: A Collection of Island Recipes, Kokua Services, 461 Aulii Dr., Pukalani, Maui, HI 96788
The Mayors' Cookbook, United States Conference of Mayors, ©1987 by Acropolis Books
    Ltd., 2400 17th St., NW, Washington, DC 20009

McComb's International Cuisine Affair, McComb Interdenominational Care Association, P.O.
    Box 7206, McComb, MS 39648
Mountain Laurel Encore, Bell County Extension Homemakers, P.O. Box 430, Pineville, KY 40977
Mountain Measures: A Second Serving, Junior League of Charleston, P.O. Box 1924,
    Charleston, WV 25327
Nebraska Feeders Auxiliary Cookbook, Route 2, Madison, NE 68748
Necessities and Temptations, Junior League of Austin Publications, 5416 Parkcrest, Suite
    100, Austin, TX 78731
Not By Bread Alone, Holy Trinity Episcopal Church, 95 Folly Rd., Charleston, SC 29407
Noteworthy, a collection of recipes from the Ravinia Festival, Noteworthy Publications,
    1575 Oakwood Ave., Highland Park, IL 60035
Offerings Past and Present, St. Luke's Episcopal Church Women, St. Luke's Episcopal
    Church, 211 North Church St., Salisbury, NC 28144
Oregon Sampler: Resorts and Recipes, Assistance League® of Corvallis, 534 NW Fourth St.,
    Corvallis, OR 97330
Our Country Cookin', Junior Social Workers of Chickasha, P.O. Box 355, Chickasha, OK 73023
Our Special Blend, Rehabilitation Center of Eastern Fairfield County, 226 Mill Hill Ave.,
    Bridgeport, CT 06610
Out of Our League, Too, Junior League of Greensboro Publications, 220 State St.,
    Greensboro, NC 27408
The Overlake School Cookbook, Overlake School Parents Club, 20301 NE 108th, Redmond, WA 98053
Palette to Palate, Junior League of St. Joseph and Albrecht Art Museum, 301 North 8th
    St., St. Joseph, MO 64501
Peachtree Bouquet, Junior League of DeKalb County, P.O. Box 183, Decatur, GA 30031
Perennials, Junior Service League of Gainesville, P.O. Box 32, Gainesville, GA 30503
Philadelphia Homestyle Cookbook, Norwood-Fontbonne Academy Home & School, 8891
    Germantown Ave., Dept. C, Philadelphia, PA 19118
Pig Out, Junior League of Waterloo-Cedar Falls, P.O. Box 434, Waterloo, IA 50704
A Pinch of Salt Lake, Junior League of Salt Lake City, P.O. Box 6163, Salt Lake City, UT 84106
Plain & Fancy, Junior League of Richardson, P.O. Box 835808, Richardson, TX 75083
Prescriptions for Good Eating, Greenville County Medical Society Auxiliary, P.O. Box 9254,
    Greenville, SC 29604
The Pride of Peoria: Recipes and Reminiscences, Junior League of Peoria, 256 NE Randolph
    Ave., Peoria, IL 61606
Private Collection 2, Junior League of Palo Alto, 1102 Elder Ave., Menlo Park, CA 94025
Purple Sage and Other Pleasures, Junior League of Tuscon, 2099 East River Rd., Tucson, AZ 85718
Putting on the Grits, Junior League of Columbia, 4600 Forest Dr., Suite 4, Columbia, SC 29206
Rare Collection, Junior League of Galveston County, 210 Kempner, Galveston, TX 77550
Recipes from Woodruff Place, Woodruff Place Civic League, 720 West Dr., Woodruff Place,
    Indianapolis, IN 46201
Remembering Our Heritage, Covenant Women of Herndon Covenant Church, Route 1,
    Herndon, KS 67739
Rockport Collection, Rockport Art Association, P.O. Box 987, Rockport, TX 78382
Sampler, Women's Art Guild, Laguna Gloria Art Museum, P.O. Box 5705, Austin, TX 78763
San Francisco Encore, Junior League of San Francisco, 2226 Fillmore St., San Francisco,
    CA 94115. Recipes used by permission of Doubleday, a division of Bantam,
    Doubleday, Dell Publishing Group, Inc.
Santa Barbara: 200 Years of Good Taste, Santa Barbara Historical Society—Docent Council,
    136 East De La Guerra St., Santa Barbara, CA 93102
Sassafras!, Junior League of Springfield, 2574 East Bennett, Springfield, MO 65804
Savoring the Southwest, Roswell Symphony Guild Publications, P.O. Box 3078, Roswell, NM 88201
Silver Soirees, Service Guild of Birmingham, P.O. Box 9172, Birmingham, AL 35213
Simply Southern, DeSoto School, Inc., Parents-Teachers Club, P.O. Box F, West Helena, AR 72390

Some Enchanted Eating, Friends of the Symphony Publications, P.O. Box 1603, Muskegon, MI 49443

Some Like It South!, Junior League of Pensacola, P.O. Box 87, Pensacola, FL 32591

Sounds Delicious!, Volunteer Council of the Tulsa Philharmonic Society, Inc., 8177 South Harvard, Suite 431, Tulsa, OK 74137

Steeped in Tradition, Junior Service League of DeLand, P.O. Box 1372, DeLand, FL 32721

The Steinbeck House Cookbook, Valley Guild, 132 Central Ave., Salinas, CA 93901

The Stenciled Strawberry Cookbook, Junior League of Albany, 419 Madison Ave., Albany, NY 12210

Stir Crazy!, Junior Welfare League of Florence, P.O. Box 3715, Florence, SC 29502-0715

Sugar Beach, Junior League of Ft. Walton Beach, P.O. Box 24, Ft. Walton Beach, FL 32549

Suncoast Seasons, Dunedin Youth Guild, Inc., 1059 Broadway, Dunedin, FL 34698

Superlatives, Junior League of Oklahoma City, 6300 N. Western, Oklahoma City, OK 73118

A Taste of Aloha, Junior League of Honolulu, P.O. Box 10513, Honolulu, HI 96820

A Taste of California, San Francisco Home Economists in Business, Neva Lee, 191 Plymouth Circle, Daly City, CA 94015

Taste of Today, Brandeis University National Women's Committee, North Shore Illinois Chapter, P.O. Box 8117, Northfield, IL 60062

Taste of the South, Symphony League of Jackson, P.O. Box 1967, Jackson, MS 39215-1967

Taste the Seasons, Woodside-Atherton Auxiliary to Children's Hospital at Stanford, P.O. Box 4152, Menlo Park, CA 94026

Temptations, Junior Service League of Rome, P.O. Box 5542, Rome, GA 30161

Temptations, Junior League of Lansing, P.O. Box 1782, East Lansing, MI 48823

Temptations, Presbyterian Day School, 1100 West Sunflower Rd., Cleveland, MS 38732

There Once Was a Cook . . . , Wesley Institute, Inc., 243 Johnston Rd., Pittsburgh, PA 15241

Tidewater on the Half Shell, Junior League of Norfolk-Virginia Beach, P.O. Box 956, Norfolk, VA 23501

To Market, To Market, Junior League of Owensboro, P.O. Box 723, Owensboro, KY 42302

Treat Yourself to the Best, Junior League of Wheeling, 907½ National Road, Wheeling, WV 26003

Unbearably Good!, Americus Junior Service League, 125 East Forsyth St., Americus, GA 31709

Upper Crust: A Slice of the South, Junior League of Johnson City, P.O. Box 1082, Johnson City, TN 37605

Uptown Down South, Junior League of Greenville, 17 West North St., Greenville, SC 29601

The Vermont Symphony Cookbook, Vermont Symphony Orchestra Association, 77 College St., Burlington, VT 05401

Victuals and Vignettes, Herkimer County Historical Society, 400 North Main St., Herkimer, NY 13350

Vintage Vicksburg, Vicksburg Junior Auxiliary, P.O. Box 86, Vicksburg, MS 39180

Virginia Seasons, Junior League of Richmond, 205 West Franklin St., Richmond, VA 23220

What's Cooking at Woodlawn?, United Methodist Women, Woodlawn United Methodist Church, 1st Ave. North at 55th St., Birmingham, AL 35210

Wild Rice, Star of the North, The 1006 Summit Avenue Society, 1006 Summit Ave., St. Paul, MN 55105

Winners, Junior League of Indianapolis, 3050 N. Meridian St., Indianapolis, IN 46208

Winning at the Table, Junior League of Las Vegas, 1100 East Sahara, Suite 311, Las Vegas, NV 89104

Index